Languages of the World: Cataloging Issues and Problems

Languages of the World: Cataloging Issues and Problems

Martin D. Joachim, MA, MA
Editor

The Haworth Press, Inc.
New York · London · Norwood (Australia)

Languages of the World: Cataloging Issues and Problems has also been published as *Cataloging & Classification Quarterly,* Volume 17, Numbers 1/2 1993.

The development, preparation, and publication of this work has been undertaken with great care. However, the publisher, employees, editors, and agents of The Haworth Press and all imprints of The Haworth Press, Inc., including The Haworth Medical Press and Pharmaceutical Products Press, are not responsible for any errors contained herein or for consequences that may ensue from use of materials or information contained in this work. Opinions expressed by the author(s) are not necessarily those of The Haworth Press, Inc.

The Haworth Press, Inc., 10 Alice Street, Binghamton, NY 13904-1580 USA

Library of Congress Cataloging-in-Publication Data

Languages of the world : cataloging issues and problems / Martin D. Joachim, editor.
     p. cm.
    Published also as v. 17, no. 1/2, 1993 of Cataloging & classification quarterly.
    Includes bibliographical references (p.) and index.
    ISBN 1-56024-520-4
    1. Cataloging of foreign language publications. I. Joachim, Martin D., 1938- .
Z695.1.F66L36 1993
025.3′2–dc20   93-38632
                                                            CIP

INDEXING & ABSTRACTING

Contributions to this publication are selectively indexed or abstracted in print, electronic, online, or CD-ROM version(s) of the reference tools and information services listed below. This list is current as of the copyright date of this publication. See the end of this section for additional notes.

- *Current Awareness Bulletin*, Association for Information Management, Information House, 20-24 Old Street, London EC1V 9AP, England

- *Foreign Library and Information Service*, China Sci-Tech Book Review, Library of Academia Sinica, 8 Kexueyuan Nanlu, Zhongguancun, Beijing 100080, People's Republic of China

- *Index to Periodical Articles Related to Law*, University of Texas, 727 East 26th Street, Austin, TX 78705

- *Information Science Abstracts*, Plenum Publishing Company, 233 Spring Street, New York, NY 10013-1578

- *INSPEC Information Services*, Institution of Electrical Engineers, Michael Faraday House, Six Hills Way, Stevenage, Herts SG1 2AY, England

- *Library & Information Science Abstracts (LISA)*, Bowker-Saur Limited, c/o. Reed Information Services, Ltd., Windsor Court, East Grinstead, East Sussex RH19 1XA England

- *Library Hi Tech News*, Pierian Press, P. O. Box 1808, Ann Arbor, MI 48106

- *Library Literature*, The H.W. Wilson Company, 950 University Avenue, Bronx, NY 10452

- *Referativnyi Zhurnal (Abstracts Journal of the Institute of Scientific Information of the Republic of Russia)*, The Institute of Scientific Information, Baltijskaja ul., 14, Moscow A-219, Republic of Russia

- *The Informed Librarian*, Infosources Publishing, 140 Norma Road, Teaneck, NJ 07666

(continued)

SPECIAL BIBLIOGRAPHIC NOTES

related to indexing, abstracting, and library access services

☐ indexing/abstracting services in this list will also cover material in the "separate" that is co-published simultaneously with Haworth's special thematic journal issue or DocuSerial. Indexing/abstracting usually covers material at the article/chapter level.

☐ monographic co-editions are intended for either non-subscribers or libraries which intend to purchase a second copy for their circulating collections.

☐ monographic co-editions are reported to all jobbers/wholesalers/approval plans. The source journal is listed as the "series" to assist the prevention of duplicate purchasing in the same manner utilized for books-in-series.

☐ to facilitate user/access services all indexing/abstracting services are encouraged to utilize the co-indexing entry note indicated at the bottom of the first page of each article/chapter/contribution.

☐ this is intended to assist a library user of any reference tool (whether print, electronic, online, or CD-ROM) to locate the monographic version if the library has purchased this version but not a subscription to the source journal.

☐ individual articles/chapters in any Haworth publication are also available through the Haworth Document Delivery Services (HDDS).

For Sarah and Lisa

ABOUT THE EDITOR

Martin D. Joachim, MA, MA, is Principal Cataloger at Indiana University Libraries, where he was Head of the Cataloging Department for eleven years. He has been active in the American Library Association and chaired or served on various committees. He chaired the RLMS Committee on Bibliographic Control of Microforms for four years and has managed three grant-funded projects to catalog large microform sets at Indiana University. A member of the editorial board of *Cataloging & Classification Quarterly,* Mr. Joachim has published articles in various library, microform, and history journals.

Languages of the World: Cataloging Issues and Problems

CONTENTS

NON-SPECIFIC LANGUAGES

VIEWPOINT OF THE PATRON

INTRODUCTION

Issues and Problems in Cataloging the Languages of the World

Martin D. Joachim

SUMMARY. The number of languages in which libraries receive materials often presents challenges and difficulties for catalogers. Included in this volume are articles that deal with issues such as cataloging in languages in which library staffs have no expertise, authority work, descriptive and subject cataloging, classification, transliteration, backlogs, cooperative and shared cataloging, and collection-level and minimal-level cataloging. Articles from academic, national, and public libraries as well as an article from the patron's viewpoint present different perspectives on these topics.

INTRODUCTION

When one considers how many languages are or have been spoken, it is clear that no single volume can possibly include discussions on cataloging materials in all the world's languages. Merritt Ruhlen's *Guide to the*

[Haworth co-indexing entry note]: "Issues and Problems in Cataloging the Languages of the World." Joachim, Martin D. Co-published simultaneously in *Cataloging & Classification Quarterly* (The Haworth Press, Inc.) Vol. 17, No. 1/2, 1993, pp. 1-14; and: *Languages of the World: Cataloging Issues and Problems* (ed: Martin D. Joachim) The Haworth Press, Inc., 1993, pp. 1-14. Multiple copies of this article/chapter may be purchased from The Haworth Document Delivery Center [1-800-3-HA-WORTH; 9:00 a.m. - 5:00 p.m. (EST)].

World's Languages offers "a complete classification of the world's roughly 5,000 languages."[1] George L. Campbell points out in the introduction to his *Compendium of the World's Languages* that some languages are spoken by millions, others by thousands, and some by only hundreds.[2] In her article on American Indian languages in this volume, Mary Russell Bucknum discusses a 1953 survey that identified languages spoken by even fewer than 100 people, some by fewer than ten, and a handful by only one or two persons.

As the last speakers of these languages die, so also do the languages. Other factors, in addition, affect how many of these languages will become "dead." The prognosis is not good. Nancy Morris states in her article that linguists predict that 90 percent of the world's languages will disappear within a century because of what Pacific language expert George Grace has called the "growing world monoculture."

A major difficulty in the planning of this special collection of *Languages of the World: Cataloging Issues and Problems* was to determine which language groups or individual languages as well as what types of libraries should be featured. I believe that the result is an excellent mixture of major groupings, which can include hundreds of languages (e.g., languages of Africa, of Central and Southeast Asia, of Eastern Europe, of the Pacific, and American Indian languages), of small groupings (e.g., languages of India, classical languages, and Arabic, Persian, and Turkish), and of individual languages (e.g., Icelandic, Hebrew, and Spanish). In addition, the perspective of national and public libraries is represented: the National Library of Canada, which is officially bilingual; the Bibliothèque Nationale to illustrate a library where English is not the first language; and the Cleveland Public Library, which serves a large number of ethnic constituencies.[3]

The articles in this volume cover virtually the entire world. As far as I know, no other single volume is as broad in scope. Mohammed M. Aman edited a valuable collection of articles, published in 1980, on cataloging and classifying non-Western works.[4] The major focus of this volume, however, is languages of Africa and Asia; it also includes an article on Slavic publications. It predates the adoption of *AACR2* and widespread use of local online systems. Catalogers today face a broad range of issues which were unknown or unfamiliar little more than a decade ago.

Special effort has been made in this volume to avoid the use of the term "foreign languages." One certainly cannot call American Indian or native Alaskan languages or the Hawaiian language "foreign." Canadians would offend a large part of their population if they were to speak of French as a "foreign" language. India has seventeen official languages. Which of these are "foreign?"

Marie Zielinska, Chief of the Multilingual Biblioservice at the National Library of Canada, has praised ALA's efforts to eliminate language that is sexist, racist, or otherwise biased. "But one area has been totally overlooked. It is the use of the expression 'foreign language' in relation to collections in languages other than English. It is repeatedly used both in ALA and other library journals, in library nomenclature and daily professional jargon without any notice that it is biased and smacks of the supposedly long eliminated policy of the 'melting pot.'"[5] Zielinska offers as alternatives a wide array of terms that includes "ethnic," "minority," "language of origin," "ancestral," "non-official," "heritage," or "community" languages and suggests that ALA should lead the fight to eliminate "the last bastion of the old-fashioned 'waspishness' in library technology."[6]

The eighteen articles in this issue cover a variety of issues in diverse ways. The comments and observations that follow are not intended to include all the points discussed in the articles. My intention is to highlight many of the sorts of problems with which catalogers deal on a daily basis.

LANGUAGE ISSUES

What Language Is It?

Most catalogers work with languages with which they are familiar. What do catalogers do, however, when they have no idea what languages they have before them? This problem is common for materials from many parts of the world. Ann Bein discusses the problem that Africana catalogers face on a regular basis: What language is this? Nancy Morris and Mary Russell Bucknum also describe the puzzling array of unfamiliar languages that catalogers encounter when dealing with Pacific and American Indian languages.

Large Africana collections can include materials in hundreds of vernacular languages. Bein directs her essay to catalogers with little or no expertise in these languages. She offers clues to identifying certain languages by examination of orthography, diacritics, or special letters or letter combinations. One of the helpful appendices in her article lists languages by place of publication.

Pacific-area languages present problems similar to African languages in that few American catalogers are familiar with them. Although some catalogers might recognize the Hawaiian or Maori languages, it is unlikely that many have even heard of such languages as Chamorro, Kapingama-rangi, or Puluwat. Morris presents background material on the three major language groups of Melanesia, Micronesia, and Polynesia. In addition, she offers advice and suggests reference sources to aid in the cataloging of these largely unknown languages and particularly emphasizes that "cata-logers have an important social role to play in documenting, preserving, and providing proper access to the Pacific island language materials that pass through their charge."

In her discussion of American Indian languages, Bucknum identifies a different type of problem. Languages often have to be determined by listen-ing to spoken or musical recordings. The sound quality of early recordings exacerbates the problem. If collectors of these field recordings were non-linguists, their notes often eliminated mention of the language(s) on the recordings. Yet it is essential that these recordings with such languages as Siksika (or Blackfoot), Nez Perce, or Chukchansi be preserved and cata-loged since they contain a wealth of unique information.

Bilingual Cataloging

As the library for an officially bilingual country, the National Library of Canada (NLC) must provide cataloging records in English or French and sometimes in English and French. There are even situations when as many as four bibliographic records might be prepared for the same item. Virgin-ia Ballance states in her essay, however, that NLC does not maintain a truly bilingual catalog. Technological enhancements of NLC's automated system DOBIS makes complete double cataloging unnecessary. The sys-tem contains a built-in language equivalence relationship that links both English and French bibliographic or authority records online. The catalog user, for example, can input a subject search in either French or English and retrieve records in both languages.

This type of technological advancement could resolve the difficulties that non-native speakers of English often encounter in using library cata-logs. Marielena Fina describes her experience and frustration as a Spanish-speaking patron wishing subject access to information. She cites models such as *Bilindex*, a bilingual Spanish-English subject heading list based on *LCSH*, as a means to promote subject access.

Not so easy to remedy, on the other hand, are situations where models such as *Bilindex* do not exist. Libraries with large ethnic constituencies have patrons who experience the same frustration that Fina describes. Ballance, for example, describes the Multilingual Biblioservice (MBS), which operates within the Public Services Branch of the National Library of Canada. The MBS provides materials in thirty-two heritage languages spoken in Canada. Edward Seely describes in his article the forty-five separate language collections within the Cleveland Public Library. Bilingual access to materials in each of these languages, however, is, at least for the near future, an unattainable goal.

PUBLICATION ISSUES

The history of publication in certain countries affects the work of the cataloger. Kerry A. Keck and Barbara Stewart describe the cataloging of non-English government publications in developing countries. Third World countries often have poor internal bibliographic control, which in turn hinders acquisition of materials and also restricts sources of information that are used to catalog these items. Bein also mentions the same problem with African publications, which are often small editions from small presses. By the time libraries learn of the existence of such items, they are usually out of print and unavailable. Furthermore, national libraries in these countries either do not exist or, if they do, are so underfunded that bibliographic control is not possible.

AUTHORITY WORK

Many of the authors in this volume discuss name authority problems. Bein gives an excellent description of the difficulties that catalogers encounter with African names. They can be forenames, simple or compound surnames, include patronymics or honorifics, have indigenous, European, and/or Islamic elements, contain animal names, plant names, or names of things, indicate caste, ethnic affiliation, place of origin, birth order, day or month of birth, or genealogy. They can be entered under first element, medial, or last element and can consist of one or many elements. The cataloger who does not know African languages often faces a monumental task in determining how to handle certain names, whose rules of entry can vary from language to language and from country to country.

Usha Bhasker describes some of the problems confronting the cataloger of materials from India. There are seventeen official languages in a variety of scripts. Certain name elements can be honorifics, enclitics, suffixes, or can stand alone. It is common in classical Sanskrit for multiple authors to have the same name. Modern headings, likewise, present a multitude of problems. Westernization and transliteration of names often result in large numbers of variants. Authors who write in English or who become known in the West, for example, can have many variant forms of names. Bhasker includes an appendix that gives a sampling of Indian names with their variants.

Catalogers of Tibetan and Mongolian materials often have little more than the items in hand on which to base headings. Michael Walter discusses the problems of cataloging works in these languages where there are virtually no vernacular reference sources. Authors' names change with initiation into new spiritual levels, but it is almost unknown to identify together all of an author's writings based on each name used. With Mongolian materials, also, there are few reference works for literary and scholarly writers.

From Central Asia we move to a discussion of names in Iceland. Martha Crowe defines the legal requirements for Icelandic names, which have varied greatly over the years in the way in which they have been established. Iceland produces more books per capita than any other country in the world and provides thorough and reliable bibliographic and biographical resources to support cataloging operations. Conflicts with multiple occurrences of the same name can usually be easily resolved.

The Bibliothèque Nationale (BN) provides different levels of fullness in authority records for French and non-French headings. Nicole Simon and Monique Choudey describe the procedures at BN where complete authority records are created for French names. BN's local system automatically generates incomplete authorities from the 1XX fields in the bibliographic records for non-French headings. There are, however, exceptions to this policy. Full records are routinely created for compound names, for authors writing in non-roman scripts, for non-unique headings, and for names appearing to be based on non-roman scripts (e.g., a Vietnamese name for an author who is really French). In addition, if the library receives works in French by authors with incomplete authority records, those records will be upgraded to full level.

The bilingual requirements of the National Library of Canada (NLC) demand that all language-specific access points in authority records be established both in English and French. Furthermore, NLC makes certain exceptions to the usual Anglo-American procedures. For example, naturally inverted names such as Vietnamese, Japanese, Chinese, or Hungarian are established without insertion of commas between surname-forename elements.

Corporate and jurisdictional headings have been discussed in articles by William McCloy and Keck and Stewart. McCloy describes the almost overwhelming confusion in trying to distinguish among the seven different LC headings for the various governments on the Chinese mainland and for the provincial government of Taiwan. Keck and Stewart, in their examination of corporate names for government documents, note that frequent reorganization of governments, with resulting name changes, occurs not only because of political upheaval but also often by design.

DESCRIPTIVE CATALOGING

Lack of Chief Sources of Information

Special formats lacking title pages or other chief sources of information often require creativity on the part of the cataloger to describe the items in hand. Since the field recordings of American Indian languages described by Bucknum do not have titles, the Archives of Traditional Music at Indiana University has devised a consistent approach to information for the title field in bibliographic records. Titles are derived based on the geographic and cultural description of the recordings; these titles begin with countries, including states or provinces, cities or villages, culture groups and dates of recordings.

Uniform Titles

Crowe describes the need for additional authority work for uniform titles for Old Norse, or Old Icelandic, literature. Works of this period from the ninth through the fifteenth centuries are usually of unknown authorship and thus require uniform titles. Although uniform titles do exist for large numbers of these early works, authorities are lacking for numerous parts of the Eddas.

When the same languages are written in different scripts (e.g., Serbian and Croatian), there are special problems with uniform titles. In describing this problem, Walter uses as an example a text written both in Cyrillic-script Uzbek and in Arabic-script Uzbek. This situation is likely to become even more confusing as former Soviet republics adopt new scripts. Walter notes that he has already seen Arabic-script works in former Cyrillic-script languages such as Kazakh and Azerbaijani.

Keck and Stewart detail the frustration of dealing with non-unique titles and frequent title changes in government publication serials–a situation, unfortunately, not unique to government documents.

Calendars and Dating

Non-Western calendars and dating systems present a special challenge to catalogers. Edward Jajko describes four different systems with which the Middle Eastern cataloger must be familiar: Gregorian calendar, Muslim calendar, Iranian calendar, and Turkish civil calendar.

SUBJECT CATALOGING

Several authors address issues of subject cataloging. LC subject headings are often inadequate for libraries that have major collections in certain areas. Some believe that subject headings are confusing, and others feel that headings are biased. There are special problems with bilingual cataloging.

The Cornell University Libraries have the largest collection of Icelandic materials in the United States and the world's largest collection of non-Icelandic works on Icelandic subjects and of translations of Icelandic and Old Norse literature. For this reason Cornell has, for example, expanded the range of period sub-divisions under **ICELAND–HISTORY, ICELAND–POLITICS AND GOVERNMENT,** and **ICELAND–DESCRIPTION AND TRAVEL.**

The unique nature of the extensive collection of field recordings of American Indian languages in the Indiana University Archives of Traditional Music (ATM) requires broader subject coverage than can be provided by such standard LC headings as **SONGS, ARAPAHO.** The ATM supplements these headings with their own list of genre terms such as **HEALING SONGS, EAGLE DANCE,** etc.

For Central Asian materials, subject headings are usually adequate except for Tibetan works. The Tibetan collections in the Indiana University Libraries support one of the few Ph.D. programs in Tibetan in the United States, and bibliographic records often include expanded subject access. Buddhist literature is one area for which LC does not provide adequate subject analysis. There is frequent inconsistency and lack of specificity in headings dealing with Buddhism.

One area of unending confusion is with subject headings dealing with India and with American Indians. Bhasker proposes a number of changes to resolve this confusion. She suggests, for example, that **EAST INDIANS** become **ASIAN INDIANS** and that **INDIANS OF NORTH AMERICA** become **NATIVE AMERICANS (NORTH AMERICA).** Adjectival designations such as **INDIAN** and **INDIC** often result in incorrect subject headings. **COOKERY, INDIAN,** for example, is intended to describe Native American cooking but has also been widely used in database records to describe cooking of India. Bhasker also suggests that **INDIC LITERATURE (ENGLISH)** be changed to **INDO-ENGLISH LITERATURE,** a term which is widely used in India and by Indian authors throughout the world.

LC has made great strides in recent years to eliminate bias and ethnocentrism in subject headings. There is, however, still work to be done. Fina laments the use of the term **LIBRARIES AND THE SOCIALLY HANDICAPPED** to describe materials for non-native speakers of English. As discussed above, Marie Zielinska comments at length on LC's use of the term **FOREIGN LANGUAGES**. On the other hand, Nancy Morris thanks LC for dropping the pejorative term **BECHE-DE-MER JARGON** and substituting **BISLAMA LANGUAGE**.

A non-equivalent relationship that may exist between English and French headings creates special problems for the National Library of Canada. Topical headings in English, for example, may become geographic headings in French. Headings in one language may require two headings in the other language; for example, **ORFEVRES** in French becomes **GOLDSMITHS** and **SILVERSMITHS** in English.

CLASSIFICATION

Discussions of classification focus primarily on inadequate or non-existent schedules for certain areas. Jajko, for example, notes particularly three problem areas in classification: history of Palestinian Arabs, Persian and Turkish literature, and Islamic law. Islamic law, especially, needs development. As one of the main pillars of Islamic principles, materials on Islamic law constitute a vast corpus of literature on this subject.

Because of its extensive collections of Islandica, Cornell has expanded on LC's single class number for nineteenth and twentieth century works of individual authors. Cornell uses a range of four numbers including further division with a series of decimal numbers for individual authors. Another area needing expansion is the PL schedule for certain Central Asian languages such as Kazakh, Kirghiz, and Tatar where the literatures of entire languages have only single cutter numbers.

George Johnston has prepared a detailed analysis of the PA schedule for Greek and Latin literature. For classifying classical literature, LC makes a distinction between language and subject of text. A Greek text of a philosophical work by Aristotle, for example, is classed in PA whereas a translation of the same text is classed in B. Likewise, a Greek text of Hippocrates is in PA and a translation in R. Johnston analyzes the impact that this policy has on classical literature collections in libraries.

In a similar vein, materials in lesser known African languages are often classified in PL8000+ regardless of subject matter. A botany text in Bozo, for example, might be classed in PL8087 in the belief that the work is more important because of the language rather than the subject matter of the text. Some libraries might include a subject heading to provide language access: **BOZO LANGUAGE–TEXTS.** Classifying such materials in PL is also a means of making many African texts available when catalogers, who do not know the languages, cannot determine the subject matter.

TRANSLITERATION

A majority of the authors in this volume speak about transliteration issues. A wide range of topics includes systematic romanization versus commonly known forms of names, availability of online access to vernacular scripts, lack of standardized romanization for some languages, problems with different transliterations for the same language, and difficulties that library patrons have with romanized bibliographic records.

Bhasker discusses a major problem for personal names in India. Systematic romanization according to transliteration tables often varies greatly from forms of names that have become widely known and accepted. She notes also that there are LC transliteration tables for twenty-one scripts of India including Arabic, Tibetan, and Urdu. Because of the variety of languages and scripts, uniformity of rules is impossible. Catalogers must not only consider each language individually but must also consider early, medieval, and modern names separately within each language.

Although minor inaccuracies do exist for diacritics in certain languages, she feels that existing tables are for the most part precise, thorough, and accurate. These languages do rely heavily on diacritics because of the abundance of retroflex and long vowel sounds in the languages. The diacritics, furthermore, result in a considerable decrease in database input time.

Heidi Lerner discusses the results of a survey of academic and Judaica libraries in the United States to determine policies about vernacular versus romanized records for Hebrew-script materials. She analyzes the arguments for and against romanization. Future directions that will influence the vernacular/romanization debate, according to Lerner, include the use of the Internet as a cataloging tool, exchange of American and Israeli cataloging, cooperative cataloging arrangements among American libraries, and multi-script capability in American online systems.

Walter details the difficulty of romanizing languages for which there are no transliteration tables. To catalog a large set of dictionaries, grammars, and other works in Manchu, for example, he was forced to improvise and adapt romanization from a standard Manchu-English dictionary. Walter must also at times deal with incomplete tables. Although there is a transliteration table for Mongolian, it lacks equivalents for some letters used in Inner Mongolia.

Catalogers of Middle Eastern materials, however, need more than just transliteration tables. Whereas one should theoretically be able to romanize most non-roman scripts by following the appropriate table, catalogers of Arabic, Persian, Ottoman Turkish, or Hebrew must have thorough knowledge of the languages and be able to determine the meaning of words from the context. These languages do not have written vowels, which must be supplied in romanization. Incorrect vocalization can affect not only the meaning of a text but also retrievability in an online or card catalog.

Another difficulty is the variety of local usages within the Arab world; certain letters are written differently, for example, in the Maghreb, the Levant, or Egypt. Jajko also notes that a main problem with Persian is that LC has chosen to romanize it as if it were Arabic. Ottoman Turkish has its own special problems, according to Jajko, because the Arabic alphabet is totally unsuited to the Turkish language.

Different transliteration schemes for the same language can lead to mass confusion. McCloy notes the differences between the standard Wade-Giles romanization for Chinese, used in the United States and Canada, and pinyin romanization, used in the rest of the world. An example is the word for **China**. In Wade-Giles it is romanized **Chung-kuo** and in pinyin as **Zhongguo**.

If one is not familiar with the different romanizations and policies on word division, it is easy to see that the catalog user might be unable to locate records in the database and assume that they do not exist. Since Chinese is not an alphabetic language, its romanization is based on pronunciation; the problem here is that there are hundreds of dialects and regional accents in China. The library user is not well served when faced with retrieving a record in romanization. Fe Susan Go confirms that romanized records create great difficulties. She notes, for example, the dilemma confronting a Burmese or a Thai or a Khmer when trying to read their own languages in transliteration.

Libraries handle non-roman script languages in different ways. Many OCLC and RLIN libraries, for example, have special terminals to provide access to Chinese, Japanese, and Korean. Lerner points out that a number of libraries is using Hebrew script in online records. With technological advancements more and more vernacular scripts will be available on line. The Bibliothèque Nationale awaits these advancements in its future automation system. Books in non-roman scripts acquired by purchase, gift, or exchange at BN are still cataloged manually on cards in the vernacular scripts because, as Simon and Choudey state, they well know "the Tower of Babel that can result from works in transliteration only." There is, however, an exception to this policy. Works acquired on legal deposit are transliterated for input into the *Bibliographie nationale française* and into BN's local system.

Ballance states that the first principle of cataloging in the Multilingual Biblioservice (MBS) at the National Library of Canada is to provide bibliographic records in language and script of publication. MBS has developed a system interface that allows access to data in non-roman scripts. Scripts currently available are Greek, Cyrillic, Arabic, Devanagari (Hindi), and Gurmukhi (Panjabi). In development are Urdu, Gujarati, Chinese, and Japanese. Main entries and titles in bibliographic records are transliterated and provided in note fields.

The Cleveland Public Library, on the other hand, provides no vernacular access to its non-roman script languages. Materials at CPL are arranged separately by language where patrons can browse in small collections. The library relies on its staff to know the collections in order to serve its users.

BACKLOGS

Backlogs, according to Jacqueline Byrd, are like death and taxes; they are inevitable. She speaks of backlogs in Slavic and East European languages and the non-Slavic languages of the former Soviet Union. Backlogs in these languages have grown because there has not been sufficient staff to deal with them and because catalogers often have to deal with a multitude of languages which they do not know.

Susan Go has another viewpoint on the growth of backlogs, especially in Southeast Asian materials. She states that catalogers are so obsessed with rules and so concerned with doing "perfect" cataloging that they are willing to allow unprocessed materials to accumulate in backlogs to the point of being unable to be stored.

COOPERATIVE AND SHARED CATALOGING

Byrd proposes a detailed plan for cooperative cataloging of Slavic materials. She discusses goals and division of responsibilities and compares the plan to existing NCCP and CONSER programs. Following the CONSER model, participants would determine standards and how all libraries, regardless of bibliographic utility used, would benefit from the cataloging. Agreed upon standards would mean greater sharing of others' cataloging.

Go argues for greater cooperation in the area of Southeast Asian studies. Cooperation so far has been primarily in collection development. She states that actual technical cooperation is often stimulated from outside sources and cites as an example a grant for cataloging of Vietnamese materials. A project known as the Vietnam Union Catalog resulted from cooperation between the Committee on Research Materials on Southeast Asia (CORMOSEA) and the Australian National Library.

Shared cataloging is another topic on which Go has strong feelings. Libraries must be more accepting of cataloging from other institutions. Too many libraries are suspicious of all cataloging except their own. Until this attitude changes, she says, libraries will continue to founder under the weight of their backlogs.

Libraries do take advantage of the work of their colleagues in other libraries, especially when those institutions have outstanding collections in certain areas. Morris cites the University of Hawaii Pacific Collection, the most comprehensive collection of Pacific Island language materials in any American library, as an example.

COLLECTION-LEVEL CATALOGING

Richard Phillips describes a project at the University of Colorado Libraries to catalog a large collection of Spanish-language plays. Approximately 3700 plays were processed using the archival and manuscripts control format. Phillips recommends this approach for libraries that have collections with limited accessibility but do not have the resources to provide full cataloging.

MINIMAL-LEVEL CATALOGING

Minimal-level cataloging (MLC) is widely used in a variety of libraries. Go states that the University of Michigan Libraries are comfortable with minimal-level cataloging of Southeast Asian materials. She believes that the need to move materials from backlogs to library shelves outweighs the arguments of librarians who argue that MLC denigrates the profession and impairs patron access. She also argues that keyword searching provides adequate access. National libraries, too, use minimal-level cataloging. The Bibliothèque Nationale routinely uses MLC for non-French books. Simon and Choudey note that the MLC standard used at the Bibliothèque Nationale is widely used in academic and public libraries in France. Finally, the Cleveland Public Library also uses minimal-level cataloging for certain categories of materials. MLC records are created for fiction and for nonfiction of minor research value.

CONCLUSION

The authors in this volume have taken a varied approach to their subjects. Major issues and problems in cataloging are discussed in beneficial and informative ways. Some essays from academic libraries provide broad discussions, and others give a narrow focus to language-specific topics. Articles from national and public libraries not only relate issues that are unique to their operations but also examine issues that all libraries have in common. This collection asks and answers many questions. It gives advice on how to answer certain questions. It leaves some questions unanswered and makes proposals for further discussion and resolution.

NOTES

1. Merritt Ruhlen, *A Guide to the World's Languages*, 3 vols. (Stanford, Calif.: Stanford University Press, 1987), 1:1.
2. George L. Campbell, *Compendium of the World's Languages*, 2 vols. (London: Routledge, 1991), 1:vii.
3. The original plans for this volume included an article from the University of Malaya to give the perspective of a non-Western library. The article, unfortunately, did not materialize.
4. Mohammed M. Aman, ed., *Cataloging and Classification of Non-Western Material: Concerns, Issues, and Practices* (Phoenix: Oryx Press, 1980).
5. Marie Zielinska, "Collections in 'Foreign Languages'–Foreign? For Whom?: A Discussion Paper," *EMIE* [Ethnic Materials Information Exchange] *Bulletin* 9:4 (Summer 1992): 4. I wish to thank Virginia Ballance of the National Library of Canada for providing this citation.
6. Ibid.

SPECIFIC LANGUAGES
OR GROUPS OF LANGUAGES

Cataloging Field Recordings
of American Indian Languages

Mary Russell Bucknum

SUMMARY. Cataloging field recordings of American Indian languages presents many challenges. The cataloger may deal with antiquated physical formats as well as with problems determining contents and applying appropriate subject headings. The Archives of Traditional Music (ATM) at Indiana University, Bloomington, is a repository of such recordings and has been cataloging them on OCLC since 1983. A general description of the ATM precedes a discussion of two specific collections that exemplify the recordings held at the Archives as well as some of the difficulties inherent in cataloging such materials.

Mary Russell Bucknum is Associate Director/Librarian of the Archives of Traditional Music at Indiana University, Bloomington.

The author wishes to thank David Bucknum, Terry Chasteen, Marilyn Graf, Karen Jung, and Richard Torgerson for their assistance.

[Haworth co-indexing entry note]: "Cataloging Field Recordings of American Indian Languages." Bucknum, Mary Russell. Co-published simultaneously in *Cataloging & Classification Quarterly* (The Haworth Press, Inc.) Vol. 17, No. 1/2, 1993, pp. 15-27; and: *Languages of the World: Cataloging Issues and Problems* (ed: Martin D. Joachim) The Haworth Press, Inc., 1993, pp. 15-27. Multiple copies of this article/chapter may be purchased from The Haworth Document Delivery Center [1-800-3-HAWORTH; 9:00 a.m. - 5:00 p.m. (EST)].

15

INTRODUCTION AND HISTORY

The Archives of Traditional Music at Indiana University is the largest university-based ethnographic sound archives in the United States. Its holdings cover a wide range of cultural and geographical areas and include commercial and field recordings of vocal and instrumental music, folktales, interviews, and oral history, as well as videotapes, photographs, and manuscripts. As a research and teaching facility, the Archives serves a wide community of scholars, students, musicians, and teachers, on campus and throughout the world.

The underlying intellectual structure of the Archives reflects the vision of its founder, George Herzog (1901-1983), Hungarian-born anthropologist, linguist, and ethnomusicologist. Herzog was educated in Budapest and Berlin, where he served as an assistant to Erich M. von Hornbostel at the Berlin Phonogramm-Archiv during the early 1920s. He studied at Columbia University under Franz Boas and conducted fieldwork with Native Americans in the southwestern United States for the American Museum of Natural History and in Liberia for the University of Chicago. Herzog's synthesis of the Berlin school of comparative musicology (with its focus on detailed and systematic analysis of music sound) and American ethnology (characterized by careful attention to field observation and historical processes) became the foundation for the emerging discipline of ethnomusicology.

Herzog regarded archiving as an essential ingredient for the development of an American school of comparative musicology. During the 1930s he undertook a survey of collections of recordings of folk and primitive music for the American Council of Learned Societies. With support from Franz Boas, Herzog began to assemble the Archives of Folk and Primitive Music at Columbia University, using recordings that were based on his own work and on the work of colleagues in the field. When he joined the faculty of Indiana University as a professor of anthropology in 1948, he brought this collection with him. Subsequent directors have been George List, Frank Gillis, Anthony Seeger, and the current director, Ruth M. Stone.

Since the arrival of the first collections of sound recordings in 1948, the Archives holdings have grown to include 7,000 cylinders, 250 wires, 3,700 cassettes, 70,000 discs, 35,000 tape reels and 250 video tapes, representing over 200,000 hours of recording time. Listening copies are available for approximately 65 percent of the cataloged recordings. In addition to the audio-visual recordings, the collections include original manuscripts, transcriptions, correspondence, and field material from a number of early collectors, as well as pamphlets, articles, piano rolls, linguistic slip files, photographs and slides, films, computer storage media, historic recording devices, and books.

Archives holdings document the history of ethnographic sound recording from early wax cylinders made during museum expeditions in the 1890s to recent commercial releases on compact disc. The core of the collection consists of 1,800 field (non-commercial) collections, unique and irreplaceable material recorded in many of the world's culture areas. Extensive holdings of Native American, African, and Latin American music and spoken word and several large collections of early jazz and blues 78s reflect the research interests of the faculty and students at Indiana University.

Important historic collections include cylinders from the Edward S. Curtis Collection of American Indian Music, the Berthold Laufer Collection of cylinders made in China in 1901-1902, the George Herzog Collection, the Laura Boulton Collection, Hoagy Carmichael memorabilia, and linguistic data from the Archives of the Languages of the World. Collectors such as Franz Boas, Edward Sapir, George Dorsey, Helen Roberts, and Alan Lomax are well represented.

The Archives Listening Library provides audio and video workstations for public use. The ATM began cataloging all new acquisitions on OCLC in 1983. In 1986 and 1988, grant funding was obtained from the National Endowment for the Humanities for retrospective cataloging of all field collections. All collections are entered into OCLC and downloaded to Information Online (IO), the NOTIS-based Indiana University library system. Access to the collection is facilitated by a card catalog (closed in 1990) and two terminals for IO. When patrons locate material of interest in the catalog or database, they are provided with listening copies dubbed from the original recording in either reel-to-reel or cassette format and printed documentation to accompany the recordings. Original recordings are shelved in the vault according to format and accession number. No Library of Congress classification scheme is used.

GRINNELL COLLECTION (1897-1898)

This paper will focus on the cataloging and processing of Native American field recordings found at the Archives of Traditional Music. The Archives collection includes both music and spoken word recordings of American Indians. As examples, I shall discuss two of our collections[1] in detail: the George Bird Grinnell collection and the Morris Swadesh Penutian Vocabulary Survey collection, a part of the Voegelin Archives of the Languages of the World (ALW).[2]

George Bird Grinnell recorded at least fifty wax cylinders of Siksika, Cheyenne, and Arapaho materials between 1897 and 1898 in Montana. Grinnell, best known for his work as a naturalist, is credited with founding the first chapter of what came to be known as the National Audubon Society. Traveling throughout the West in search of fossils, Grinnell came in contact with and recorded various Native Americans over a span of forty years.

The documentation for Grinnell's collection of recordings is generally complete. Information taken from cylinder box inscriptions, occasional spoken announcements on the actual recordings, and entries in the American Museum of Natural History Phonograph Recordings Catalog help to identify genres, dates, and informants' names. There are, however, significant problems in matching the information to the proper cylinder. "The collector's numbers are not consecutive and, through the years, some cylinders were placed in the wrong boxes."[3]

The lack of reliable information to describe field recordings is a common concern. Field recordings do not come with chief sources of information. Sometimes they contain little or no information whatsoever! Cylinder box inscriptions, recorded announcements, or collectors' field notes should all be considered as chief sources of information. Aside from these primary sources, any additional information is helpful, even if it comes from a recording technician. Conflicting information sometimes surfaces, especially with older collections. When this occurs, listening to the recording may help to clarify the confusion. Major discrepancies may be listed in the notes area.

Also, field recordings do not have titles. In order to provide some useful and consistent information for the title field, the Archives of Traditional Music derives a title based on the geographic and cultural description of the recording–beginning with the country, and including state or province, city or village, culture group, and date of recording. For instance, one of Grinnell's collections has received the following title: [United States, Montana, Piegan Agency, Blackfoot Indians, 1897] (see Figure 1). This pattern for deriving a title is loosely based on George Murdoch's *Outline of World Cultures*[4] and has been used at the ATM since 1955.

Describing the physical characteristics of these early recordings can also be challenging. Most of the ATM's earliest recordings of Native Americans are on cylinders. Cylinder recordings (ca. 1890-1920) were made on a simple, easily portable, spring-driven mechanism (see Photo). Cylinder machines were not regulated to operate at a specific speed. Most machines recorded at between 120 and 160 rotations per minute. If the machines were not frequently rewound between recordings, a cylinder would begin to slow down, even in the middle of a song. Hence, when played back, the pitch steadily rises throughout the song, providing a false representation of the actual song.

Later, electrically-driven cylinder machines with variable speed could sometimes compensate for this pitch problem. It is, however, often difficult to determine the correct speed of cylinders, especially if the music is unfamiliar. We continue to find cylinders in the ATM collection which were, at one time, misidentified due to improper play-back speed. Songs

Cylinder machine, early 1900's

FIGURE 1. Record for one of Grinnell's collections

```
OCLC: 15087409          Rec stat:  c
Entered:  19870119      Replaced:  19930303      Used:  19870119
Type: j      Bib lvl: c      Source: d      Lang: bla
Repr:        Enc lvl: I       Format: n      Ctry: xx
Accomp: z    Mod rec:         Comp: fm       LTxt:
Desc: a      Int lvl:         Dat tp: s      Dates: 1897, ¶

▲ 1  040     IJZ ǂc IJZ ¶
▲ 2  007     s ǂb e ǂd i ǂe a ǂf s ǂg s ǂh n ǂi n ǂj i ǂk w ǂl h ǂm n ǂn ¶
▲ 3  033 0   189710-- ǂb 4250 ¶
▲ 4  041 0   ǂd bla ǂg eng ¶
▲ 5  043     n-us-mt ¶
▲ 6  090     ǂb ¶
▲ 7  049     IULA ¶
▲ 8  245 00  [United States, Montana, Piegan Agency, Blackfoot Indians, 1897]
   ǂh sound recording / ǂc collected by George Bird Grinnell. ¶
▲ 9  300     25 cylinders : ǂb 150 rpm, coarse groove ; ǂc 2 1/8 in. x 4 1/4
   in. + ǂe documentation ¶
▲ 10 500     Blackfoot songs and music. ¶
▲ 11 511 0   Performed by George Starr, Black-Looks, Cross-Guns, Jim White-
   Calf, Rides-at-the-Door, Wipes-His-Eyes, Chews-Black-Bones, Mrs. Ground and
   Mary Evans. ¶
▲ 12 518     Recorded by Grinnell in October, 1897 at Piegan Agency, Montana;
   sound quality fair. ¶
▲ 13 500     Accompanied by item description sheets; listed in Dorothy Sara
   Lee, Native North American Music and Oral Data (I.U. Press, 1979) and Indiana
   University, Bloomington, Archives of Traditional Music, Early Field Recordings
   (I.U. Press, 1987). ¶
```

▲ 14 500   Deposited at the Archives of Traditional Music by the American Museum of Natural History under Option 2. ¶
▲ 15 505 0 Parted Hair Society dance songs -- Women's love song -- War song -- Smoking song of beaver medicine -- Three lizard songs, diving duck songs, scalping songs from beaver medicine -- Crow and Piegan water songs from beaver medicine -- Sioux song and two camp songs -- Crazy Dog Society songs -- Wolf song -- Songs sung during building of medicine lodge -- Fox trapping songs -- Cree dance song -- Bull dance -- Eagle dance -- Social gathering (tea dance) songs -- War party songs -- Beaver pipe and medicine songs -- Two weasel songs -- Dance songs -- Piegan tea songs -- Blacktail Deer Society songs -- French, English and Italian songs sung on test cylinders by collector. ¶
▲ 16 650 0 Siksika Indians. ¶
▲ 17 650 0 War songs ‡z Montana. ¶
▲ 18 650 0 Hunting songs ‡z Montana. ¶
▲ 19 650 0 Love songs, Siksika. ¶
▲ 20 651 0 Montana. ¶
▲ 21 700 00 Black-Looks. ¶
▲ 22 700 00 Cross-Guns. ¶
▲ 23 700 00 Rides-at-the-Door. ¶
▲ 24 700 00 Wipes-His-Eyes. ¶
▲ 25 700 00 Chews-Black-Bones. ¶
▲ 26 700 20 White Calf, James. ¶
▲ 27 700 20 Ground, ‡c Mrs. ¶
▲ 28 700 10 Evans, Mary. ¶
▲ 29 700 10 Starr, George. ¶
▲ 30 700 10 Grinnell, George Bird, ‡d 1849-1938. ¶
▲ 31 710 20 American Museum of Natural History. ¶
▲ 32 710 20 Indiana University, Bloomington. ‡b Archives of Traditional Music. ¶

labeled as being sung by one sex are often, in reality, sung by the opposite sex. Thus the cylinder was being played back either too fast or too slowly.

Once the physical attributes of the recording have been identified, one must realize that, with the publication of *AACR2*, rules for cylinder description have been dropped. Rules for cataloging cylinders are available in *AACR1*. The Association for Recorded Sound Collections has published a set of guidelines for applying *AACR2* to sound recordings.[5] This publication does specifically address cylinders and suggests describing them with four measurements: outside diameter, inside diameter at edge, inside diameter at runoff, and length. For example, a cylinder might be described as follows: 5.5 cm × 4.7 cm × 4.4 cm × 10.5 cm. These measurements are in centimeters even though other sound recordings are described in inches. However, the ATM provides physical description in inches for the outside diameter and length of the cylinder only.

Once the physical characteristics of the cylinders have been determined, one can begin to analyze the content of the material recorded. Assigning a culture group heading to a collection is not always as simple and straightforward as it might at first seem. Library of Congress subject headings for culture groups do not always correspond to names used by field collectors or even by the groups themselves. For example, Grinnell uses **BLACKFOOT INDIANS**, while the proper LC heading is **SIKSIKA INDIANS**. When a term used in the documentation does not correspond with any LC heading or cross-reference, additional research is necessary. Murdoch's *Outline* provides alternate names and groupings of cultures and has often been helpful for determining the correct LC headings. It is also likely that field collectors have written and published monographs or dissertations on their research. If one can find books or bibliographic records for the written material, one might use the same subject headings for the recordings as applied to the written material.

Many culture groups, including Native Americans, borrow materials from other groups. For instance, a Cheyenne Indian may sing a song of Arapaho origin. Although the heading, **SONGS, ARAPAHO** is applicable, it is important for scholars of culture to be aware of this cross-cultural borrowing. I have often been questioned about using this heading by those who consider it to be misleading. While I do not consider it to be misleading, I have always attempted, in the contents or note field, to indicate when material of one culture group is performed by members of another group.

Assigning anything other than very general headings for intellectual content can be difficult. *LCSH* provides the standard headings **SONGS, ARAPAHO** or **ARAPAHO INDIANS–RITES AND CEREMONIES**, etc. Traditional Native American music does not have song titles in the same sense that popular music does. Songs are grouped, instead, by genre categories, such as **GREEN CORN SONGS, HEALING SONGS, EAGLE DANCE**, etc. Because its collection of Native American music is so extensive, the ATM finds it useful to provide local subject access via such genre terms.

Some Native American materials may be of a sensitive nature and may need to be restricted. Some songs were intended to be heard only by members of the same family or tribe, while other songs were meant to be heard by members of one sex or the other, or are appropriate to specific times of the day or year. Unfortunately, examples of recorded materials which were obtained under false pretenses do exist. Archivists and librarians should became aware of these ethical issues, be familiar with the recordings in their collections, and treat all materials with appropriate respect.

SWADESH PENUTIAN SURVEY (1953)

The Penutian Vocabulary Survey, conducted by Morris Swadesh, presents for the cataloger some of the same challenges found in the Grinnell Collection and some different ones (see Figure 2). Generally containing spoken rather than sung materials, the Swadesh collection does not present the same ethical concerns as songs and rituals but is challenging to analyze and describe. Recorded on reel-to-reel tape in 1953, the Penutian survey compared vocabulary of twenty-two west coast American Indian languages, to see how closely they were related. Morris Swadesh and his assistant, Robert Melton, visited Washington, Oregon, and northern California to study the languages which the linguist Edward Sapir had classified as the Penutian language phylum. Swadesh designed his survey to find data which would demonstrate an historical connection among members of the phylum. Using a list of 1,000 words and expressions in twenty-four hours of recordings, he surveyed twenty-two Penutian languages, including Nez Perce, Umatilla, Yakima, Warm Springs Sahaptin, Wishram and Milluk Coos, Siuslaw and Lower Umpquaw, Molale, Northern Wintu, Nomlaki, Patwin, Concow, Nisenan, Lake and Sierra Miwok, Klamath, and Chukchansi. Three-quarters of the languages were spoken by fewer than 100 people at the time of the survey: Nisenan, Wasco, and Wishram were spoken by fewer than ten; Kalapuya by perhaps only one or two. In the announcement at the beginning of the Siuslaw and Lower Umpquaw recording, the elicitor comments that all the remaining speakers of those languages are probably in the room. The informant for the Molale recording, Fred Yelkes, was the last speaker of that language; Molale is

FIGURE 2. Record from Swadesh Penutian Survey

```
OCLC: 19121763            Rec stat:  c
Entered:  i  19890209     Replaced: 19930303      Used: 19890209
▲ Type: i    Bib lvl: c    Source: d     Lang: nai
  Repr:      Enc lvl: I    Format: n     Ctry: xx
  Accomp:    Mod rec:      Comp: nn      LTxt:
  Desc: a    Int lvl:      Dat tp: s     Dates: 1953, ¶

▲ 1  040     IJZ ǂc IJZ ¶
▲ 2  007     s ǂb t ǂd m ǂe m ǂf n ǂg c ǂh m ǂi a ¶
▲ 3  033 0   1953----- ǂb 4290 ¶
▲ 4  043     ---msu-u ¶
▲ 5  090     ǂb ¶
▲ 6  049     IULA ¶
▲ 7  245 00  [United States, Northwest Coast, Penutian, 1953] ǂh sound
  recording / ǂc collected by Morris Swadesh and Robert Melton. ¶
▲ 8  300     28 sound tape reels : ǂb analog, 3 3/4 ips, 1 track, mono. ; ǂc
  7 in. ¶
▲ 9  511 0   Numerous named informants. ¶
▲ 10 518     Recorded in 1953 in California, Oregon and Washington by Morris
  Swadesh and Robert Melton. ¶
▲ 11 500     Deposited by F.M. Voegelin at the Archives of Traditional Music
  in 1985, as part of the C.F. and F.M. Voegelin Archives of the Languages of the
  World, under option 1. ¶
▲ 12 500     Penutian and Athabaskan linguistic material. ¶
▲ 13 500     Lexical elicitations in Nez Perce, Sahaptin, Yakima, Chinook,
  Tsimshian, Santiam, Galice, Dootoodn, Coos, Suislaw, Molale, Paiute, Chinook
  (upper), Klamath, Wintun, Concow, Nomlaki, Patwin, Miwok, Chukchansi, and
  Nisenan languages. ¶
```

▲ 14 500 Related publications: Swadesh "On the Penutian Vocabulary Survey" in IJAL 20:123-133; Pierce. "The Status of Athabaskan Research in Oregon" in IJAL 30:137-143; Swadesh. "Kalapuya and Takelma" in IJAL 31:237-240; Swadesh. "Problems of Long-Range Comparison in Penutian" in Language 32: 17-41; Pierce. "Hanis and Miluk" in IJAL 31:323-325; Pierce. "Genetic Comparisons of Hanis, Miluk, Alsea and Siuslaw" in IJAL 32:379-387; Hymes. "Some points of Siuslaw Phonology" in IJAL 32:328-342; Haijer. "Galice Athapaskan" in IJAL 32:320-327. ¶

▲ 15 650 0 Penutian languages ‡x Vocabulary. ¶
▲ 16 650 4 Penutian languages ‡x Elicitation. ¶
▲ 17 650 0 Athapascan languages ‡x Vocabulary. ¶
▲ 18 650 4 Elicitations ‡x Penutian. ¶
▲ 19 700 10 Swadesh, Morris, ‡d 1909-1967. ¶
▲ 20 700 10 Melton, Robert. ¶
▲ 21 700 10 Voegelin, F. M. ‡q (Florence Marie), ‡d 1927- ¶
▲ 22 700 10 Voegelin, Charles Frederick, ‡d 1906- ¶
▲ 23 710 20 Indiana University, Bloomington. ‡b Archives of the Languages of the World. ¶

now extinct. Swadesh also recorded two Athabaskan languages, Coquille and Dootoodn, which are probably no longer spoken.[6]

As with many of the materials of the Archives of the Languages of the World, it is difficult to distinguish between language and dialect. Terms referred to by the collector as language are often treated as dialects of a larger language group by *LCSH*. Sometimes LC provides no hint as to what heading should be applied. When a collector's language is not used as an LC heading or cross-reference, one must consult other reference sources. Particularly applicable to ALW recordings is the Voegelins' *Classification and Index of the World's Languages* (1977).[7] However, the *Classification*'s usefulness is sometimes limited, as it occasionally differs greatly from LC's language subject heading classification.

The ALW collections are somewhat unusual in that the collectors were generally linguists. Most ATM collections were recorded by non-linguists who often neglected to provide any information regarding languages(s) recorded. Perhaps the collectors felt that the languages were obvious; perhaps they forgot to notate them in the midst of providing so much other information; or perhaps the collectors were not familiar with the languages. Occasionally a subsequent listener will identify an unknown language, but this is the exception. Archives or other repositories which collect field recordings must insist on full documentation to accompany their recordings at the time of deposit. Without this supplementary information, the recordings cannot be properly cataloged and are of little use to future researchers, regardless of the value of the recorded contents.[8]

The Penutian survey presents various linguistic concepts that are not readily covered by standard Library of Congress subject theory, particularly in the area of applicable subdivisions. I have found that such subdivisions as **ELICITATION, CONVERSATIONS, PHONEMES,** and **UTTERANCES**, when supplied with the language heading, afford researchers a much greater degree of specificity and accuracy in their searching of Archives of the Languages of the World collections. Such subdivided headings are tagged as local headings in the online database and have 690 notes in their authority records, alerting other catalogers to the fact that these headings are not constructed according to standard Library of Congress practice.

CONCLUSION

Every field collection presents the cataloger with a new challenge. Sometimes the challenge comes in the form of an early physical format or combination of formats. Other times, the cataloger is faced with more perplexing challenges of determining specifics about the intellectual content of a recording without the aid of any printed liner notes or foreword or assigning the most useful, if not always proper, subject heading.

Despite these concerns, the wealth of unique, irreplaceable information which exists in non-published formats must not be left uncataloged, and, therefore, unavailable to the public. Many facets of the fast-disappearing cultural heritage of Native Americans exist only on these sound recordings from the early twentieth century. The Archives of Traditional Music has initiated a mutually-beneficial outreach program to assist Native American communities in obtaining copies of recordings of their own music from the ATM and to help the Archives of Traditional Music improve the documentation of those recordings.[9]

NOTES

1. The ATM generally defines a collection as a group of recordings made by the same person or group on one specific field trip.

2. The ALW was established in 1954 by Drs. Charles and Florence Voegelin as an organized repository for the sound of language. It currently represents some 300 languages.

3. Anthony Seeger and Louise Spear, eds., *Early Field Recordings: A Catalog of Cylinder Collections.* (Bloomington: Indiana University Press, 1987), 45.

4. George Peter Murdoch, *Outline of World Cultures* (New Haven: Human Relations Area Files, 1983).

5. *Rules For Archival Cataloging of Sound Recordings.* (S.l.: Association For Recorded Sound Collections, 1980).

6. Bonnie Urciuoli, "Preserving the Archives of the Languages of the World," *Resound: a Quarterly Publication of the Archives of Traditional Music* 6:3 (July 1987): 1-5.

7. C.F. and F.M. Voegelin, *Classification and Index of the World's Languages* (New York: Elsevier, 1977).

8. For further information on documentation, see: Society for Ethnomusicology, *Handbook for Field Recording* (in publication as this article is being written).

9. For more information on the outreach program, please contact the Archives of Traditional Music, Morrison Hall 117, Indiana University, Bloomington, IN 47405 (812-855-4679).

Cataloging Icelandic Materials

Martha J. Crowe

SUMMARY. This paper addresses issues in descriptive cataloging, subject analysis, and classification of Icelandic materials. It includes an extensive discussion of Icelandic personal names, particularly their formulation and its implications for establishing entries according to *AACR2*. Subsequent sections of the paper deal with uniform titles in Old Norse, subject headings, and classification with descriptions of current practice and with reflections on needed enhancements. It concludes with a consideration of the availability and usefulness of various cataloging aids and includes a bibliography of helpful reference sources.

The cataloging of Icelandic (and, in its earlier form, Old Norse) materials involves a number of idiosyncracies not normally encountered in the more widely spoken Germanic and Scandinavian languages. These include the establishment of personal names in accord with Icelandic conventions, the need for additional subject access, and the adaptation of the Library of Congress classification schedule for Icelandic literature to the purposes of a more extensive research collection of Icelandic materials than the current schedule can easily accommodate.[1]

Martha J. Crowe, MLS, MA, is Germanic and Icelandic Cataloger, Catalog Department, John M. Olin Library, Cornell University, Ithaca, NY 14853 (e-mail: Z63Y@cornellc.edu).

The author thanks Patrick J. Stevens for his thoughtful reading and constructive comments on this paper.

[Haworth co-indexing entry note]: "Cataloging Icelandic Materials." Crowe, Martha J. Co-published simultaneously in *Cataloging & Classification Quarterly* (The Haworth Press, Inc.) Vol. 17, No. 1/2, 1993, pp. 29-46; and: *Languages of the World: Cataloging Issues and Problems* (ed: Martin D. Joachim) The Haworth Press, Inc., 1993, pp. 29-46. Multiple copies of this article/chapter may be purchased from The Haworth Document Delivery Center [1-800-3-HAWORTH; 9:00 a.m. - 5:00 p.m. (EST)].

PERSONAL NAMES

Elements of Icelandic Names

The form of Icelandic names had varied little from the time of the original settlement of the country in the ninth century until the mid-nineteenth century. The basic pattern included a single forename and a patronymic (or, rarely, a matronymic), and there were no surnames until the beginning of the seventeenth century. From 1850 on, however, the number of surnames began to increase (encouraged by travel between Iceland and the Continent and intermarriage with foreign nationals, often Danes) to the point that concern arose over the erosion of the old patronymic tradition.

That concern led to a series of federal laws (Lög um mannanöfn) that have regulated Icelandic naming practice since 1913. The first law allowed either the traditional patronymic or the adoption of a surname. The second law, enacted in 1925, negated the option allowed by the law of 1913 and prohibited adopting a surname as an adult or giving one to a child. Instead, all Icelanders were to be "named by one or two Icelandic names [meaning first names], and to identify themselves further according to their father, mother, or adoptive father [a patronymic or matronymic] and to write their first names and patronymic in the same style for their entire lives."[2] The most recent law, enacted in 1991, prescribes no more than three forenames and a patronymic if no surname exists. Established surnames may be perpetuated, but no new family names may be introduced. The law does, however, contain some exceptions, for example, in cases of marriage to foreign nationals and divorce.[3]

Thus the historical linguistic pattern of Icelandic names, that is, forename(s) with patronymic, continues to exist side by side with first name/surname forms and combinations of the two. In addition, it is not uncommon for an Icelander to further identify himself or herself by adding a place name. The International Federation of Library Associations and Institutions (IFLA), in its *Names of Persons: National Usages for Entry in Catalogues*, distinguishes four elements normally forming Icelandic names.[4]

Element	Type	Examples
1. Forename(s)	simple	Snorri
		Guðrún
	compound, not joined by a hyphen	Ólafur Jóhann
2. Patronymic	masculine, ending in -*son*	Sigurðsson
	feminine, ending in -*dóttir*	Jakobsdóttir

Element	Type	Examples
3. Family name	simple	Laxness
4. Place name	preceded by a preposition	úr Kötlum
		frá Lundi

The combinations of these elements follow five basic patterns:

forename(s) + patronymic	Svava Jakobsdóttir
forename(s) + patronymic + place name	Davíð Stefánsson frá Fagraskógi
forename(s) + patronymic + family name	Guðmundur Gíslason Hagalín
forename(s) + family name	Halldór Laxness
forename(s) + preposition + place name	Jóhannes úr Kötlum

Order of Elements

The guidelines set forth in *Names of Persons* for determining the entry of names were developed in accordance with the principle adopted by the International Conference on Cataloguing Principles, Paris, 1961: "When the name of a personal author consists of several words, the choice of entry word is determined as far as possible by agreed usage in the country of which the author is a citizen, or, if this is not possible, by agreed usage in the language which he generally uses."[5] In Icelandic usage the forename is of primary importance and is the entry element in all alphabetical listings.[6] Some publications (such as the telephone book) add a second listing, and the national bibliography includes a cross-reference from the family name if there is one.

Practices of entering Icelandic names have varied over the years, however, both at the National Library of Iceland (Landsbókasafn Íslands) and abroad according to the various cataloging codes. It is therefore necessary to be aware of those practices when using older printed bibliographies and even when searching the bibliographic utilities for modern imprints, for the *AACR2* rules that apply to Icelandic names have been interpreted in two different ways.

National Library of Iceland Entries

The National Library of Iceland, until the publication of the first national bibliography, for 1974,[7] entered Icelanders under the patronymic, as though it were a conventional surname–a practice totally at variance with the linguistic structure of names proper to the Icelandic language and with all other domestic bibliographies and reference sources. One can only assume that the reason was the force of convention and convenience in accommodating Icelandic practice to that of the rest of the world. The library had long wanted to break with that practice, especially as it meant that public and other libraries in the country had not been able to use its catalog cards directly, but had been creating their own with entry under the forename. The appearance of an official national bibliography gave the impetus and opportunity to implement the reform and enter all Icelanders under forenames, even if they had surnames.

AACR Entries

None of the cataloging codes in use in the United states before *AACR2* gave any special instructions for Icelandic names, although *AACR* contained two provisions that could have resulted in entry under forename but which were not originally applied to Icelandic. The introductory notes to the section "Entry of Names" instruct: "If the name by which a person is identified consists of several elements, it is necessary to determine which of these is to be the first or entry element. This element is normally that part of the name or title by which a person is entered or would be entered in alphabetical lists in his language." Rule 49.A.1 reads: "Enter a person whose name does not include a surname and who is not primarily identified by a title of nobility under the part of his name by which he is primarily identified in reference sources, normally the first of the names that he uses."

In 1974 the Library of Congress issued a statement in *Cataloging Service* on its entry practice:

> Several years ago the Library of Congress reviewed its practice of entering Icelandic personal names under the last element of the name, concluding that this practice was not warranted. . . . Not only is entry under a patronymic contrary to sound principles of establishing personal names for cataloging purposes, it is also contrary to standard Icelandic usage. Therefore, it was decided to adopt the provisions of the *Anglo-American Cataloguing Rules* (cf. "Introductory notes," p. 80, and rule 49) under which such names are entered under the personal name followed by the patronymic and the toponym, if any, in running form. . . . Those exceptional names containing a surname are, of course, entered under the surname. When the name of a person established under the patronym is used in connec-

tion with new cataloging it is revised to the correct form, and all main entries under the name are reprinted.[8]

Implementation of that practice still ignored the fact that standard Icelandic usage was to enter under first name even if a surname was present. Moreover, it allowed for multiple practices to develop with the adoption of *AACR2*, because the formulation of the new rule allowed two interpretations.

AACR2 Entries

A close literal reading of *AACR2* rules 22.8A1 and 22.8B1 in the 1988 revision (unchanged in content from those rules numbered 22.8A and 22.8C in the original edition of *AACR2*) would indicate a continuation of the practice established by the Library of Congress instructions of 1974. Rule 22.8A1 prescribes: "Enter a name that does not include a surname and that is borne by a person who is not identified by a title of nobility under the part of the name under which the person is listed in reference sources. Include in the name any words or phrases denoting place of origin, domicile, occupation, or other characteristics that are commonly associated with the name in works by the person or in reference sources. Precede such words or phrases by a comma unless the name is Icelandic and the words denote a place." Rule 22.8B1 instructs: "If a name consists of one or more given names and a patronymic, enter it under the first given name, followed by the rest of the name in direct order. . . . If in an Icelandic name a phrase naming a place follows the patronymic, treat it as an integral part of the name. Refer from the patronymic."
Since 22.8A1 deals with names that do not include surnames and 22.8B1 speaks only to names including patronymics (and, possibly, place names), by default the cataloger is left to establish Icelandic names containing surnames under the surname. Some catalogers continued in that vein; others, seemingly the majority, began entering all Icelandic names under the forename. The result was that the national utilities showed a confusing mixture, and as late as June 1990 the National Coordinated Cataloging Operations (NACO) project at the Library of Congress rejected a Cornell University record with the name heading under the forename because it contained a surname.
By that time the Library of Congress began considering issuing a rule interpretation, and the Joint Steering Committee for Revision of AACR (JSC) discussed a rule revision, maintaining that all Icelandic names must be entered under the first name, with only an occasional exception for internationally known writers, such as Halldór Laxness.[9] The rule inter-

pretation finally appeared in *Cataloging Service Bulletin* in winter 1991: "Enter an Icelandic name under the first given name, followed by the other given names (if present), by the patronymic, and by the family name, in direct order. If a phrase naming a place follows the given name(s), patronymic, or family name, treat it as an integral part of the name. Refer from the patronymic and from the family name."[10]

At that point even the former major exception, Halldór Laxness, was given as an example for entry under forename. A proposed new rule (to be numbered 22.9B) with the same formulation is being considered by the JSC.[11] Thus personal name entries are now established in accord with Icelandic usage, but there remain a few artifacts to be updated in the national utilities.

Western Icelanders

During the half century from about 1855 to 1900 over fourteen thousand Icelanders emigrated to North America, settling mostly in North Dakota, Manitoba, Saskatchewan, and Alberta. Those so-called Western Icelanders (*Vestur-Íslendingar*) actively sought to maintain their literary tradition in their native tongue by establishing newspapers and by publishing a significant number of literary works, memoirs, and correspondence. Establishing entries for such authors is a judgment call, as the utilities show a mixture of forename entries and surname entries in which the patronymic has been treated as a surname and used as the entry element.

Entry under the forename for émigrés publishing in Icelandic would be in accord with *AACR2* rule 22.4A: "If a person's name . . . consists of several parts, select as the entry element that part of the name under which the person would normally be listed in authoritative alphabetic lists in his or her language or country of residence or activity. In applying this general rule, follow the instructions in 22.5-22.9. If, however, a person's preference is known to be different from the normal usage, follow that preference in selecting the entry element." It would seem wisest to judge on the basis of both form and function–if the name still appears to function as a patronymic and is spelled in the work in its Icelandic form, including the diacritics, it should be treated as an Icelandic name. In addition, a number of émigré works were and continue to be published in Iceland–since many of them consist of correspondence with relatives back home, travel memoirs, and accounts by repatriates of their adventures abroad–further supporting a choice of forename entry.

The question of changing usage becomes more complicated, however, when establishing name entries not for authors but for the subjects of family histories, genealogies, and biographies. In those cases it is often obvious from the captions to illustrations and from biographical data that the persons had acculturated and were using the patronymic as a surname (for example, a woman identified as Svanfridur Kristjanson, having adopted her husband's patronymic) and that it should be established as such.

For modern-day émigrés rule 22.4A can be applied equally well to establish entries under the patronymic as a surname. For example, the Icelanders Magnus Magnusson, a television journalist and an author of popular nonfiction who has long lived in Scotland, and Halldór Hermannsson, the first curator of the Fiske Icelandic Collection at Cornell University, both took up permanent residence abroad and published the majority of their works in English.

Old Norse Names

Old Norse personal names pose no particular problem. They not uncommonly include epithets, such as *helgi, fróði, rauði* (*the holy, the learned, the red*). A point of special attention is that names ending in -*ur* in modern Icelandic were spelled -*r* in Old Norse, and it is the Library of Congress practice to retain the original orthography. Thus the spelling of Oddr Snorrason (a twelfth-century author) is to be found regularized in modern Icelandic as Oddur Snorrason. The cataloger must take care to refer from modernized spellings in authority records.

UNIFORM TITLES

Old Norse, or Old Icelandic, literature comprises the literature of Norway and Iceland composed from the ninth through the fifteenth century and appearing in written form from the twelfth century on. In its multiplicity of genres (ranging from pre-Christian mythological poetry through the accounts of the discovery of America, heroic historical sagas, translations of classical Roman historians, and stylized medieval court poetry, to translations of late medieval Continental literature), it is counted as one of the most significant literatures of the Middle Ages.

Apart from a few notable exceptions (for example, the works of Snorri Sturluson), the majority of Old Norse literature is of unknown authorship. Fortunately, uniform titles for a large number of even the lesser-known works were established in pre-*AACR2* form, and the *AACR2* authority records that have been created online thus far seldom differ from them. Important deviations here are the uniform titles for individual parts of the poetic compilations known as the Eddas. *AACR2* entries under rule 25.6A1 differ distinctly in that the title of the part itself is now used as the uniform title, rather than the title of the whole work with the title of the part as a subheading as under *AACR*. Thus the *AACR* entry **Edda Sæmundar. Hávamál** is now **Hávamál** in *AACR2* form.

Online authorities for many titles (and particularly for the numerous parts of the Eddas) are still lacking and need to be created whenever a new edition of a work is cataloged. Most of the works a cataloger would encounter are listed in the classifications PT 7263-7323 in the new schedule, published in 1992, but it is important to note that those forms are still pre-*AACR2*. Rule 25.4A1 comes into play here: "Use the title, or form of title, in the original language by which a work created before 1501 . . . is identified in modern sources. If the evidence of modern reference sources is inconclusive, use (in this order of preference) the title most frequently found in: (a) modern editions (b) early editions (c) manuscript copies."

In considering the form of a uniform title and the necessary cross-references, apart from using the PT schedule as a starting point, a cataloger would do well to consult the old pre-*AACR2* form in the *National Union Catalog, Pre-1956 Imprints*, Stefán Einarsson's *A History of Icelandic Literature*, Simek's *Lexikon der altnordischen Literatur*, and the appropriate bibliography in the series Islandica (see the appended bibliography of reference sources), all of which indicate the titles of the works in Old Norse orthography. When a choice arises in reference sources, the Library of Congress records online show a preference for the Old Norse rather than modern Icelandic orthography.

It is not within the scope of this paper to treat in detail the many facets of establishing online authority records for the large corpus of uniform titles. They remain an area that would profit from a concentrated review and revision.

SUBJECT CATALOGING

Period Subdivisions

The *Library of Congress Subject Headings*, 16th ed., 1993, provides limited period subdivisions for Iceland. **HISTORY** is subdivided into **TO 1262** and **1918-1945**, and **POLITICS AND GOVERNMENT** into **18TH, 19TH**, and **20TH CENTURY**. Changes in colonial authority that affected politics and government from 1262 to 1918, which do not necessarily correlate with historical periods, account for a divergence in the period subdivisions recommended under the two headings. The following is suggested as a more-detailed breakdown to encompass an in-depth collection of research materials:[12]

HISTORY

–TO 1262	(end of the Republic)
–TO 1550	(Reformation [*siðaskipti*])
–16TH CENTURY	
–17TH CENTURY	
–18TH CENTURY	
–19TH CENTURY	
–20TH CENTURY	
–1918-1944	(independent in union with Denmark)
–1944-	(establishment of the Republic)

POLITICS AND GOVERNMENT

–TO 1262	(end of the Republic)
–1262-1383	(Norwegian rule)
–1383-1918	(Danish rule)
–16TH CENTURY	
–17TH CENTURY	
–18TH CENTURY	
–19TH CENTURY	
–20TH CENTURY	
–1918-1944	(independent in union with Denmark)
–1944-	(establishment of the Republic)

It is important to note that the most significant political and historical event for Iceland in this century–the end of the union with Denmark and the establishment of the Icelandic Republic–occurred in 1944, not in 1945. It would be appropriate for the Library of Congress to change that date in the subdivision.

Similarly, a full range of period subdivisions is lacking for **DESCRIPTION AND TRAVEL**. Currently only **1945-1980** and **1981-** are provided, and the Library of Congress is no longer establishing date subdivisions for earlier time periods. Because the Icelandic collection at Cornell contains a wealth of travel accounts and diaries from the late eighteenth and early nineteenth centuries, the library is using the following scheme to accommodate them:[12]

DESCRIPTION AND TRAVEL

–17TH CENTURY
–18TH CENTURY
–19TH CENTURY
–20TH CENTURY

–1945-1980
–1981-

Topical Subject Headings

As might be expected, the existing topical subject headings of the type **[SUBJECT], ICELANDIC** or **ICELANDIC [SUBJECT]** are often inadequate for a comprehensive collection. For example, although there is **ART, ICELANDIC,** there is no **ARCHITECTURE, ICELANDIC.** Particularly for subject headings that follow a predictable pattern, it is a simple procedure to send a request to the Library of Congress to include them. There can, however, be a considerable lag in response time.

In recent years the number of headings applying to Old Norse literature has increased, but there is in particular a need for more specific headings for literary genres. It is puzzling that there exist specific headings for poetry (**EDDAS; LAUSAVÍSUR; RÍMUR; SCALDS AND SCALDIC POETRY; RELIGIOUS POETRY, OLD NORSE**), about which much less has been published, while appropriate headings for the distinctly identifiable and numerous genres of the sagas are still lacking. Currently only the one generic heading **SAGAS** is available for family sagas, kings' sagas, mythical-heroic sagas, romantic sagas, and a number of saga types of religious content. Distinguishing the major saga genres would allow more specific access points both for history and criticism and for collections.

Here again, as in the area of uniform titles, the issue cannot be adequately dealt with in the framework of this article. A thorough review resulting in the creation of additional headings for Old Norse literary history and criticism would facilitate access and improve the organization of that area of the catalog.

CLASSIFICATION

The Library of Congress classification schedule for modern Icelandic literature provides only one class number for both nineteenth- and twentieth-century works of individual authors (PT7511). The author numbers listed were established during the period when personal names were entered under surname if one existed. Thus the cutters for authors with surnames no longer correspond to the entry element (for example, Halldór Laxness still has the author number .L3 and Guðmundur Kamban, .K3). The most efficient practice (to avoid having to recutter) is to continue to cutter according to the established author numbers even though the headings in the catalog have been revised.

The provision of only one class number for two centuries of modern Icelandic authors was not sufficient for conveniently cataloging an in-depth collection such as that at Cornell, and for that reason the library has departed from the schedule in this area. It has consistently used

PT	7508	Anonymous works. 1800-1960 (XXVIII)
	7509	Authors, A-Z. 1800-1960 (XL)
	7510	Anonymous works. 1960- (XXVIII)
	7511	Authors, A-Z. 1960- (XL)

In addition, because the practice of entry under first name meant that the conventional cuttering system created such long author numbers in the cases of common first names, the Cornell University Library devised an in-house table to be applied exclusively to modern Icelandic authors. It divides PT7509 and PT7511 further by a series of decimal numbers for the first name and then determines an author number by cuttering for the second letter of the first name or, in the case of a very common first name, by cuttering for the second element of the name. For example, PT7509.1 (or PT7511.1) is used for all first names beginning with A, and PT7509.1 .D12 is the name Aðalbjörg, PT 7509.1 .D15 is Aðalbjörn, etc.:

PT7509

.1	.D12	Aðalbjörg
	.D15	Aðalbjörn
	.E28	Ægir
	.G83	Ágúst

CATALOGING AIDS

Icelandic Sources

The cultural environment in which the Icelandic publishing trade and the National Library of Iceland operate is unique and provides catalogers with unusually thorough and reliable bibliographic and biographical resources.[13] Chief among these is the national bibliography of Iceland (*Íslensk bókaskrá*). Entries are established according to the *Anglo-American Cataloguing Rules*, and descriptions are in accordance with the IFLA International Standard Bibliographic Description (ISBD) standards. Dewey decimal classification is provided, with only a few variations that are common practice in Icelandic libraries, and there is a separate section arranged by class number in each issue. Other useful Icelandic publications, such as biographies and directories, are appended to this article in a select bibliography of reference sources.

National Databases

Name and series authority records are not plentiful, making the national databases of limited use except for the most common authors and publications.[14] Because of the Icelandic patronymic naming practice, common first names often result in multiple occurrences of the entire name. When a single occurrence of a personal name has been established with no dates because there was no conflict, it has interfered with creating unique authority records for additional occurrences of that name. For example, the Library of Congress has one online authority record for Jón Jónsson, no dates, whereas the Cornell database has ten, all with dates; the Library of Congress has no Sigurður Guðmundsson or Sigurður Jónsson, while Cornell has eight and ten respectively.

The Library of Congress rule intepretation to rule 22.17 now mandates adding dates to personal names whenever they are known, even when there is no conflict, thus making it possible to avoid the problem.[15] As Icelandic documentation is excellent, dates are often readily available.

CONCLUSION

Icelandic and Old Norse materials challenge catalogers in ways that publications in the other Germanic and Scandinavian languages do not. The establishment of personal names reflects a national usage virtually unique in Western Europe. Uniform titles stem from a literary tradition that has experienced subtle orthographic changes, and authority records for many of those works are lacking. Subject analysis and classification deserve revision with an eye to providing more-detailed access to the significant elements of Icelandic culture.

Although additional work needs to be done to provide more access points for Icelandic materials, recent clarification of the rules for the entry of personal names and the availability of reliable Icelandic bibliographical and biographical reference sources to support cataloging efforts make the challenges easier to meet.

REFERENCES AND NOTES

1. The issues discussed in this paper are those that have arisen in cataloging the Fiske Icelandic Collection at Cornell University, one of the three major collections of Islandica, currently comprising approximately 37,500 volumes. Although the National Library of Iceland and the Danish Royal Library hold more titles in Icelandic, the Fiske Collection ranks first in holdings of non-Icelandic works on Icelandic subjects and in translations of Icelandic and Old Norse literature. The intention is that the collection be a resource for the study of Iceland in every respect–literature, language, culture, history, politics, economics, and the natural history of the country itself.

Current collecting is at the advanced research level, but until World War I it was the practice to acquire everything published in Iceland. In fact, the original printed catalog of the collection (Halldór Hermannsson, comp., *Catalogue of the Icelandic Collection Bequeathed by Willard Fiske* [Ithaca, N.Y., 1914]) and its two supplements, covering additions through 1942, are a standard bibliographic reference in the field and are often cited by antiquarian book dealers in their catalogs. The comprehensiveness of this collection thus presents some cataloging situations that would not surface in libraries with fewer Icelandic materials (for example, identifying and creating unique authority records for many personal authors with the same name, whereas a smaller collection might offer only one occurrence of that name, or the need for additional period subdivisions for the subject headings **HISTORY** and **POLITICS AND GOVERNMENT** that are not provided in the *Library of Congress Subject Headings*).

2. Hermann Pálsson, *Íslenzk mannanöfn* (Reykjavík: Heimskringla, 1960), 15.

3. The complete text of the latest version of the law is contained in Guðrún Kvaran and Sigurður Jónsson frá Arnarvatni, *Nöfn Íslendinga* (Reykjavík: Heimskringla, 1991), 81-86.

4. IFLA International Office for UBC, *Names of Persons: National Usages for Entry in Catalogues*, 3d ed. (London: IFLA International Office for UBC, 1977), 65.

5. International Congress on Cataloging Principles, Paris, 1961, *Report* (London: International Federation of Library Associations, 1963), 96.

6. In alphabetizing lists of names, it is the practice in Iceland to ignore a second forename, a patronymic, or a second forename plus patronymic given before a family name or patronymic unless two entries bear the same first forename, and patronymic or family name. For example, the second name (the initial) is not considered in the filing order of the following:

Sigurður J. Grétarsson
Sigurður Gunnarsson
Sigurður B. Haraldsson

7. That year saw the first publication of the *Íslensk bókaskrá* (Reykjavík: Landsbókasafn Íslands), the national bibliography per se. For the years 1944 to 1973 the library had been publishing an annual bibliography, "Íslenzk rit," as part

of its *Árbók* (Reykjavík: Landsbókasafn Íslands), and for the years 1887 to 1943 it had been issuing its *Ritaukaskrá Landsbókasafnsins* (Reykjavík: Landsbókasafn Íslands), basically an acquisitions list.

8. *Cataloging Service* 110 (Summer 1974): 2-3.

9. Cf., memoranda to the committee 3JSC/Chair/31/Chair addendum/2, June 17, 1991, and 3JSC/Chair/31, November 24, 1990.

10. *Cataloging Service Bulletin* no. 51 (Winter 1991): 37-38.

11. Cf., memorandum 3JSC/Chair/31/LC revision), October 9, 1991.

12. The Cornell University Library practice is to use these subdivisions, tagging the entry as "other subject heading."

13. The literacy rate in Iceland is 99.9%, and Icelandic society fosters creative writing and a lively interest among the general population in the country's cultural and literary history, with the result that Icelanders produce more books per capita than any other nation. In 1989 the population of Europe (including the U.S.S.R.) produced 455,000 titles, or 584 titles per million inhabitants (source: *UNESCO Statistical Yearbook,* 1991). In comparison, the total population of Iceland (254,788) produced 935 titles per approximately ¼ million (source: *Íslensk bókaskrá,* 1990), or more than six times as many books per capita as all of Europe.

The Icelandic literary involvement extends through all levels of the population. It is a rare Icelandic farmhouse that does not have a collection of books including a number of volumes of contemporary poetry; people regularly listen to broadcasts of literary readings on the state radio, and the writing of poetry is practiced in the schools (P. M. Mitchell, "The Scandinavian Literary Engagement," in *Scandinavian Studies, Essays Presented to Dr. Henry Goddard Leach on the Occasion of His Eighty-fifth Birthday,* ed. by Carl F. Bayerschmidt and Erik J. Friis (Seattle: University of Washington Press, 1965), 333-334). This intense interest on the part of Icelanders in their cultural and personal heritage extends to a preoccupation with its scrupulously accurate and detailed documentation: their bibliographies, biographies, and bio-bibliographical dictionaries are exhaustive, and genealogies abound.

14. Currently Cornell University, which catalogs locally on NOTIS, is uploading bibliographic records, but not authority records, into RLIN. It does request corrections and updates of existing authority records through NACO and may begin submitting its own in the future.

15. *Cataloging Service Bulletin* no. 44 (Spring 1989): 47. Libraries that are not sure about dates for specific persons may contact the Cornell University Library, which has extensive resources for verification.

SELECT BIBLIOGRAPHY OF REFERENCE SOURCES

Bibliographies

Bókmenntaskrá Skírnis. Reykjavík: Íslenzka bókmenntafélag.

A bibliography of Icelandic belles lettres and literary criticism, published annually since 1968. It gives full names and dates of authors and includes critical reviews of the works.

Hermannsson, Halldór, comp. *Catalogue of the Icelandic Collection Bequeathed by Willard Fiske*. Ithaca, N.Y.: Cornell University Library, 1914-1943.

A bibliography of the original collection and additions through 1942. Meticulous bibliographic descriptions and annotations with a subject index. The classification scheme and subject headings were developed by the compiler.

Islandica.

A reprint edition of the first thirty-six volumes of this series was published in New York by Kraus Reprint Corporation in 1966. The following bibliographies, all compiled by Halldór Hermannsson, are extremely useful in establishing uniform titles: I. *Bibliography of the Icelandic Sagas and Minor Tales*; III. *Bibliography of the Sagas of the Kings of Norway and Related Sagas and Tales*; IV. *The Ancient Laws of Norway and Iceland*; XIII. *Bibliography of the Eddas*; XXIV. *The Sagas of Icelanders (Íslendinga sögur)*; XXVI. *The Sagas of Kings (konunga sögur) and the Mythical-heroic Sagas (fornaldar sögur)*. In addition, refer to the original editions by Jóhann S. Hannesson: XXXVII. *Bibliography of the Eddas* (Ithaca: Cornell Unversity Press, 1955) and XXXVIII. *The Sagas of Icelanders (Íslendinga sögur)* (Ithaca: Cornell University Press, 1957) and by Marianne E. Kalinke and P. M. Mitchell: XLIV. *Bibliography of Old Norse-Icelandic Romances* (Ithaca: Cornell University Press, 1985).

Íslensk bókaskrá. Reykjavík: Landsbókasafn Íslands.

The national bibliography of Iceland. Published since 1974, it includes items produced in Iceland or printed abroad for Icelandic publishers. New serials titles and maps and charts are listed in separate sections.

Íslensk hljódritaskrá. Reykjavík: Landsbókasafn Íslands.

A bibliography of Icelandic sound recordings, an annual supplement to the national bibliography since 1979.

Landsbókasafn Íslands. *Árbók*. Reykjavík: Landsbókasafnið.

The yearbook of the National Library of Iceland. For the years 1944 to 1973 it included a bibliography of Icelandic imprints, "Íslenzk rit," and a section of foreign imprints by Icelandic authors or containing material on Iceland, "Rit á erlendum tungum eftir íslenzka menn eða um íslenzk efni."

Landsbókasafn Íslands. *Ritaukaskrá Landsbókasafnsins.* Reykjavík: Ísafoldarprentsmidja.

The acquisitions list of the National Library of Iceland from 1887-1943.

Ólafur F. Hjartar. *Vesturheimsprent, skrá um rit á íslensku prentuð vestan hafs og austan af Vestur-Íslendingum eða varðandi þá.* Reykjavík: Landsbókasafn Íslands, 1986.

A bibliography of publications in Icelandic printed in North America or printed elsewhere but written by, or relating to, the Icelandic settlers in North America.

Biographies and Bio-Bibliographies

Brynleifur Tobiasson. *Hver er maðurinn.* Reykjavík: Fagurskinna, 1944.

Contemporary biographies, 3,735 entries. Preferred forms of names are indicated. Includes bibliographies.

Hannes Pétursson and Helgi Sæmundsson. *Íslenzkt skáldatal.* Reykjavík: Bókaútgáfa Menningarsjóðs og Þjóðvinafélagsins, 1973-1976.

A bio-bibliographical dictionary of literary authors from Old Norse through contemporary times. Preferred forms of names are indicated.

Jón Guðnason. *Íslenzkir samtíðarmenn.* Reykjavík: Bókaútgáfan samtíðarmenn, 1965-1970.

Contemporary biographies, 2,342 entries. Preferred forms of names are indicated. Includes bibliographies.

Páll Eggert Ólason. *Íslenzkar æiskrár.* Reykjavík: Hið Íslenzka bókmenntafélag, 1948-1976.

The only biographical compendium covering the period from the settlement of the country to contemporary times (1965). Preferred forms of names are indicated. Includes bibliographies.

Torfi Jónsson. *Æviskrár samtíðarmanna.* Hafnarfjörður: Skuggsjá, 1982-1984.

> Contemporary biographies, over 4,000 entries. Preferred forms of names are indicated. Includes bibliographies.

Who's Who in Icelandic Business & Government 1990-1991. Reykjavík: Forskot, 1990.

> Short biographies of the majority of leading personalities in business and government.

Directories

Íslensk fyrirtæki. Reykjavík: Frjálst framtak, 1984.

> A directory of firms, associations, institutions, societies, municipal authorities, and federal government departments.

Símaskrá. Reykjavík: Póst- og símamálastofnunin.

> The telephone book for the entire country.

Skrá um stofnanaheiti. Reykjavík: Hagstofa Íslands, 1972.

> A directory of offices, societies, institutions, and associations. With Danish and English translations.

Skrá yfir dána. Reykjavík: Hagstofa Íslands.

> The official annual mortality register, issued by the Statistical Bureau of Iceland. Gives birth and death dates.

Encyclopedias, Handbooks, etc.

Birgir Thorlacius, ed. *Ríkishandbók Íslands 1986.* Reykjavík: Ríkisstjórn Íslands, 1986.

> More than a government handbook, this manual includes all government offices plus schools, national organizations, and institutions related to the state or state supported, as well as offices of international and foreign agencies represented in Iceland.

Íslenska alfræðiorðabókin. Reykjavík: Örn og örlygur, 1990.

An invaluable cataloging aid. Although this is intended to be a general encyclopedia, it contains a wealth of Islandica. Useful for biographical data, Icelandic place names and political jurisdictions, institutions, and Icelandic history.

Kulturhistorisk leksikon for nordisk middelalder fra vikingetid til reformationstid. København: Rosenkilde og Bagger, 1956-1978.

The standard encyclopedic resource for medieval Scandinavian literary and cultural history.

Simek, Rudolf, and Hermann Pálsson. *Lexikon der altnordischen Literatur*. Stuttgart: Alfred Kröner, 1987.

An excellent handbook for identifying anonymous Old Norse literary works and authors and establishing uniform title entries. Includes bibliographical references for secondary literature on each entry.

Stefán Einarsson. *A History of Icelandic Literature*. New York: Johns Hopkins Press for the American-Scandinavian Foundation, 1957.

A valuable overview with a thorough index. Useful for establishing uniform title entries.

The Spanish *Comedias* Project
at the University of Colorado:
A Case for Collection-Level Cataloging

Richard F. Phillips

SUMMARY. This paper reviews a project at the University of Colorado at Boulder Libraries utilizing the AMC format to upgrade the accessibility of a collection of Spanish plays cataloged in 1956 as an unanalyzed set. The project used the original finding aid as a tool to create records providing access at box level to a collection of 3700 plays kept in 145 boxes. Results show 58 percent of authors traced in the project are unique to Colorado's on-line holdings, while another 12 percent are represented by just one other entry. Therefore, an enrichment of the coverage of Spanish literature at CU has been accomplished.

INTRODUCTION

In the 1950s the University of Colorado at Boulder Libraries acquired a collection of nineteenth and twentieth century Spanish plays from the firm of García Rico. Numbering about 3700 items, these plays represent excellent coverage of the *comedia chica* genre of Spanish literature which

Richard F. Phillips was Head, Catalog Department, University of Colorado at Boulder Libraries when this article was written. He is now Director of the Latin American Collection, University of Florida Libraries, Gainesville, FL (e-mail: ricphil@nervm.nerdc.ufl.edu).

[Haworth co-indexing entry note]: "The Spanish *Comedias* Project at the University of Colorado: A Case for Collection-Level Cataloging." Phillips, Richard F. Co-published simultaneously in *Cataloging & Classification Quarterly* (The Haworth Press, Inc.) Vol. 17, No. 1/2, 1993, pp. 47-68; and: *Languages of the World: Cataloging Issues and Problems* (ed: Martin D. Joachim) The Haworth Press, Inc., 1993, pp. 47-68. Multiple copies of this article/chapter may be purchased from The Haworth Document Delivery Center [1-800-3-HAWORTH; 9:00 a.m. - 5:00 p.m. (EST)].

thrived during the years ca. 1850-1920. CU's collection of these plays was cataloged and processed in 1956 using an unanalyzed set record. An alphabetical finding aid was also prepared. Items were classed as a whole, boxed in 145 containers, and shelved in public stacks. Use was minimal over the many years since, as might have been predicted, given the limited access that the manual card catalog environment offered.

In 1990 it was decided to upgrade cataloging and access to these materials using a collection-level approach. The *comedias* were moved to the Special Collections Department, and the Archives and Manuscript Control (AMC) format was utilized on OCLC, with application of the PRISM feature of constant data overlay[1] being a critical element in the success of the project.

This paper discusses the CU Libraries Spanish *comedias* project and outlines the rationale and methodology implemented. CU Libraries recognize that the access created to this body of materials is by no means total, but there is agreement that the finished project has enhanced user access to and knowledge of this collection. The success of the project also suggests that other applications of collection-level cataloging can be made in the processing and reprocessing of large accumulations of special-interest library materials.

BACKGROUND

Like many ARL members, CU Libraries have often made bulk purchases, such as the García Rico collection of *comedias*. This has continued, and in the last periods of the 1980s CU Libraries acquired several large and notable private collections of Spanish and Latin American literature and literary criticisms. These private collections (three from Spain and one other from Barranquilla, Colombia) number about 30,000 volumes and are heavily concentrated in their coverage of the literatures and literary histories of Iberia and Ibero-America.

The acquisitions of these private collections have come on top of heavy regular mainstream buying. Counter to national trends, CU Libraries in the late 1980s were enjoying healthy materials budgets (and fortunately have continued to do so). On the other hand, however, the cataloging and processing of the most recently purchased private Spanish collections were predictably going to strain Technical Services workflows as they and the large amounts of regular purchase receipts received processing. Consequently, CU's Acquisitions, Cataloging, and Binding/Marking units have frequently needed to review standards and efficiency as they handle such large infusions of special purchase materials as additions to their regular routines.

Downstream, public shelving areas became a concern almost immediately as the first trickles of the special purchase Spanish items emerged from Technical Services. A review of shelf space in the PQ class areas (Spanish-Latin American literatures) showed little room for housing such concentrated collection growth. It was here, therefore, that the presence of Colorado's boxed *comedias chicas* (from the 1950s), held in that area and on those shelves, were first identified as a ready option for solving recognizable shelf space needs in the PQ areas.

The *comedias* are for most part at least 100 years old or older. Boxed as they were meant that all were unbound, and many were clearly showing signs of deterioration and were in need of special care in a controlled environment. Also, their unique nature as an accumulation of a genre meant that these items most likely would receive only highly specialized use. In concert with the head of Cataloging, who also serves as a Spanish/Latin American specialist, a complete and appropriate review was given to these points by the literature bibliographer and the special collections librarian. The decision to move the *comedias* to the Special Collections Department was thus arrived at, thereby accomplishing two things: the PQ areas were given room to grow, and CU's *comedias* project was born.

REVIEW

The literary genre of the *comedia chica* has been well covered and discussed in critical writings on Spanish literature. These short plays were quite popular in Spain and elsewhere in the nineteenth and early twentieth centuries. Often absurd in theme, they were commonly presented in small cafe-theatres as a means to attract customers and business.[2]

The phenomenon reached a peak in the 1880s-1890s during which dozens of cafe-theatres and thousands of plays sprang forth in Madrid alone. The advent and acceptance of motion pictures and movie houses as the years of the twentieth century began to unfold soon siphoned off audiences from the *comedias*. However, they do remain as portraits of Spanish popular culture from a bygone era, and they are attracting scholarly attention on a regular basis.

The CU Libraries collection of *comedias* is central to the needs of the campus. Colorado's Department of Spanish and Portuguese has for many years focused on Spain and its civilization. There is a strong interest in

Latin America as well, but collecting and research in the Libraries have long supported the advanced study needs of scholars of Spain and Spanish themes. CU's recent special purchases from Spain continue this priority and attest to this point.

WORKFLOW

Of the several large special purchases made by the CU Libraries in the late 1980s, the most significant was the Ricardo Gullón Collection. Gullón was, for many decades, a distinguished critic and scholar[3] of Spanish civilization, and his personal library was a major acquisition by Colorado. In addition to the many books and journals contained within the collection, there is a large number of personal papers and miscellaneous matter in need of appraisal and organization.

The placement within the Libraries of a resource person with advanced subject expertise from the CU Spanish Department to work with the head of Cataloging to facilitate the organization of these personal items was arranged. Gullón's papers were thus reviewed and processed, with final organization being a collection of 57 boxes. A finding aid was prepared and the entire lot was collection-level cataloged using the AMC format on OCLC.

As an outgrowth of this activity, a second project was designed to take on CU's newly-moved boxes of *comedias*. The subject resource person was again invited to work as part of a collection-level cataloging project. His initial examination of the boxes and items led to the general opinion that the collection was worthy of reprocessing to upgrade its cataloging. At this point some consideration was given to doing full catalog records for each play, but cost was deemed prohibitive.

Reasons for this decision include the sheer number of the *comedias* and the already fully-taxed workflows within CU's Technical Services from regular purchases. As mentioned, Colorado has run counter to the national trend of less buying; ARL monographic purchases have shrunk 15 percent since 1986[4] while CU has shown growth virtually every year. Thus, the use of the AMC format for cataloging the *comedias* as a collection (at the box level) was entertained and determined feasible.

The *comedias* project drew from resources on hand. A team of several individuals was involved in the execution of the work as the project went forward. Also, the original finding aid (prepared in 1956) provided a reliable tool in several phases of the work.

The first step following the decision to start project work was to inventory the boxes to determine holdings. A sweep through the containers resulted in the removal of extraneous matter that had built up over the past thirty-five years of shelving in public stacks areas. This included slips of note paper left behind by library users as well as odd pieces of other material (i.e., gum wrappers, paper clips, etc.). A number of the plays was misfiled, and many boxes needed reordering. Likewise, a number of items not belonging to the *comedias* collection was found wrongly inserted into the containers. These were returned to regular shelving areas after checks on their status as lost or missing items were completed.

After the determination that the collection was for the most part sound and intact, the resource person began a more detailed review of each box to appraise contents as to scholarly import, relevance to the genre, and physical condition. It was verified that the collection was a well created one; virtually all items did belong to the *comedias* phenomenon and thus deserved to remain in the accumulation. Physical condition was more uneven, however, and it was noted as such. Given that the boxes were already moved to the controlled environment of the Special Collections Department, it was recommended that archival containers and envelopes be utilized for future storage. This activity has now been carried out.

A next step in the processing involved probably the most difficult and sensitive portion of the project. As mentioned, cost prohibited the full cataloging of each piece. The decision to use AMC format cataloging led to discussions concerning what information to include in each catalog record. The suggestion to include a full contents note was made by the support staff member of the project team as everyone prepared for the actual keying of records on OCLC. It was also decided that only one author added entry per box would be made as a concession to time limitations (a recognition that time can work against the best intentions). Again, working in favor of and supporting that logic were the heavy workflows on hand that offered little discretionary time other than perhaps a slot of about one hour per day for OCLC input. Therefore, it was decided that just one added name entry would be generated for each box cataloged.

The determination of which playwright to trace was made by the subject resource person, working in close contact with the head of Cataloging. As stated, both are subject specialists in Spanish and Latin American studies and usually arrived easily in agreement as to which author to name. Their decision was based on merit of the playwright's work, and they did no prior checking of local on-line catalog holdings to influence this. Once that was done, the keying of records began.

CONSTANT DATA RECORDS

The advent of OCLC PRISM service is being hailed widely as a step for efficiency and as a matter of technological achievement across the library community.[5] One salient feature of PRISM is the possibility of overlays of pattern records in the processing of accumulations of similar materials. The CU Libraries Spanish *comedias* project would have been much more difficult without the constant data overlay feature of PRISM.

On OCLC's old system, called now the First System, creation of cataloging records for similar materials offered little in expediency. With the "new" command, certain fields could be gleaned from existing records with like bibliographic elements but only to a certain point. Fixed field data, for example, had to be rekeyed entirely in all situations. PRISM, however, offers the overlay capability that includes both fixed and variable fields data. This basic word processing characteristic clearly represents a major breakthrough in the processing of materials in the AMC format.

Figure 1 shows the cataloging record for box 49. Figure 2 represents the collection-level record used in this project. Few areas other than the 505 contents note needed complete keying/rekeying, while call numbers, dates, and collation specifics needed only adjustments.

The span of dates of the contents of each box was captured by glancing through the original finding aid that was used for the 505 input. Records were keyed by the project team staff member and placed on "save" for review by CU's head of Cataloging, the project's cataloging coordinator, who scanned the saved record against the original finding aid to ascertain accuracy and completeness. He then verified each author chosen for added entry tracing against the national on-line name authority file and other bibliographic sources as need dictated to ensure compliance with AACR2 standards. Records were thus produced on OCLC and later tape-loaded into CU's local automated catalog PAC.

CONCLUSION

Below is an analysis of the result of the *comedias* project (see Tables 1 and 2). One can see that some 58 percent of the names traced were unique to Colorado's on-line holdings; another 12 percent were represented by just one other entry. Therefore, an enrichment of the scope of the CU's coverage of Spanish literature has been accomplished.

On the other hand, some 21 percent of the playwrights entered in the project were well represented, having many hits in PAC: i.e., four or more entries retrieved via name search on PAC in the Libraries. This result

FIGURE 1. Catalog Record at Box Level

```
OCLC: 252869231              Rec stat:   n              Used:    19920217
Entered: 19920217            Replaced: 19920217         Lang:    spa
▲ Type: b        Bib lvl: c      Source: d              Ctry:    xx
Repr:            Enc lvl: K                              Dates: 1852,1933 ¶
Desc: a          Mod rec:        Dat tp:  k
▲  1  040        COD #c COD ¶
▲  2  090        PQ6226 #b .C6 Box-49 ¶
▲  3  090        #b ¶

▲  5  110 2      Garc´ia Rico (Firm) ¶
▲  6  245 10     Colecci´on de comedias espa˜nolas de los siglos XIX y XX #f 1852-
1933 ¶
▲  7  300        25 items ¶
▲  8  505 0      1174. El se˜nor duque / Antonio Fern´andez Lepina -- 1175. El
valiente capit´an / A. Fern´andez Lepina -- 1176. La escuela de los maridos /
Leandro Fern´andez de Morat´in -- 1177. El s´i de las ni˜nas / L. Fern´andez de
Morat´in -- 1178. La casa de socorro / Manuel Fern´andez Palomero. ¶
```

53

FIGURE 1 (continued)

▲ 9 505 0 1179. El guitarrico / Manuel Fern´andez de la Puente -- 1180. El
lego de San Pablo / M. Fern´andez de la Puente -- 1181. Loreto-Fr´egoli / M.
Fern´andez de la Puente -- 1182. Ninon / M. Fern´andez de la Puente -- 1183.
Si las mujeres mandasen / M. Fern´andez de la Puente. ¶
▲ 10 505 0 1184. Una perla en el fango / Federico Fern´andez San Rom´an --
1185. "Las ermitas" / Luis Fern´andez de Sevilla -- 1186. "Estudiantina" / L.
Fern´andez de Sevilla -- 1187. Madre Alegr´ia / L. Fern´andez de Sevilla --
1188. La bendici´on / Carlos Fern´andez Shaw -- 1189. No somos nadie / C.
Fern´andez Shaw. ¶
▲ 11 505 0 1190. El tirador de Palomas / C. Fern´andez Shaw -- 1191. La
venta de Don Quijote / C. Fern´andez Shaw -- 1192. Pascual Cordero / Emilio
Fern´andez Vaamonde -- 1193. La casa de los p´ajaros / Jos´e Fern´andez del
Villar -- 1194. La caseta de la feria / J. Fern´andez del Villar -- 1195. El
clavo / J. Fern´andez Villar. ¶
▲ 12 505 0 1196. Constantino Pla / J. Fern´andez Villar -- 1197. El huerto
de los rosales / J. Fern´andez Villar -- 1198. Mujeres y flores / J. Fern´andez
Villar. ¶
▲ 13 650 0 Spanish drama ‡y 19th century. ¶
▲ 14 650 0 Spanish drama ‡y 20th century. ¶
▲ 15 700 22 Fern´andez Shaw, Carlos, ‡d 1865-1911. ‡t Selections. ¶

FIGURE 2. Catalog Record for Collection

```
OCLC: 246177983           Rec stat:      n
Entered: 19911024         Replaced:      19911024      Used:    19911024
Type: b        Bib lvl: c      Source:     d           Lang:    spa
Repr:          Enc lvl: K                               Ctry:    xx
Desc: a        Mod rec:        Dat tp:  k               Dates:   1800,1941 ¶
  1  040       COD ‡c COD ¶
  2  090       PQ6226 ‡b .C6 ¶
  3  090       ‡b ¶

  5  110 2     Garc´ia Rico (Firm) ¶
  6  245 10    Colecci´on de comedias espa~nolas de los siglos XIX y XX ‡f 1800–
1941 ¶
  7  300       3763 items ¶
  8  351       Kept in boxes ¶
  9  555       Inventory ‡b available in library : ‡c box level control ¶
 10  650  0    Spanish drama ‡y 19th century. ¶
 11  650  0    Spanish drama ‡y 20th century. ¶
```

Table 1. Profile of Project Playwrights in CU's PAC

# traced only by project		81 (58%)
# held with just 1 representation	17	(12%)
# with 2 or 3 prior entries	12	(9%)
# well represented prior		
to project (4 or more entries)	29	(21%)
	--	
sub-total	139	
authors with multiple boxes	6	
	---	
total boxes	145	(100%)

testifies to the strength of the CU Libraries Spanish collection in place prior to the start of this project and underscores the value of efforts like this to reinforce a collection and its strength. This is evident when one realizes that authors selected for tracing in the project were chosen from among many possibilities of those contained in the boxes. Virtually every box had more than one author represented. The fact that authors with many hits were given additional entry points from this project's cataloging is notable in that users may now find access to other plays by these important and noted authors that may not have been otherwise available. The duplication rate of individual plays now accessible with those previously accessible is beyond the current range of this project; this follow-up work will be undertaken as a second review. A second phase of this project could also add tracings for other playwrights from each box.

This project's success is a strong argument in favor of collection-level cataloging since many ARL libraries have resources with limited accessibility that could gain in use if they were processed with the AMC format as Colorado has done with the *comedias*. With few exceptions, CU Libraries does all its cataloging on OCLC to full national standards and will continue to do so as a responsible member of the national bibliographic community. However, collection-level project cataloging such as this *comedias* endeavor should be recognized as a viable way to make specialized materials accessible and considered an attractive and affordable means to increase user service in these demanding times of escalating need and ever-tighter budget realities.

Table 2. Collection-Level Cataloging: Enriching the Database

AUTHOR TRACED IN PROJECT	STATUS IN PAC AT CU
Box 1	
Joaquin Abati	project catalog record only
Box 2	
Juan de Alba	project catalog record only
Box 3	
Vicente Almela Mengot	project catalog record only
Box 4	
Nicasio Alvarez de Cienfuegos ..	2 other hits
Box 5-6	
Alvarez Quintero Brothers	many hits
Box 7	
Leonid Andreyev	many hits
Box 8	
José M. Aparici y Valparda	project catalog record only
Box 9	
Juan de Ariza	1 other hit
Box 10	
Carlos Arniches y Barrera	many hits
Box 11	
Victor Ducange	3 other hits
Box 12	
Eusebio Asquerino	project catalog record only
Box 13	
Victor Balaguer	2 other hits
Box 14	
Mariano Barranco	1 other hit

TABLE 2 (continued)

Box 15

Juan Belza . . . . project catalog record only

Box 16

Jacinto Benavente . . . . many hits

Box 17

Ildefonso Antonio Bermejo . . . . . project catalog record only

Box 18

Gerardo Blanco . . . . project catalog record only

Box 19

Eusebio Blasco . . . . 2 other hits

Box 20

Vicente Blasco Ibáñez . . . . many hits

Box 21-23

Manuel Bretón de los Herreros . . many hits

Box 24

Angel Caamaño . . . . project catalog record only

Box 25

Antonio Calero Ortiz . . . . project catalog record only

Box 26

Ramón de Campoamor . . . . many hits

Box 27

Francisco Camprodón . . . . project catalog record only

Box 28

Gonzalo Cantó . . . . project catalog record only

Box 29

Bartolomé Carcassona . . . . project catalog record only

Box 30

Pelayo del Castillo .... project catalog record only

Box 31

Juan Catalina .... project catalog record only

Box 32

Juan Antonio Cavestany .... 1 other hit

Box 33

Gaspar Fernando Coll .... project catalog record only

Box 34

Luis Cortés y Suaña .... project catalog record only

Box 35

Manuel Cuartero .... project catalog record only

Box 36

Júlio Dantas .... 3 other hits

Box 37

Sinesio Delgado .... 2 other hits

Box 38

José Maria Diaz .... project catalog record only

Box 39

Joaquin Dicenta .... many hits

Box 40

Antonio Dominguez .... project catalog record only

Box 41

José Echegaray .... many hits

TABLE 2 (continued)

Box 42

Miguel Echegaray . . . . project catalog record only

Box 43

Luis de Eguilaz y Eguilaz . . . . . . 1 other hit

Box 44

Juan B. Enseñat y Morell . . . . . . 1 other hit

Box 45

Pedro Escamilla . . . . project catalog record only

Box 46

José Estremera . . . . project catalog record only

Box 47

Luis Fernández Ardavín . . . . 2 other hits

Box 48

Antonio Fernández Lepina . . . . . . project catalog record only

Box 49

Carlos Fernández Shaw . . . . many hits

Box 50

José Fernández del Villar . . . . . project catalog record only

Box 51

Francisco Flores García . . . . 3 other hits

Box 52

José Fola Igúrbide . . . . 1 other hit

Box 53

Carlos Frontaura y Vázquez . . . . 1 other hit

Box 54

Adolfo García . . . . project catalog record only

Box 55

Enrique Garcia Alvarez .... 1 other hit

Box 56

Manuel Garcia González .... project catalog record only

Box 57

Antonio Garcia Gutiérrez ...... many hits

Box 58

Rafael Garcia y Santisteban .... project catalog record only

Box 59

Enrique Gaspar .... 1 other hit

Box 60

Constantino Gil .... project catalog record only

Box 61

Casimiro Giralt .... project catalog record only

Box 62

Valentín Gómez .... project catalog record only

Box 63

Salvador Maria Granés .... project catalog record only

Box 64

Angel Guimerá .... many hits

Box 65

José Maria Gutiérrez de Alba ... 1 other hit

Box 66

Juan Eugenio Hartzenbusch .... many hits

TABLE 2 (continued)

Box 67

Antonio Hurtado .... project catalog record only

Box 68

Alberto Insúa .... many hits

Box 69

Eduardo Jackson Cortés .... project catalog record only

Box 70

José Jackson Veyán .... project catalog record only

Box 71

Gonzalo Jover .... project catalog record only

Box 72-73

Luis Mariano de Larra .... project catalog records only

Box 74

Mariano José de Larra .... many hits

Box 75

Salvador Lastra .... project catalog record only

Box 76

Rafael María Liern .... project catalog record only

Box 77

Manuel Linares Rivas .... many hits

Box 78

Adelardo López de Ayala .... many hits

Box 79

Enrique López Marín .... project catalog record only

Box 80

José López Pinillos .... many hits

Box 81

José López Silva .... 1 other hit

Box 82

Tomás Luceño y Becerra .... project catalog record only

Box 83

Adolfo Llanos y Alcaraz .... 2 other hits

Box 84

José Marco .... project catalog record only

Box 85

Emilio Mario .... project catalog record only

Box 86

Pedro Marquina .... project catalog record only

Box 87

Gregorio Martínez Sierra ...... many hits

Box 88

Manuel Matoses .... project catalog record only

Box 89

Miguel Mihura .... many hits

Box 90

Luis Millá .... project catalog record only

Box 91

Eduardo Montesinos .... project catalog record only

Box 92

Pantaleón Moreno Gil .... project catalog record only

TABLE 2 (continued)

Box 93

Emilio Mozo de Rosales .... project catalog record only

Box 94

Pedro Muñoz Seca .... many hits

Box 95

Ramón de Navarrete .... project catalog record only

Box 96

Calixto Navarro .... project catalog record only

Box 97

Eduardo Navarro Gonzalvo ..... project catalog record only

Box 98

Gaspar Núñez de Arce .... many hits

Box 99

Luis Olona .... many hits

Box 100

César Ordás-Avecilla

de Urrengoechea .... project catalog record only

Box 101

Manuel Ortiz de Pinedo .... project catalog record only

Box 102

Ceferino Palencia .... project catalog record only

Box 103

Pablo Parellada .... project catalog record only

Box 104

Antonio Paso .... 1 other hit

Box 105

Emilio Sánchez Pastor .... project catalog record only

Box 106

Miguel Pastorfido .... project catalog record only

Box 107

Felipe Pérez Capo ....J.... 1 other hit

Box 108

Enrique Pérez Escrich .... 3 other hits

Box 109

Felipe Pérez y González .... 1 other hit

Box 110

Eloy Perillán Buxó .... project catalog record only

Box 111

Guillermo Perrin .... project catalog record only

Box 112-113

Mariano Pina Domínguez .... project catalog records only

Box 114

José Ma. Pous .... project catalog record only

Box 115

Enrique Prieto Enriquez .... project catalog record only

Box 116

Ricardo Puente y Brañas ...... project catalog record only

Box 117

Miguel Ramos Carrión .... many hits

Box 118

Francisco Luis de Retes ...... project catalog record only

TABLE 2 (continued)

Box 119

Juan Rico y Amat   . . . . 1 other hit

Box 120

Juan Rodriguez Rubi . . . . project catalog record only

Box 121

Tomás Rodriguez Rubi . . . . project catalog record only

Box 122

Cayetano Rosell . . . . 2 other hits

Box 123

Eugenio Rubi . . . . project catalog record only

Box 124

Eduardo Sainz Noguera . . . . project catalog record only

Box 125

Laureano Sánchez Garay . . . . project catalog record only

Box 126

Antonio Sánchez Pérez . . . . project catalog record only

Box 127

Felipe Sassone . . . . many hits

Box 128

Antonio María Segovia . . . . project catalog record only

Box 129

Narciso Serra . . . . 1 other hit

Box 130

Francisco Serrano Anguita . . . . . project catalog record only

Box 131

Eusebio Sierra .... project catalog record only

Box 132

Ceferino Suárez Bravo .... project catalog record only

Box 133

Manuel Tamayo y Baus .... many hits

Box 134

Angel Torres del Alamo .... project catalog record only

Box 135

Rafael Torromé .... project catalog record only

Box 136

Luis Valdés .... project catalog record only

Box 137

Aurelio Varela .... project catalog record only

Box 138

Ricardo de la Vega .... 3 other hits

Box 139

Ventura de la Vega .... many hits

Box 140

Francisco Villaespesa .... many hits

Box 141

Fiacro Yráyzoz .... project catalog record only

Box 142

Marcos Zapata .... 1 other hit

Box 143-144

Enrique Zumel .... project catalog records only

Box 145

Vital Aza .... many hits

NOTES

REFERENCES

1. OCLC, Inc., *Cataloging User Guide: PRISM Service* (Dublin, Ohio: OCLC Online Computer Library Center, 1990), 7:73-82.

2. Nancy J. Membrez, "The Mass Production of Theater in Nineteenth-Century Madrid," in *The Crisis of Institutionalized Literature in Spain*, ed. Wlad Godzich and Nicholas Spadaccini (Minneapolis: Prisma Institute, 1988), 310-343.

3. *Diccionario de autores iberoamericanos*, s.v. "Gullón, Ricardo."

4. Sarah Pritchard, "ARL Statistics Show Shift from Ownership to Access," *ARL: A Bimonthly Newsletter of Research Library Issues and Actions* 161 (2 March 1992): 3.

5. Nita Dean, "Users Say PRISM Works Better, Faster," *OCLC Newsletter* 195 (Jan./Feb. 1992):16-25.

The Literature of Classical Antiquity and the PA Schedule

George F. Johnston

SUMMARY. This article evaluates the Library of Congress PA schedule as to how well it classifies classical literature. To do this, we take a two-pronged approach. After outlining the various types of material published in the area of classical literature, we examine PA to see how well it classifies these various types of material. Finally we examine the format of the PA schedule and discuss its usefulness to the cataloger. We arrive at the conclusion that most types of material are well treated by the schedule, except that LC's policy of separation of non-literary materials may be a hindrance to some libraries in their shelving of translations and commentaries. We also find that PA is an old schedule which is in desperate need of revision.

INTRODUCTION

Ancient Latin and Greek are now considered by many to be "dead" languages. After all, how many people speak them any more? But the literature on these languages and on the literature generated by those who once spoke and wrote them is very much alive. It is hard to get a picture of

George F. Johnston, BA, MDiv, MLS, is Cataloger of classics materials at the University of Cincinnati.

The author wishes to thank his colleagues Jeff Crawford, Jacquelene Riley, and Jean Wellington for their many fine suggestions on earlier drafts of this document. Any weaknesses that remain are, of course, his own.

[Haworth co-indexing entry note]: "The Literature of Classical Antiquity and the PA Schedule." Johnston, George F. Co-published simultaneously in *Cataloging & Classification Quarterly* (The Haworth Press, Inc.) Vol. 17, No. 1/2, 1993, pp. 69-85; and: *Languages of the World: Cataloging Issues and Problems* (ed: Martin D. Joachim) The Haworth Press, Inc., 1993, pp. 69-85. Multiple copies of this article/chapter may be purchased from The Haworth Document Delivery Center [1-800-3-HAWORTH; 9:00 a.m. - 5:00 p.m. (EST)].

the amount of material published in classical studies each year. The *Bowker Annual* each year gives the total number of books from U.S. publishers broken down by subject, but classical studies is not listed among the subjects. Even if it were, however, this would cover only a fraction because a large percentage of the output in the classics comes from foreign publishers. At the University of Cincinnati, where we collect rather broadly, our purchases of classics books in the fiscal year 1991-92 totaled 2570 volumes. This figure includes only firm orders and books received on various approval plans. It does not include standing orders, which would add another 25 to 33 percent to this figure. This is only a small portion of what is actually published and reflects the purchases of only one institution.[1]

Because there is such a large amount of material published in the area of classical literature, it is important that a classification for this area be one well suited for the type of literature published. The Library of Congress developed the PA schedule to organize its material on classical literature, and thousands of libraries nationwide have adopted the Library of Congress Classification for their own use. Therefore, it is fitting that we evaluate the PA classification both in terms of its organization of the material in this subject area and in terms of the format of the schedule itself.

Before we go any further, it is important that we define our terms. In this article we shall use the term *classical studies*, or *classics*, to refer to studies on the art, literature, and culture of the ancient Greeks and Romans, as well as to the supporting studies of ancient history, archaeology, numismatics, etc. We shall use the term *classical literature* to refer not just to the literature generated by the ancient Greeks and Romans but also to books written about that literature.

Scope

Any good classics collection will include not just books on the texts of the classical authors but will also obtain a significant amount of supporting material in other areas of classical studies, such as ancient history and culture, civilization, etc.; the archaeology of sites in the classical world, and on archaeological expeditions to these sites; numismatics of the period; and books on Greek and Roman art. Though these topics form an important part of a classics collection, I shall not be considering them in this paper because they would be classed outside the PA schedule.

It should be noted that the PA schedule includes a classification for the Latin and Greek languages as well as Latin and Greek literature. Most of my comments in this paper, however, will be limited to a discussion of its classification of Latin and Greek literature. This decision is based on the assumption that the core of any good classics collection is the texts of the Latin and Greek authors and books about these texts. Books on the languages themselves will form a much smaller, albeit important, part of the collection.

I shall also limit myself to evaluating The Library of Congress PA schedule on its own merits; I have not attempted to compare it with other classification schemes such as the Dewey Decimal.

Classical Literature

Before we can evaluate the PA schedule, we must first understand the kind of material that is common in the area of classical literature. Any classification of classical literature needs to take these types of literature into account and provide a good, coherent organization for all of them. There are seven basic kinds of material published in the area of classical literature:

1. *Textual series.* Series which are designed to present the original Latin or Greek texts of the whole corpus of classical literature. These series may include critical apparatus, and they may or may not include translations. Two such series are the Loeb Classical Library and the Bibliotheca Teubneriana.
2. *Collections of (a) several works of one author or (b) several examples of one particular genre, such as drama.* These collections may include only the original texts, the originals plus translations, or only translations. They may or may not be accompanied by introductions to each of the works included.
3. *Texts of individual works, or portions of works, in the original Latin or Greek.* These may or may not be accompanied by textual apparatus and may or may not include translations.
4. *School texts.* These give the original texts of works, usually without translations. Included, however, are introductions to the works and extensive notes which give the student help with translation and historical and cultural background information.
5. *Translations of individual works, usually with introductions to the works.* These are usually designed to enable lay persons who are not familiar with Latin or Greek to read the great works of old without getting them involved in the intricacies of the ancient languages.
6. *Commentaries on individual works.* These may or may not include the original texts and may or may not include translations. Provided are extensive commentaries giving the meaning of the works on an almost line by line basis. The difference between this

group of material and the school texts discussed above is that the notes in school texts usually concentrate on assisting the student with translation, whereas commentaries are more concerned with textual information–e.g., the meaning of a particular phrase, where it originated, other places in classical literature where it is used, etc.

7. *General discussions of an author and his works.* In this category we can also include general discussions of particular genres–for example, Greek drama. Some books in this category may discuss particular subjects covered in the classical texts–for example, slavery in Greek poetry or the poetic style of the Greek historian Thucydides.

Now that we have an understanding of the kinds of material published on classical literature, we are ready to begin our discussion of the PA schedule in particular. We shall first discuss the general, overall organization of the schedule and examine various parts of it in more detail. We shall discuss the split of non-literary material by classical authors between PA and subject classifications. We shall conclude by discussing the format of the PA schedule and improvements that can be made to make it more useful to the cataloger.

GENERAL ORGANIZATION OF PA

The cataloger must be aware that the PA schedule comes in two parts: the basic PA schedule itself and the PA *Supplement.* When PA was first published in 1928, it excluded medieval and modern Latin literature and Byzantine and modern Greek literature except in outline form. It was not until forty years later that the full classification for these periods of Latin and Greek literature was published as the PA *Supplement.* I am including here my own outline of the PA schedule. This outline is a modified version of Synopsis I, found in PA. It includes numbers not originally a part of the schedule but now published in cumulated additions and changes by Gale Research and incorporates numbers from the PA *Supplement* into it.[2] When I refer to PA or the PA schedule I shall be referring to PA and the PA *Supplement* as a whole.

OUTLINE OF THE PA SCHEDULE

PA–Greek and Latin Philology and Literature

1- 199   Classical Philology (General)

201-1179	Greek Philology and Language
201- 591	Classical
601- 691	Hellenistic
695- 791	Biblical. Septuagint
801- 895	New Testament
1000-1179	Medieval and Modern
2001-2915	Latin Philology and Language
2001-2390	Classical
2391-2550	Ancient Dialects of Italy (Etruscan, etc.)
2600-2748	Vulgar Latin
2801-2899	Medieval
2901-2915	Modern
2901-2905	1350/1500-
2911-2915	19th Century-
3000-3049	Classical Literature (General)
3050-5665	Greek Literature
3050-4500	Classical (to ca. 600 A.D.)
3050-3291	History
3300-3681	Collections
3818-4500	Individual Authors, A-Z, Through 700 A.D.
4505	Medieval & Modern Authors Writing in Classical Greek, A-Z
5000-5665	Byzantine and Modern
5000-5040	History and Criticism
5050-5075	Collections
5101-5298	Special Periods
5101-5198	Medieval. Byzantine
5201-5298	Modern (Including Renaissance)
5301-5610	Individual Authors or Works

5301-5395	Byzantine to 1600, A-Z
5609-5610	Modern, 1600-1960, A-Z
5611-5637	Modern, 1961- , A-Z
5650-5665	Modern Greek Authors Outside of Greece
6000-8595	Latin Literature
5000-6971	Roman (to ca. 700 A.D.)
6000-6098	History
6100-6191	Collections
6202-6971	Individual Authors, A-Z
8001-8595	Medieval and Modern
8001-8096	History and Criticism
8101-8149	Collections
8155-8199	Translations from Latin into Other Languages
8200-8595	Individual Authors or Works
8200-8445	Medieval to 1350
8450-8595	Modern, 1350-

Several points regarding the general organization of PA need to be made.

1. Note that classical literature in general comes first, followed by Greek literature, and finally Latin literature.

2. Greek and Latin literature are then divided into two major time periods: classical, and Medieval and modern. In the prefatory note to PA, the classical period is defined for Greek literature as ending with the reign of Justinian I, or 527-565 A.D., and for Latin literature as ending about 600 A.D. It is with the definition of these periods that we run into a slight discrepancy, for later in the schedule when it begins listing individual authors, it gives, under classical Greek, the heading **Individual authors to 700 A.D.** The outline at the beginning of PA (Synopsis I) at this point gives the caption **Classical (to ca. 600 A.D.).** This, at least, is more consistent with dating it with the reign of Justinian I, who died in 565 A.D. The intention of the schedule is to have classical Greek literature include everything up to the beginning of the Byzantine period. The question then becomes: when does classical Greek literature end and Byzantine literature begin? To answer that question here would take us well beyond the

scope of this paper. At this point, however, we should note that the basic PA schedule includes several Greek authors who flourished during the sixth century, whereas the PA *Supplement* includes at least two authors who lived in the seventh century.[3] It appears that LC's intention is to make the break between classical and Byzantine Greek at about 600 A.D. This would be consistent with placing it at the reign of Justinian I and would agree with the statement in the outline. If this assessment of LC's intention is correct, then the date of 700 A.D., given on page 83 of the schedule, is in error.

It should also be noted that the definition of classical Latin provides its own discrepancy. The preface to PA states that "the beginning of the seventh century marks the end of the Roman literature." This would place it at 600 A.D. The outline, however, gives the caption **Roman (to ca. 700 A.D.)**. At least this discrepancy is not a major one and has not caused any real problems in cataloging.

3. Within each period there is the recurring pattern of (a) **History and criticism**, (b) **Collections**, and (c) **Individual authors**.[4] The history and criticism sections include general works on the literary history of the period and literature concerned and special topics relating to the literature of that period as a whole. They then usually include sections on the various genres of literature, such as poetry, drama, and prose. See, for example, the section on classical Latin literature (PA6000-6098). Note that LC prefers to place all periodicals, serial collections, and other generalities other than literary history together in either classical philology (PA1-85), or if specific to Latin, in Latin philology (PA2001-2067).

It is interesting to note that similar publications that are specific to Greek are not classed with Greek philology but rather with classical philology. In the schedule, PA3050 is in parentheses,[5] and the heading reads "Generalities; Serial publications, etc., *see* PA1-85. If desired reference may be made here; *see also* PA3061." As we examine the schedule, we find that it is not uncommon for LC to group the history of Greek literature together with classical literature in general but to give the history of Latin literature its own place in PA6000-6098. See, for example the following numbers given in parentheses in PA:

(3065)	Literary landmarks, etc., *see* PA3006
(3066)	Iconography, *see* PA3006.9
(3069)	Relations to history, civilization, culture (in general). Prefer PA3009.

Other topics in the areas of Greek literature, however, receive their own number and are not grouped together with classical literature. Exactly why

LC did this is not certain. It is possible, however, that at the time the PA schedule was created, LC may have felt that its collections in the areas grouped together with classical literature were not large enough to warrant giving them their own numbers; but place was made for them so that LC could begin to use these numbers in the future if the collections grew. It is possible too that LC's collection strength in Latin literature was much stronger, and so it was not grouped together with classical literature. There are other parts of the LC classification, however, where we find this practice of classing one subject with more general works while a subject corollary to the first is given its own place and number.[6]

After the history and criticism sections, within each period, come the sections designed for collections. These provide for collections either of the entire corpus of Latin or Greek literature or of particular genres. This section is self-explanatory and needs no special mention.

The individual authors sections, especially for the classical period, are quite long and extensive. They include nearly every author, whether major or minor. In the prefatory note to PA, LC explains its reasoning in this way:

> The schedules for Greek and Roman literature contain an extensive list of authors, designed to aid the classifier in distinguishing homonymous writers and in the occasionally difficult arrangement of names. The inclusion of many more or less obscure names may seem unnecessary; it is justified, nevertheless, because it enables the classifier to avoid cumbersome and injudicious notation. Inasmuch as the classical literature practically presents a closed *fond,* the extent of possibilities may be very nearly indicated, whereas with modern literature this is obviously impracticable.

This was a wise decision on LC's part because it has meant that the cataloger rarely if ever encounters a classical author who is not listed in the schedule. This statement, however, is much more true of PA itself than of the PA *Supplement.* The original PA schedule is much more detailed than the *Supplement.*

SEPARATION OF NON-LITERARY MATERIAL

Statement of the Problem and LC's Approach

In classifying works by literary writers, it is obvious that their works will go into the appropriate literature schedule in P. In the case of non-literary writers, however, especially those who are well known, the cataloger must decide where to classify their works. Should they be classed according to subject or with literature? For modern authors, this is usually not an issue–they are classed by subject. For classical writers, however, this is an important question; not only have they made contributions to their particular subject areas, but they are also known for their overall contributions to their language and literature. It should also be noted that many of the publications about these writers are of a technical nature: original texts, with or without translations, school editions, etc.

It is obvious that the Library of Congress has wrestled with this issue as well. LC has opted for a both/and rather than an either/or approach. Some items are classed by subject, others with literature. LC has developed a policy that outlines which kinds of materials go where. This policy is stated in both schedules B and D. The B schedule (4th ed., 1989) states at B165:

> At the Library of Congress the distinction in use between classes B and PA in classifying philosophical works by Greek and Roman writers is as follows:
>
> In class B:
>
> 1. Translations with or without original text, except translations into Latin (PA). Tables I-V give the arrangement for translations.
> 2. Original text with commentaries, if the editor's purpose is interpretive. These are classified with the criticism of the work or works. Tables I-V give the arrangement for criticism.
>
> In class PA:
>
> 1. Original Greek and Latin texts (except as noted above).
> 2. Latin translations.
> 3. Texts with textual criticism.

It should be emphasized that, though this passage refers specifically to the distinction between B and PA, the Library of Congress applies this principle much more broadly. We could easily substitute the phrase "In a subject classification" for "In class B." The fact that this same passage is quoted almost verbatim in a footnote to D58 in the D schedule underscores this fact. Indeed, footnotes with similarly worded statements have been added at the beginning of the Greek authors and Latin authors sections of the additions and changes to the PA schedule and state explicitly that individual works by Greek and Latin authors are classified "in classes B-Z, according to the topic of the work."

When we examine this statement closely, we find the following general principle behind it: non-literary works that are textual in nature are classed in PA; books that are interpretive are classed in the appropriate subject classification. To use the categories of material published in classical literature listed above, we find that in general school texts will be classed in PA whereas commentaries will be in the appropriate subject classification. Texts alone, with or without textual apparatus, will be classed in PA whereas texts with translations will be in the appropriate subject classification. It appears that LC's goal is to classify items of primary interest to the classical scholar–the original texts, textual criticism, etc.–in PA. Scholars in other subject areas, philosophy for example, may want to consult the works of Plato and Aristotle but not want to be overwhelmed by the original Greek and the notes one generally finds, for example, in school texts. These scholars may want only translations, whether or not the original texts are present, and perhaps interpretive commentaries. These books will be found in the B classification where they would be doing most of their work.

Examples of LC's Practice

There are numerous examples of this practice. We find works by Aristotle in both B and PA. Caesar's *Gallic Wars* can be found in both DC and PA. Works by the Greek physician Hippocrates can be found in both R and PA. Figures 1 and 2 show LC bibliographic records that illustrate this split. Figure 1 is a record for a Greek text of Plato's *Republic* with notes and is classed in PA. Figure 2 is a record for an English translation of *The Republic* and is classed in JC.

Figures 3 and 4 are another matched pair of LC records that illustrate this split. Figure 3 is for a Greek edition of Aristotle's *Nicomachean Ethics*. The title statement indicates that it was "edited with a commentary." What kind of commentary is not specified, but it appears that either it was not "interpretive," or else the commentary was minor when compared to the text, for LC classed this work in PA. Figure 4 is for an English translation of selections of the *Nicomachean Ethics* and is classed in B.

Evaluation of This Practice

These examples illustrate the distinction which LC makes between classical books to be classed by subject and those to be classed in PA. Is this a useful practice that should be maintained, or should it be altered in some way or dispensed with entirely? The answer to this question really

FIGURE 1. Greek text of Plato's *Republic* classified in PA

```
OCLC:  14933110        Rec stat:    c
Entered:    19861120   Replaced:    19871219    Used:     19920827
Type: a         Bib lvl: m     Source:         Lang:  eng
Repr:           Enc lvl:       Conf pub: 0     Ctry:  nyu
Indx: 1         Mod rec:       Govt pub:       Cont:
Desc: a         Int lvl:       Festschr: 0     Illus:
                F/B:      0    Dat tp:   r      Dates: 1987,1894
   1  010    86-29610//r872
   2  040    DLC  c DLC
   3  020    0824069218 (alk. paper) :  c $155.00
   4  041 0  enggrc
   5  050 0  PA4279  b .R4 1987
   6  082 0  321/.07  2 19
   7  090    b
   8  049    CINN
   9  100 0  Plato.
  10  240 10 Republic
  11  245 10 Plato's Republic /  c edited by Lewis Campbell and Benjamin
Jowett.
  12  260    New York :  b Garland,  c 1987.
  13  300    3 v. ;  c 24 cm.
  14  440 0  Greek & Roman philosophy ;  v 22
  15  500    Text in Greek, notes and essays in English.
  16  500    Reprint. Originally published: Oxford : Clarendon Press, 1894.
  17  500    Includes indexes.
  18  650 0  Political science  x Early works to 1800.
  19  650 0  Utopias.
  20  700 10 Cambell, Lewis,  d 1830-1908.
  21  700 10 Jowett, Benjamin,  d 1817-1893.
```

depends on the individual library. Each has its own individual characteristics and needs.

A general undergraduate library with a small classics collection may find this separation satisfactory. Patrons doing research in any subject area will find in the appropriate section of the LC classification books that will be of interest to their research. The classics major would find books on textual criticism of the original text of Aristotle in PA. The philosopher would find translations and commentaries of Aristotle in B.

Other libraries with medium to large size classics collections may find this separation undesirable, but they opt to live with it because they do not have the time and resources to develop their own policy and change the call numbers on LC and member copy records that this policy would require.

At the University of Cincinnati (UC), however, where we have a separate Classics Library with a collection of about 140,000 volumes, serving the Classics Department, this was determined to be an undesirable separation of materials. Texts generally wind up in PA, whereas translations of the texts and commentaries on them generally are scattered by subject.

FIGURE 2. English translation of Plato's *Republic* classified in JC

```
OCLC:  11159955          Rec stat:    c
Entered:    19840831     Replaced:    19920114        Used:    19921229
Type: a          Bib lvl: m        Source:            Lang:  eng
Repr:            Enc lvl:           Conf pub: 0        Ctry:  nyu
Indx: 0          Mod rec:           Govt pub:          Cont:  b
Desc: a          Int lvl:           Festschr: 0        Illus:
                 F/B:      0        Dat tp:    s        Dates: 1985,
     1   010     84-20565//r872
     2   040     DLC  c DLC
     3   020     0393019721 :  c $19.95
     4   020     039395501X (pbk.)
     5   041 1   enggrc
     6   050 0   JC71  b .P35 1985
     7   082 0   321/.07  2 19
     8   090     b
     9   049     CINN
    10   100 0   Plato.
    11   240 10  Republic.  l English
    12   245 14  The Republic /  c Plato ; a new translation by Richard W.
Sterling and William C. Scott.
    13   250     1st ed.
    14   260     New York :  b Norton,  c c1985.
    15   300     317 p. ;  c 22 cm.
    16   500     Translation of: Respublica.
    17   504     Includes bibliographical references.
    18   650 0   Political science  x Early works to 1800.
    19   650 0   Utopias.
    20   700 10  Sterling, Richard W.
    21   700 10  Scott, William C.  q (William Clyde),  d 1937-
```

FIGURE 3. Greek text of Aristotle's *Nicomachean Ethics* classified in PA

```
OCLC:  14932973          Rec stat:    p
Entered:    19861117     Replaced:    19870706        Used:    19921102
Type: a          Bib lvl: m        Source:            Lang:  gre
Repr:            Enc lvl:           Conf pub: 0        Ctry:  nyu
Indx: 0          Mod rec:           Govt pub:          Cont:
Desc: a          Int lvl:           Festschr: 0        Illus:
                 F/B:      0        Dat tp:    r        Dates: 1987,1878
     1   010     86-29529
     2   040     DLC  c DLC  d m/c
     3   020     0824069013 :  c $80.00
     4   041 0   grelat
     5   050 0   PA3893  b .E6 1987
     6   082 0   171/.3  2 19
     7   090     b
     8   049     CINN
     9   100 0   Aristotle.  w cn
    10   245 10  Nicomachean ethics /  c Aristotle ; edited with a commentary by
G. Ramsauer.
    11   260     New York ;  a London :  b Garland Pub.,  c 1987.
    12   300     viii, 740 p. ;  c 22 cm.
    13   440 0   Greek & Roman philosophy ;  v 2
    14   500     Reprint. Originally published: Leipzig : Teubner, 1878.
    15   650 0   Ethics  x Early works to 1800.
    16   700 10  Ramsauer, G.  q (Gottfried),  d 1827-1904.  w cn
```

FIGURE 4. English translation of Aristotle's *Nicomachean Ethics* classified in B

```
OCLC:  22240353        Rec stat:    p
Entered:   19900731    Replaced:   19910223    Used:      19920902
Type: a      Bib lvl: m      Source:          Lang:  eng
Repr:        Enc lvl:        Conf pub: 0      Ctry:  cau
Indx: 0      Mod rec:        Govt pub:        Cont:  b
Desc: a      Int lvl:        Festschr: 0      Illus:
             F/B:     0      Dat tp:   s      Dates: 1991,
   1  010    90-45138
   2  040    DLC  c DLC
   3  020    0874848954
   4  041 1  eng  h grc
   5  050 00 B430.A5  b B5413 1990
   6  082 00 171/.3  2 20
   7  090    b
   8  049    CINN
   9  100 0  Aristotle.
  10  240 10 Nicomachean ethics.  l English.  k Selections
  11  245 12 A guided tour of selections from Aristotle´s Nicomachean ethics
/  c [edited by] Christopher Biffle.
  12  260    Mountain View, Calif. :  b Mayfield Pub. Co.,  c c1991.
  13  300    vii, 167 p. ;  c 24 cm.
  14  500    Translation of selections from: Nicomachean ethics.
  15  504    Includes bibliographical references (p. 167).
  16  650  0 Ethics.
  17  700 10 Biffle, Christopher.
```

Classics scholars then wanting original texts and translations and commentaries may find themselves looking in two different places. Since most of the patrons using the Classics Library are faculty members in the department, graduate students, and classics majors, they will want to obtain as much on a particular work as possible. Having works scattered proves to be a hindrance. To rectify this situation, we at UC have opted to class all items relating to a particular classical non-literary work, whether they be translations or commentaries, with the text of that work in PA. The only items in a subject classification are biographies of an author and books dealing with several of an author's works in general. This policy, however, has proved to be a burden on the catalogers and has meant that more of the material in the classics has had to be given to higher level staff than would be the case with books in other subject areas.

Each library, then, will have to decide for itself whether to stay with LC's practice or not. Some will follow it because there is no compelling reason for them to do differently. Many will decide to follow it for economic reasons alone; the cost of not doing so would be prohibitive, whether or not they find the practice desirable. Others may find that they have a compelling enough reason to bear the costs of following a different policy.

NEED FOR A NEW EDITION OF PA

As stated above, the PA schedule was first published in 1928. Since then, there has not been a new edition although LC did republish it in 1968 with supplementary pages of additions and changes added at the end. The PA schedule is thus an old one, and this fact has caused numerous problems for the cataloger in its use:

1. The division between PA and the PA *Supplement,* though not an insurmountable problem, is at the very least an inconvenience.

2. The schedule does not give explicit instructions on how to subdivide many of the entries. For example, see PA3867 (Andocides, fl. 411-391 B.C.). The schedule outlines this number as follows:

.A1	Editions. By date.
.A13-19	Separate Orations.
	De mysteriis.
	De pace.
	De reditu.
	In Alcibiadem.
.A2-69	Translations.
.A7-Z3	Criticism (including criticism of particular orations).
.Z8	Lexicography: Glossaries, indices, etc. By date.

Individual orations are to be classed in the .A13-19 range, but the schedule does not assign cutter numbers for each one. For this reason, each library has to assign its own cutters for each oration. As a result, catalogers will find different cutter numbers for any given title in the bibliographic utilities, making it important for them to check their own shelflists before unquestioningly using numbers on a database record.

3. The schedule lacks table numbers by which to subdivide the entries. When PA was first published, there was merely an appendix with a few tables, but these have long since been abandoned in favor of the language and literature tables now used for the all of the P-PZ language and literature schedules. It is understandable that these table numbers, which were not developed until much later, do not appear in the PA schedule. It does underscore the fact, however, that PA is badly in need of revision. Catalogers must now guess which of the language and literature tables is most useful for the author and title with which they are dealing. Sometimes they may fortunately choose the same table which LC uses; often, however, they will not. Here again there is room for different libraries to use differ-

ent tables, making it difficult to use another library's call number without checking one's own shelflist.

4. The language and literature tables present another problem. Some of these tables do not make clear how commentaries on individual titles are to be shelved. For example, let's examine Table XXXVIII, which is designed for authors who are assigned a cutter number in the schedule. In abridged form, the table looks like this:

Collected works	.xA1-19
Translations (Collected)	.xA2-59
Selected works. Selections. By date	.xA6
Separate works. By title	.xA61-78
Biography and criticism	
Dictionaries, indexes, etc. By date	.xA79
Autobiography, journals, memoirs. By title	.xA8-829
Letters (Collections). By date	.xA83
Letters to and from particular	
individuals. By correspondent	.xA84-849
General works	.xA85-Z

Nowhere does this table provide room for commentaries on a particular title, let alone commentaries on selected portions of a title. The "General works" category is usually designed for works that cover the author's entire corpus. The only option is to try to fit them in with the separate works in .xA61-78. This is a small range, and since the first cutter is already needed for the author's name, one cannot cutter for the commentator. In addition, LC gives no guidance as to how to fit commentaries in with the texts. Is there a way, for example, to cutter for a commentary in the same way there is to cutter for a translation?

There are a number of possible reasons why LC has not revised the PA schedule since it first appeared in 1928. The most likely, however, is that much of the current publishing in classical literature is in areas already covered in the schedule. That is, there is little work being done in "new" areas. As a result, few numbers have had to be added to the schedule. The additions and changes to P-PA, as issued by Gale Research, total only 102 pages, and includes changes made since 1928. In addition, this update also includes additions and revisions to the P schedule, not covered in this article. It is possible, then, that LC has seen little reason for revising PA. It is my personal feeling, however, that the problems enumerated above justify a revision by LC. It is hoped that LC will soon decide to publish a second edition of P-PA, which will (a) incorporate the numbers from the PA *Supplement* into it and thus make the *Supplement* obsolete, (b) include the table numbers from the language and literature tables for each individual author, (c) make clear in the schedule how authors are to be subdivided, and (d) reconcile the discrepancy that exists in the definition of the end of both classical Greek and classical Latin literature. This revision would require much effort from LC, but it would be a great benefit to the library community at large and particularly to those of us who do classics cataloging on a regular basis.

CONCLUSION

As mentioned above, a scheme which purports to classify classical literature needs to take account of the various types of works published in the area and to provide a good, coherent organization for them. It now remains for us to evaluate the PA schedule from this point of view. Considering the types of materials discussed above, we come to the following conclusions:

1. Textual series, collections, texts of individual works, and school texts are all well treated in the classification. Their placement in the overall organization is logical, and the schedule is clear as to their treatment.

2. General discussions either of a particular genre or of a particular author are also given good treatment. Discussions of Latin poetry, for example, will be placed in the history and criticism sections of PA. General discussions of one author not limited to one particular title also receive good treatment in the language and literature tables.

3. Translations of an author's works do pose a problem. For a literary writer, there is generally no problem, as translations will appear together with the original texts in PA. For a non-literary writer, however, translations will be arranged in the appropriate subject classification. This separation of texts and translations of non-literary writers can result in inconvenience, especially for libraries with large collections of materials in the classics.

4. This same evaluation applies also to commentaries. In addition, however, commentaries suffer from a lack of specificity in the schedule as to where to classify them. Ideally, they should stand close to the works on which they comment. Neither the schedule itself nor the language and literature tables clarify exactly where to place them and with what notation.

In general, however, the Library of Congress Classification does a good job of classifying classical literature. In particular, LC is to be commended for giving such a full delineation of authors in the original PA schedule. Many of the weaknesses we found were more a matter of specificity or notation, which can be easily resolved in a new edition of PA. LC's policy of separating translations and commentaries of non-literary works from their original texts, however, does prove to be a hindrance, especially to libraries with large classics collections. Libraries with smaller classics collections, on the other hand, may find this practice desirable, or at the very least, tolerable. To conclude, I would like to reiterate my hope that LC will soon come out with a second edition of the PA schedule.

NOTES

1. These figures were provided by Michael Braunlin, Library Associate at the Classics Library, University of Cincinnati.

2. These are taken, in abridged form, from the synopsis given in the PA *Supplement*, p. v.

3. David, an Armenian philosopher (PA3948.D17), and Elias, a philosopher (PA3968.E3), both of whom lived in the sixth century A.D., are included in the basic PA schedule. On the other hand, Paul of Aegina, d. 642 (PA5319.P3), is included in the PA *Supplement*, and Georgius Pisidia, fl. 610-641, is classified in PA5317.G4 in the additions and changes to the PA *Supplement*.

4. It is interesting to note, that, in contrast to PA, the German literature schedule in PT makes the history, collections and individual authors sequence primary, and then divides by period under them. For example, see the **Individual Authors and Works** section in PT1501-2688.

5. In the PA schedule, parentheses are used to indicate numbers not used by LC but which may be used by other libraries if they wish. Usually these numbers are followed by a reference to the class number used by LC for such material.

6. See, for example, the BR-BV schedule. BS476 is the number for works on hermeneutics of the Bible as a whole. At BS1140.2, the number for hermeneutics of the Old Testament, is a reference to BS476. However, works on the hermeneutics of the New Testament are provided their own number, BS2331.

A Cooperative Cataloging Proposal
for Slavic and East European Languages
and the Languages
of the Former Soviet Union

Jacqueline Byrd

SUMMARY. This paper proposes, as a backlog reduction strategy, a national cooperative cataloging program among libraries with major collections in the Slavic and East European languages and in the languages of the former Soviet Union. The long-standing problem of cataloging backlogs is discussed, including a brief discussion of some of the other ways that have been used to address the problem. The proposal for a cooperative effort is outlined and some of the cataloging issues to be considered are discussed.

INTRODUCTION

Like death and taxes, cataloging backlogs of materials in Slavic and East European languages and the non-Slavic languages of the former Soviet Union seem inevitable.[1] Backlogs, of course, are not limited to materials in these languages. In 1987, Behrens and Smith surveyed 112 academic libraries and found that 85 percent of the responding libraries had backlogs.[2] In 1990 Rogers compared a general backlog and a Slavic

Jacqueline Byrd, BA in History, and MLS, (Indiana University), is currently Cataloger of Slavic language materials at the Indiana University Libraries.

[Haworth co-indexing entry note]: "A Cooperative Cataloging Proposal for Slavic and East European Languages and the Languages of the Former Soviet Union." Byrd, Jacqueline. Co-published simultaneously in *Cataloging & Classification Quarterly* (The Haworth Press, Inc.) Vol. 17, No. 1/2, 1993, pp. 87-96; and: *Languages of the World: Cataloging Issues and Problems* (ed: Martin D. Joachim) The Haworth Press, Inc., 1993, pp. 87-96. Multiple copies of this article/chapter may be purchased from The Haworth Document Delivery Center [1-800-3-HAWORTH; 9:00 a.m. - 5:00 p.m. (EST)].

backlog and found less available cataloging copy for materials in the Slavic backlog.[3] The lesser amount of copy means eliminating a backlog of these materials would be more difficult than eliminating a more general backlog.

There have been many attempts to reduce or eliminate Slavic backlogs, and much effort has been put into the management of them. Since it is a problem that is shared among most of the libraries with major Slavic collections in the country, those libraries may benefit from joining in a cooperative effort that would make more cataloging available for these materials and help to stop the growth of the backlogs.

BACKLOGS

Like all cataloging backlogs, the ones for materials in the Slavic languages have grown because the cataloging staffs that deal with these materials are too small to catalog the number of receipts. However, there are some unique factors that have contributed to the creation of these backlogs.

Languages

The languages of these materials are quite diverse, and many are not related to each other. Included are all of the Slavic languages (Bulgarian, Byelorussian, Czech, Macedonian, Polish, Serbo-Croatian, Slovak, Slovene, Russian, Ukrainian, and Wendic), the non-Slavic languages of the former Soviet Union (Azerbaijani, Armenian, Estonian, Georgian, Kazakh, Kirghiz, Latvian, Lithuanian, Turkmen, etc.), and the remaining languages of Eastern Europe (Albanian, Hungarian, Romanian, etc.).[4]

Very few libraries have staffs with knowledge of all of these languages, but some Slavic cataloging units are asked to catalog all or a substantial part of these languages. They have traditionally been grouped together in a single Slavic cataloging unit because of the similar political systems of the countries where these languages are spoken and because of their geographic proximity. Although it is not unusual for a cataloger to be asked to catalog material in a language in which he/she lacks a background, many catalogers of Slavic materials face this problem in the majority of their work. Because they must work with languages in which they have little or no training or expertise, their work is considerably slower, cataloging production is lower, and backlogs develop more rapidly.

Number of Receipts

For decades materials in these languages have been acquired very cheaply via exchange agreements.[5] The increased number of receipts was a leading cause in the development of cataloging backlogs. Although the recent political changes in the former Soviet Union and Eastern Europe have resulted in higher prices and lower receipts for many libraries, materials still outnumber the available cataloging records for most major Slavic collections. It remains to be seen what the political changes in the area will mean for acquisitions and cataloging of Slavic materials.

Other Factors

Crayne discussed several factors that promoted the growth of Slavic backlogs in a paper presented at the 1991 AAASS Conference in Miami, Florida. She said that an increasing emphasis on the use of copy over original cataloging and the decreasing percentage of copy for Slavic language materials has caused a large amount of Slavic language materials requiring original cataloging to be set aside. She also stated that some libraries decreased their emphasis on Slavic languages or suspended Slavic-language cataloging completely; both of these actions have resulted in smaller Slavic cataloging staffs and bigger backlogs. Finally she cited the tendency to have precatalog searching personnel separated from the Slavic catalogers as a problem that has resulted in bigger backlogs; often the searchers lacked the needed language background and failed to find available copy for Slavic-language materials which were then incorrectly deposited in the backlog for materials requiring original cataloging.[6]

EARLIER WORK ON SLAVIC BACKLOGS

Just as the Slavic backlogs are not new, neither are attempts to diminish them. In 1989 the Conference on Access to Slavic Materials in North American Libraries was held in Champaign, Illinois, at least in part to discuss this problem. Several approaches, including cooperative cataloging efforts and outside funding, were discussed.[7]

Grants to fund special cataloging projects have been used to deal with the Slavic backlog problem. In 1992 and 1993 the Social Sciences Research Council in conjunction with the American Council of Learned Societies offered grants under their "Program to Alleviate Backlogs in Soviet and East European Collections in the United States." There have also been several other kinds of grants, from both public and private sources, to individual institutions for work on their Slavic backlogs.

FACTORS LIMITING PROGRESS
ON BACKLOG REDUCTION

The combination of these efforts to reduce Slavic cataloging backlogs and the decline in acquisitions for many of the major collections should have resulted in a much improved situation with smaller backlogs. However, a few external factors have limited the progress made on Slavic backlog reduction and threaten the collections with growing backlogs.

Budget Cuts in Libraries

At the same time receipts are lower, many libraries are faced with budget crises. Positions are being cut or reassigned, and Slavic cataloging positions are not being spared. Any headway that Slavic catalogers might make during this time of lower acquisitions could be offset by the Slavic cataloging staff reductions or reassignments.

Exchanges

The period of declining acquisitions may be ending for many major Slavic collections. With the changes in Eastern Europe and the former Soviet Union comes a liberalized collection development environment for the libraries in this region. These libraries are anxious to collect materials from the West and are still willing exchange partners for U.S. libraries. The bleak economic situation in Eastern Europe and the former Soviet republics has driven up the prices of library materials drastically. Libraries in this region are forced to use exchanges as a major part of their acquisition programs. U.S. libraries in turn are able to collect more materials today via exchanges with these libraries than they would if forced to buy them at the higher prices.

COOPERATIVE CATALOGING PROPOSAL

It is important that the major Slavic collections in the U.S. not allow diminished backlogs to grow to their former size. It is also important that these libraries continue efforts to reduce and eventually eliminate the remaining backlogs. One way to work towards this goal would be to set up a cooperative cataloging program among the libraries with major Slavic collections. El-Sherbini writes positively about cooperative cataloging ventures:

> But the main positive feature of cooperative cataloging is that your materials will be cataloged by a librarian in an institution similar to your own, who has the needed language/subject/form expertise as well as a knowledge of the needs of patrons like yours. With a cooperative cataloging arrangement you not only get the job done, but you also create a deep relationship with another library based on mutual trust of each other's work.[8]

Below is outlined a proposed cooperative cataloging effort among the libraries with major slavic collections.

Each member institution would be responsible for cataloging its materials in a given language upon receipt. The assignment of languages would be based upon an institution's strength in terms of its catalogers' knowledge of languages. If, for example, a library has catalogers who have a good command of Serbo-Croatian but who struggle with Czech, then that library could accept Serbo-Croatian as its language in the cooperative program. All of the Serbo-Croatian materials with no records on a national database would be cataloged by that library upon receipt. Another library having catalogers knowledgeable in Czech but not in Serbo-Croatian would accept the responsibility for cataloging Czech-language materials.

Goals

Such an agreement among libraries would achieve several goals. First, bibliographic records would be made available for more materials at an earlier time. Second, catalogers could be more productive if they concentrate on materials in languages which they know well rather than on materials in languages which are difficult for them. Third, since the cataloging staffs of most libraries would most likely have expertise in areas and languages representing the strengths of their collections, each participating library would benefit from being able to concentrate cataloging efforts on the language or languages most heavily collected by the library and most desired by its users.

NCCP and CONSER Models

This proposal may sound similar to the National Coordinated Cataloging Program (NCCP), which has many of the same goals as the above proposal. NCCP's initial goals were:

a. to increase the timeliness of cataloging copy
b. to extend cataloging coverage
c. to reduce duplication of effort
d. to produce cataloging of a 'national level quality.'[9]

Also like the above proposal, each participating institution of NCCP is responsible for cataloging a defined group of materials that "does not overlap with that of another participant."[10]

The primary difference between the above proposal for a cooperative Slavic cataloging program and NCCP is the initial role of the Library of Congress in NCCP. In NCCP, LC has been the "host" institution which determines the cataloging standards for the program and is responsible for training and revision.

No one institution would have that role in the above proposal, but LC's NCCP role would be played by all participating institutions. NCCP's cataloging standards have been those of LC. Under a truly cooperative program, the cataloging standards would be determined by all of the institutions involved. Each participating library would be responsible for the training and revision of its own catalogers.

One of the problems cited about NCCP as initially set up is that it has not been cost-effective for the participating libraries. The University of Illinois Libraries found that it required less time to catalog a book in its normal workflow than it did to catalog a book under NCCP procedures.[11] A time study conducted in the Indiana University Libraries had the same results.[12]

A better model for the Slavic cooperative cataloging project would be the Cooperative Online Serials Program (CONSER), in which participants have gradually gained greater independence from the Library of Congress and the National Library of Canada, which initially reviewed all records. In 1984 participants were granted the authority to review their own records, and CONSER no longer had a "Center of Responsibility," but it had, instead, a cadre of equal partners.[13] The CONSER approach has been so successful that NCCP participants are looking into redesigning that project along the CONSER lines.[14]

In a program with participant-defined standards and a cataloging work-flow determined locally, the discrepancy in cataloging time (and therefore cost) should be lessened, if not entirely eliminated, depending on the current cataloging standards of a library and those adopted for the Slavic cooperative cataloging programs. Assuming that all potential participants currently provide cataloging that conforms to standards defined by the national databases, then the standards of the cooperative program should be similar to those of many of the participating libraries.

Bibliographic Utilities

Most libraries contribute their Slavic records to either OCLC or RLIN and use only one utility to make the records created by other libraries available to their patrons, either in a local online system or in a card catalog. In order to make the bibliographic records created for the cooperative cataloging program available to all participants, it is important that input from the bibliographic utilities be included when the program is set up so that all of the records created for the project are available in each national utility. An effort should be made for participating libraries to be able to catalog for this program in much the same workflow that they use for materials that are not part of the program. However, it is probably even more essential that all of the records be available to all of the participants.

STANDARDS

When an initial group of libraries is identified for the cooperative cataloging program, representatives from those libraries would need to agree on the cataloging standards for the program. It is important that the standards be high enough that records can be used with minimal editing by other participating libraries. It is also important to avoid the kind of discrepancy cited in the NCCP and non-NCCP cataloging cost studies. If cataloging for the program takes considerably longer than a library's normal cataloging, then the program would not be cost-effective.

Level of Cataloging

One can find various levels of cataloging in the national databases for materials in these languages. Some of the major collections provide full-level cataloging and some only minimal. The quality of the cataloging also varies widely. Some libraries routinely use all of the available cataloging rules and guides, including *AACR2* (2nd ed.), *Library of Congress Rule Interpretations*, *LCSH*, *Subject Cataloging Manual: Subject Headings*, and *Subject Cataloging Manual: Classification*, as well as the documentation provided by the bibliographic utilities. Many of these libraries also participate in the NACO program to provide authority records in the national databases. However, some of the other libraries also routinely provide minimal-level records which do not follow even *AACR2* rules. Some bibliographic records for new Slavic language materials are contributed with coding for pre-*AACR2* cataloging.

Since the records created as part of the cooperative cataloging program would need to be useful to all participating libraries, a required level of cataloging would have to be agreed upon by the participants. Gurevich warns about lowering standards too far:

> The trend toward lowering cataloging standards unilaterally and re-verting to various kinds of less-than-complete cataloging locally might eventually jeopardize the whole concept of shared cataloging using bibliographic utilities.[15]

However, if the standards are set too high, then some of the libraries currently providing lower level cataloging for these materials may find that participation in the program would not be cost-effective.

Upgrading and Enhancing

Part of the participation in this project could also include a commitment on the part of OCLC libraries routinely to upgrade minimal level records and, if authorized, enhance full-level records that contain errors or omissions. The aim here would be to have the records in the national databases conform to the standards set by the libraries participating in the cooperative cataloging program. The benefit to the library that upgrades or enhances a record would be OCLC's financial credit for the work. The benefit for all participating libraries would be bibliographic records of higher quality which would require less local editing. Gurevich writes:

> Slavic catalogers across the country are busy improving each other's records locally, often without being able to share the improvements with other member libraries. This leads to an enormous duplication of effort–the effort that could have been spent on cataloging new materials.[16]

By including upgrades and enhances in the cooperative cataloging program, at least part of this duplication of effort could be eliminated, and catalogers' time could be spent more efficiently.

CONCLUSION

Due in large part to grants and to diminished acquisitions resulting from the political situation in Eastern Europe and the former Soviet Union, progress has been made in the reduction of backlogs in materials from that part of the world. However, budget reductions in libraries and the continued interest in exchanges could result in further growth of these backlogs. In order to combat this problem, it is important that libraries be able to maximize the productivity of the catalogers working with these materials. A proposal has been made here for a cooperative cataloging program which would allow libraries with major Slavic collections to use their cataloging staffs more effectively and to make records more readily available in the national databases.

The presentation here is intentionally limited to only the basic components of the proposal. The primary goal is to stimulate a discussion out of which a more specific plan could grow. Many details will have to be worked out, such as what constitutes a "major Slavic collection," which library would assume the responsibility for which language(s), what cataloging standards would be adopted for such a program, how to get the records into all of the appropriate databases, and whether or not the upgrade or enhancement of contributed copy is to be included in the program.

NOTES

1. In the interest of simplicity, materials in these languages will be referred to as "Slavic" even though many of them are not Slavic languages.

2. Beth Behrens and Philip M. Smith, "Cataloging Backlogs in Academic Libraries," *Tennessee Librarian* 39 (1987): 15.

3. Sally A. Rogers, "Backlog Management: Estimating Resources Needed to Eliminate Arrearages," *Library Resources & Technical Services* 35 (1991): 33.

4. Robert H. Berger, "Slavic Technical Services," in *Technical Services Today and Tomorrow*, ed. Michael Gorman and associates (Englewood, CO: Libraries Unlimited, 1990), 130.

5. Ibid., 132.

6. Janet I. Crayne, "Processing a Slavic Backlog by Hook or by Crook" (Paper delivered at the Annual Conference of the American Association for the Advancement of Slavic Studies, Miami, FL, 23 November 1991).

7. "Conference on Access to Slavic Materials in North America, University Inn, Champaign, IL, May 7-9, 1989," *Association of College and Research Libraries Slavic and East European Section Newsletter* 6 (1990): 21.

8. Magda El-Sherbini, "Cataloging Alternatives: An Investigation of Contract Cataloging, Cooperative Cataloging, and the Use of Temporary Help," *Cataloging & Classification Quarterly* 15 (1992): 85.

9. Henriette D. Avram and Beacher Wiggins, "The National Coordinated Cataloging Program," *Library Resources & Technical Services* 32 (1988): 112.

10. Robert H. Burger, "NCCP as a National Information Policy: An Evaluation," *Technical Services Quarterly* 8 (1990): 57.

11. Ibid., 60.

12. Indiana conducted a time study as part of a cost study by Tantalus, Inc. of all participants in NCCP.

13. Linda K. Bartley and Regina R. Reynolds, "CONSER: Revolution and Evolution," *Cataloging & Classification Quarterly* 8 (1985): 55.

14. Sarah E. Thomas, "Rethinking Cooperative Cataloging," *ARL* 165 (1992): 6.

15. Konstantin Gurevich, "Russian Monographic Records in the OCLC Database: a Crisis in Shared Cataloging," *Library Resources & Technical Services* 35 (1991): 461.

16. Ibid., 460.

Cataloging of Materials in African Languages

Ann Bein

SUMMARY. In many libraries the cataloging of materials in African languages is done of necessity by librarians who have little or no background in the languages or the subject matter. Guidelines and reference tools are suggested for the non-specialist cataloger, and suggestions are made for an appropriate attitude toward the whole problem.

DEFINITIONS

1. The term "African languages" is used here to denote the indigenous languages of sub-Saharan Africa written in roman script.
2. This article is directed to the cataloger who is responsible for cataloging materials in African languages, is not a language expert, and feels overwhelmed by the magnitude of the assignment.

THE PROBLEM

There are some 2,000 languages spoken in Africa.[1] Fortunately for the cataloger, not all of them have publishing programs, written literatures, or

Ann Bein is Chair of Monographic Catalogers, University Research Library Cataloging Department, University of California, Los Angeles.

The author wishes to thank Ruby Bell-Gam, Africana Bibliographer at UCLA, for her assistance.

This article is dedicated to the memory of Elizabeth A. Widenmann, who should have been the one to write it.

[Haworth co-indexing entry note]: "Cataloging of Materials in African Languages." Bein, Ann. Co-published simultaneously in *Cataloging & Classification Quarterly* (The Haworth Press, Inc.) Vol. 17, No. 1/2, 1993, pp. 97-114; and: *Languages of the World: Cataloging Issues and Problems* (ed: Martin D. Joachim) The Haworth Press, Inc., 1993, pp. 97-114. Multiple copies of this article/chapter may be purchased from The Haworth Document Delivery Center [1-800-3-HAWORTH; 9:00 a.m. - 5:00 p.m. (EST)].

even written alphabets as yet. But even in 1986, Northwestern University, a leader in the acquisition of African language materials, reported a collection of works in 273 African languages.[2] And in the same year the Bible Society reported that Bibles, Bible stories and/or tracts had been produced in 690 African languages.[3] It is not unusual for a library to collect in over 100 languages.

All phases of a library's collecting of African-language materials are fraught with difficulties. Acquiring the materials tends to be a hit or miss affair. Publication is in small editions, by small presses, so that by the time a publication is documented, it is likely to be out of print and unavailable. National libraries may be nonexistent or seriously underfunded for the task of bibliographic control. Unsettled conditions within countries can make the job of on-the-spot book buyer rather more exciting than is good for the nerves.[4] The bibliographer's lot is not a happy one.

Once the materials arrive in the library, the cataloger's problems commence. Few libraries can afford specialists in African-language cataloging; few catalogers can spend more than a fraction of their time on African-language materials, and the field is so vast and varied that it cannot be fully mastered by the generalist. In order to deal with the problem, the non-specialist must be able to: (1) define a clear-cut target clientele, (2) tailor cataloging to the needs of the clientele and the library, (3) gain access to language and bibliographic tools, and (4) develop a network of informants who can fill in the gaps in the cataloger's knowledge.

PURPOSE OF AFRICAN LANGUAGE COLLECTIONS

Why does an institution collect African-language materials? Few are rich enough or comprehensive enough to do so indiscriminately. At UCLA, the African-language collection serves primarily (1) those seeking to learn a language in order to work in a particular country or with a particular ethnic group, (2) students and faculty working in comparative linguistics and classification of African languages, and (3) historians seeking to incorporate oral traditions and the linguistic evidence of group migrations into their work.[5] Choices are made from among materials of the following types:

1. Literacy materials for adults
2. Instructional materials for schools
3. Newspapers and recreational reading
4. Instructional manuals and other items for day-to-day living

5. Literature and belles-lettres
6. Research in African languages to preserve them and analyze them for use in education
7. Research and scholarly writing, including folklore and history
8. Government documents and proclamations.[6]

LEVEL OF CATALOGING

Because African-language collections usually serve a relatively small and specialized clientele and since cataloging can be so frustrating and time-consuming because of the multiple language barriers, many institutions take the easy way out: collection-level records (usually based on language) in the local database, sometimes supplemented with computerized or manual files with access by author and/or title. This method can serve local needs in an economical and probably satisfactory manner. It is certainly preferable to the rock-bottom minimal-level record: access by some approximation of the author's name and the title.

Still, it is well to remember that collections no longer exist in a vacuum. Libraries are dependent upon each other for help in cataloging, and with the decline of the book-buying dollar each institution needs to share the works which it has been able to acquire. This sharing can happen most easily if we put our cataloging into a national database.

UCLA is beginning to experiment with inputting materials that have been analyzed for language and correct (as far as we can determine) author entries but not for actual subject content; access will be provided by language and a classification number with the language, usually in PL8000+. This policy replaces our previous local minimal cataloging, enhancing both local and national access. It is difficult to produce cataloging for works in languages we do not understand, and we are bound to feel at least a trace of uneasiness about nearly every item. None of us likes to expose our inadequacies on the national stage, but very few of us are in a position to be critical of someone else's. I am grateful for the information that others can provide, and I would like to think they can make use of mine. If we can improve each other's records, so much the better. If we have labored long over our authority work, we should get that online as well, through NACO.

THE PROCESS OF CATALOGING

On general principles, the cataloger would do well to develop a close relationship with the selector of African-language materials for the institution and make extensive use of any expertise available there whenever it might be necessary. Either through the selector or independently, one should seek access to a network of specialist scholars, local and nationwide. African university students living in one's locality are a useful resource for language identification and a bit of cultural background. No one person can answer all the questions that will arise, but somewhere in even a rudimentary network lies the solution to many baffling problems. Ready access to a fax machine will facilitate getting a query to the far ends of the earth.

Of course, the cataloger is going to search national and local databases for copy, authority records, previous works by the same author, added editions, and all those delightful discoveries that help one's efforts along, so I need not go into that here.

Full citations for the tools referred to in the following sections will be found in the corresponding sections of the bibliography.

LANGUAGE

What language is it? If we are lucky, an item will include, somewhere on the title page or verso, "A novel in Venda," "Southern Sotho epic poetry," "The Bible in Fulani," "Translation into Swahili of the Complete Works of Hegel," or some such straightforward, unambiguous statement. These identifying phrases occur most often, though neither exclusively nor invariably, in publications from South Africa and English-speaking East Africa. If the publication itself does not specifically identify the language, the information may come from the selector(s), perhaps through annotations on acquisitions records. At UCLA, we have the language coded into the in-process record, but one has to treat it with some care. The information may have come from the Africana bibliographer (reliable) or from the book dealer (maybe), or it might have been input by an overworked student assistant (iffy). It comes in the form of the MARC language codes, which include too many "bucket" codes and too few specific African language codes. And dialects with their own names get coded under the main language: e.g., **NYA/Nyanja** for **Chewa**.

Always try to batch your work by place of publication whether or not you know what the language is. Note that place of publication is not just a matter of country but of city also; in a multi-lingual country, the city can be a key to the regional language(s). You can sometimes discern enough similarities between two different works, one each of a known and unknown language, to identify the unknown language. You could do the same thing with imprints already in the collection, published in the same place, but locating them can be a problem unless you already have a good idea of what the language ought to be, or you have a system that allows you to search on place of publication. See Appendix V for some languages and their places of publication; it can serve as a basis for your own list, which you should add to every time you have a known language and a new place of publication. You might want to make an additional list of places of publication with their respective language(s). Note that some cities publish works in several languages, so your list may merely cut down possibilities rather than pinpoint.

Search works for words and statements that look language-like. Develop a familiarity with the language names and variants you find in Library of Congress subject headings: e.g., **Sesuto**, **Chichewa**, **isiZulu**. Pay particular attention to those capitalizations in the middle of words; they indicate names of various sorts, often of peoples or languages.

Sometimes you can identify a language by means of distinctive characters or diacritics or rule out a language on that basis. The section below on diacritics and orthography points out a few languages and their attributes. Unfortunately, however, there are no characters or diacritics that are unique to a single language, and often a single language will be printed in several different ways (with and without special characters and/or diacritics, for instance, or with completely different spelling conventions, or even in completely different alphabets) depending on what country is doing the publishing or how sophisticated the printing establishment is. Mimeographing is still used in some areas, for instance, and is limited to what is available on a local typewriter keyboard.

If the publication comes out of Tanzania, it is most likely to be in Swahili, which is the national language, and too common to merit mention in the publication. Also widely spoken in other countries, it is one of the official languages of both Kenya and Uganda. By the same token, if a work is published in Rwanda it is probably in Kinyarwanda, the national language along with French.

Try to find other works by your author in the various databases and the national bibliography. Few authors write in more than one African language, though some do; many more write in one African language and one European language. You may find an author with a name similar to that of your author, one that indicates a common ethnicity, and you may get a hint about language from it. But be warned: national bibliographies do not always tell you the language.

Consult the language tools listed in Appendix I, beginning with Martin Lyon's glossary.[7] Consult your information network. And if you are unclear what the book is about at this point, which is a distinct possibility, try to get that information while you are about it.

DIACRITICS AND ORTHOGRAPHY

I have done a survey of about twenty-five languages and have come up with a few of their significant orthographic features. The arrangement is alphabetical within each grouping. Some languages fall into more than one group. Needless to say, these are probably not the only languages with these characteristics:

Languages which do not employ diacritics or altered letters:

> Kinyarwanda, Lugbara, Luo (Kenya and Tanzania), Southern Sotho, Swahili, Tsonga.

Languages which do not employ diacritics or altered letters but use capital letters in the middle of words:

> Shona, Swazi, Xhosa, Zulu.

Languages which use round or square dots under letters (which tends to be a question of typeface):

> Efik (but just as often altered letters are used instead), Igbo, Yoruba.

Languages which use specific altered letters:

> *b* (curl over or flag on the upright): Basa, Duala, Hausa.
> *d* (curl over or flag on the upright): Hausa.
> *e* (open, like a sigma): Basa, Duala.
> *k* (curl over or flag on the upright): Hausa.
> *n* (extension down on the right side; sometimes written as *n* with a tilde instead): Basa, Duala, Efik, Soninke, Wolof.

Languages which use specific diacritics:

> acute accent: Basa, Duala, Wolof, Yoruba.
> caret below letter: Venda.
> circumflex: Basa, Chewa (*w* only).
> grave accent: Basa, Wolof, Yoruba.
> ha^vcek (wedge, caron): Basa, Northern Sotho (*s* only), Tswana (*s* only).
> macron: Basa, Duala.

Languages which use profuse or unusual double letter combinations:

vowels: Lugbara, Somali, Wolof.

consonants: Lugbara (including *bb, mm, nn, ss* to begin words), Somali (including *xx* to begin words), Soninke (including *xx* to begin words), Northern Sotho (*mm* to begin words).

SOME DISCOURAGING WORDS

It is not possible to develop a title-page expertise in African languages, as one can with European language groups, with the expenditure of a year or so of study. You cannot just take a class in Swahili, for instance, and expect to fake your way through the rest. There is no reason, however, why you shouldn't study an African language; an understanding of the way even one African language is put together will strengthen your ability to deal with others.

It is generally a waste of time to try to determine the language of an item at hand by looking up words in dictionaries for several different languages. I speak from bitter experience. You will probably find just as many words in one dictionary as another, but you will not find enough in any one dictionary to clinch a choice.

If you cannot determine the language of a work, you cannot catalog it.

NAMES

African personal names are as profuse, rich, and varied as African languages. They may contain simple or compound surnames, forenames, patronymics, honorifics; include indigenous, European, and/or Islamic elements, animal names, plant names, names of things; indicate caste, ethnic affiliation, place of origin, birth order, day or month of birth, genealogy; be entered under first element, last element, or something in between; or consist of one element or many.

Sometimes there are clear guidelines right on the title page. Many South African authors use an initials-and-surname format that gives only one option for the entry element. Names with combined European and African elements usually break down into European forename(s) and African surname(s). Often Islamic-African combinations break down the same way although they are more difficult for western catalogers to analyze correctly. Publishers in francophone Africa (and France as well) often set the author's surname element(s) in all capitals, with other elements in upper and lower case.

Since at least 1972, Zaire has prohibited western-style names and mandated only Zairian names for its citizens. These names are always entered in direct order. While entry is simplified, there is sometimes the need to pull the new name together with an old one. Malou wa Kalenga, for example, used to be Felix Malou.[8]

National bibliographies can be helpful in establishing names. Look in the index; even if your author is not there, you can often get a feel for how names of the same type are entered and structured. The *South African Bibliography* gives the full names that the title-page initials stand for (there are often three), and often a date of birth as well (all helpful in establishing authority records).

The names tools (Appendix II) can help you to get a handle on the type of name with which you might be dealing and how it ought to be treated. You do need to be clear on the country of origin and, if possible, ethnic affiliation of your author and then hope that they match the information that is available in the names tools. Otherwise, it is difficult to determine which criteria to apply. My own rule of thumb is to treat a name as if it were an English-language name if I cannot figure out a more likely treatment. I make lots of cross-references on my authority records and hope for the best.

Corporate bodies do not crop up too often outside of government publications, but they can be very difficult to verify. The national databases and national bibliographies are your first resort, of course. If these fail you, consult Gail Junion's bibliography (Appendix III) for a list of guides to corporate entities that may provide useful information. Your information network should be able to help you set up plausible entries even if you cannot otherwise discover anything about the bodies.

SUBJECTS

The kind and extent of subject analysis you need to do depends on the requirements of your patrons and the policies of your library. But at the very least you need to give patrons access to African-language materials through the languages. That means either a subject heading for the language or classification in a language and/or literature number.

Certain categories of materials are simple to catalog. Indeed, these materials practically catalog themselves, once you have determined the languages and set up any names. Each title should be given a subject heading which includes the name of the language, whether or not that is the customary practice for works of the same type in other languages:

1. Belles-lettres: Usually one name on the title page; page layout (poems, a play with its speeches, the dashes signifying dialogue in novels and short stories) that is unmistakable.
2. Collections of readily-recognizable literary materials: Poems, plays, etc., with no overall author indicated. Could have a name associated with each item. A single epic poem could occupy a whole book; in fact, if you have a single poem that occupies the whole book and it does not clearly imply single authorship, it is probably an epic poem.
3. Bible (whole and parts): The books of the Bible are similar in most languages; sound them out if the spelling is unconvincing. Again, page layout is generally distinctive.
4. Dictionaries: I cannot imagine any library not giving dictionaries full cataloging.
5. Textbooks for language teaching.

If you want to give full cataloging to other categories of materials, those that are really "about" something, then it becomes more difficult, and there is less assistance available. You might, however, do the following:

1. Check national bibliographies. Most of the works in the national bibliographies section (Appendix IV) list their works in classified order, either Dewey or Universal Decimal. This arrangement is useful in determining what your work is about, provided that you can actually find your work listed in a national bibliography. A few, notably the *South African Bibliography* and the *National Bibliography of Nigeria,* give full cataloging records with subject and name added entries. The *NBN* even gives an LC call number as well.
2. Using a dictionary for the language of your item, laboriously look up every word on the title page, in the table of contents, and in the introduction, but note the discouraging words below.
3. Call upon your information network.

MORE DISCOURAGING WORDS

Heroic efforts have been made to compile and publish dictionaries in an astonishing number of African languages. But even if you know which language you are dealing with, it is almost impossible to pin down what a work is about by using the dictionary. Peculiarities of orthography, agglutination, verb conjugation, case endings, dialects, and a number of *et ceteras* militate against it. You will find some of the words, or at least terms sort of like some of the words, but it will very likely be impossible to put them together to make much sense. Even if you know that some languages (primarily in Central-East and Southern Africa) use prefixes extensively and that you have to lop off the prefix in order to locate the word in the dictionary, it is rarely clear just how much is prefix. You are likely to find (or not find) words using several different permutations of what the prefix might be with, of course, mutually exclusive meanings.

NOTES

1. Information and citations in this paragraph were drawn from Gretchen Walsh, "African Language Materials: Challenges and Responsibilities in Collection Management," in *Africana Resources and Collections: Three Decades of Development and Achievement: a Festschrift in Honor of Hans Panofsky*, ed. Julian W. Witherell (Metuchen, N.J.: Scarecrow Press, 1989), 77-107. The article and the entire book contain a great deal of interest to the Africana/African languages cataloger. This particular piece of information came from Michael F. Lofchie, "Area Needs Summaries: Africa," in *Beyond Growth: the Next Stage in Language and Area Studies*, by Richard D. Lambert, et al. (Washington: Association of American Universities, 1984), 400.

2. Andrea Stamm, "African Languages Collection at Northwestern University" (Report to the Joint Meeting of Africana Librarians and Africanist Linguists, Indiana University, Bloomington, Indiana, April 1986), 2.

3. *Scriptures of the World* (London: United Bible Societies, 1986), 49-54.

4. Conversation with Ruby Bell-Gam, UCLA Africana bibliographer, July 14, 1992.

5. Ibid.

6. Walsh, "African Language Materials," 86.

7. My thanks to Gretchen Walsh for citing this title in "African Language Materials," 92, 103, 106. She suggests that an expanded version would be an excellent project.

8. Elizabeth A. Widenmann, "Recent Developments in Africana Cataloging in the United States (1973-1988)," in *Africana Resources and Collections*, ed. Julian W. Witherell (Metuchen, N.J.: Scarecrow Press, 1989), 40.

APPENDIX I. LANGUAGE TOOLS

Dalby, David. *Language Map of Africa and the Adjacent Islands.* Manchester: Manchester University Press, 1977.

Visual counterpart to Mann and Dalby's *A Thesaurus of African Languages* (London and New York: Zell, 1987). A new edition is reported to be in the works.

Ethnologue. 11th ed. Santa Ana, Calif.: Wycliffe Bible Translators, 1988.

Universal language coverage. Organized by continent, then country, then alphabetically by language. Each entry includes all alternate language names and forms of names, dialects, number of speakers. Index by all language names and variants; under each: where spoken, dialect relationship, need for Bible translations.

Lyon, Martin, comp. *An African Language Glossary for Catalogers.* London: School of Oriental and African Studies, 1985.

A glossary of words frequently appearing on title pages for twentyseven African languages.

Mann, Michael and David Dalby. *A Thesaurus of African Languages.* London and New York: Zell, 1987.

Listing of languages (1) in linguistic classification hierarchies and (2) by state. Index by language, with cross-references from alternate names, spellings, etc. All languages throughout spelled out using African Reference Alphabet, a phonetic alphabet designed for African languages.

APPENDIX II. NAMES TOOLS

Fontvieille, Jean. *Le nom des écrivains d'Afrique Noir: essai de catalographie.* [Dakar], Université de Dakar, [1967?]

No index or table of contents, and arrangement is confusing. Covers Benin/Dahomey, Burkina Faso/Haute-Volta, Burundi, Cameroon, Central African Republic, Chad, Congo/Zaire, Gabon, Guinea, Ivory Coast, Madagascar, Mali, Mauritania, Niger, Rwanda, Togo.

IFLA International Office for UBC. *Names of Persons: National Usages for Entry in Catalogues.* 3rd ed. London, 1977.

Index by language and name of country in the official vernacular. Covers Botswana, Ethiopia, Ghana, Kenya, Nigeria, South Africa, Tanzania.

_____. *Supplement.* London, 1980.

Indexes by language and by name of country in the official vernacular. Covers Burkina Faso/Haute-Volta, Burundi, Cameroon, Ghana, The Gambia, Ivory Coast, Madagascar, Malawi, Senegal, Zambia.

APPENDIX III. GENERAL BIBLIOGRAPHY

Junion, Gail J. "A Guide to Reference Books for Cataloging Africana." *Library Resources and Technical Services* 26:2 (Apr./June 1982): 109-121.

Includes references for personal, corporate and geographic names, languages, and ethnic groups. Needs updating, but very detailed and still exceptionally useful.

APPENDIX IV. NATIONAL BIBLIOGRAPHIES

These are the bibliographies that I have found readily available at UCLA. There are doubtless more, maybe even some that have been published in the last ten years. "Latest issue" is as of August 1, 1992. Comments are based on the issues that I have examined; they may, of course, be completely in error for other, later issues. Most have lists of publishers appended, and many of those include addresses. I have specified a "Dewey-like" classification where it was unspecified in the bibliography but obviously decimal. Regarding indexes, "author/title" indicates one integrated index, while "author, title" indicates two separate ones. The "Temporarily suspended publication" notations were found in UCLA's serial records; some of the suspensions have gone on long enough for one to suspect permanence. The listing is alphabetical by the name of the country.

Benin

Bibliographie du Bénin. Porto-Novo: Bibliothèque nationale, 1978- (latest issue covers 1984)

Dewey-like classification. Separate listings for books, periodical articles, official publications, other documents. Index: author/title. Exclusively publications in French.

Botswana

National Bibliography of Botswana. Gaberones: Botswana National Library Service, 1969- (latest issue covers 1990)

Dewey classification. Index: author/title. Mostly publications in English and Tswana.

Gambia

The Gambia National Bibliography. Banjul: The Gambia National Library, 1977- (latest issue covers 1990)

Dewey classification. Index: author/editor/title/series. Exclusively publications in English.

Ghana

Ghana National Bibliography. Accra: Ghana Library Board, 1965- (latest issue covers 1978)

Listing by broad subject groupings, then alphabetically by author. Index: author. Mostly publications in English. Includes a section on Ghanaian language publications, broken down by language.

Ivory Coast

Bibliographie de la Côte d'Ivoire. Abidjan: Bibliothèque nationale, 1970- (latest issue covers 1975)

Dewey-like classification. Separate listings for books, periodical articles, official publications, other documents. Index: author/title.

Kenya

Kenya National Bibliography. Nairobi: Kenya National Library Service, 1983- (latest issue covers 1985)

Dewey classification. Index: author/title. Mostly publications in English, with some Swahili, and a sprinkling of other languages.

Madagascar

Bibliographie nationale de Madagascar = Rakitahirinkevi-Piren' i Madigasikara. Antananarivo: Bibliothèque nationale, 1970/71- (latest issue covers 1988). Temporarily suspended publication 1989-

Dewey classification. Separate listings for books, series. Indexes: authors, subjects, publications in series. Publications in French and Malagasy.

Malawi

Malaŵi National Bibliography. Zomba: National Archives, 1967-   (latest issue covers 1983) Temporarily suspended publication.

Dewey classification. Index: author/title. Mostly publications in English, some in African languages.

Nigeria

National Bibliography of Nigeria. Lagos: National Library of Nigeria, 1973-   (latest issue covers 1988)

Dewey classification. Indexes: author/title/series, subject, new serial titles. Publications in English and African languages.

Senegal

Bibliographie du Sénégal. Dakar: Archives du Sénégal, no. 40/1972- (latest issue covers 1986)

Universal Decimal classification. Indexes: author, title. Almost exclusively publications in French.

South Africa

SANB: Suid-Afrikaanse Nasionale Bibliografie = South African National Bibliography. Pretoria: State Library, 1959-   (latest issue covers 1991)

Dewey classification. Index: author/title/editor/translator/illustrator/series. Publications in English, Afrikaans, and African languages.

Swaziland

Swaziland National Bibliography. Kwaluseni: University of Botswana and Swaziland, University College of Swaziland, 1973/76-   (latest issue covers 1986/87)

Dewey classification. Separate listings for monographs and serials. Index: author/title. Mostly publications in English and Swazi.

Tanzania

Tanzania National Bibliography. Dar es Salaam: Tanzania Library Service, 1975-   (latest issue covers 1987)

Dewey classification. Index: author/title/editor/series. Publications in English (mostly) and Swahili.

Zambia

National Bibliography of Zambia. Lusaka: National Archives of Zambia, 1970/71-   (latest issue covers 1983)

Dewey classification. Index: author/title. Mostly publications in English, with a few in African languages.

Zimbabwe

Zimbabwe National Bibliography. Salisbury: National Archives, 1979- (latest issue covers 1989)

Dewey classification. Indexes: author/title, subject, new periodicals. Mostly publications in English, some noted in Ndebele and Shona.

APPENDIX V. LANGUAGES BY PLACE OF PUBLICATION

Not included are European or American places of publication, which do not help in differentiating languages.

Bambara
Mali
    Bamako
    Faladye
Upper Volta
    Bobo-Dioulasso

Chewa
Malawi
    Blantyre
    Limbe
    Zomba
Zambia
    Lusaka

Duala
Cameroon
    Douala
    Yaounde

Hausa
Morocco
    Rabat
Nigeria
    Ibadan
    Kaduna
    Kano
    Lagos
    Mubi
    Zaria/Bello Zariya

Igbo
Nigeria
    Enugu
    Ibadan
    Ikeja
    Onitsha
    Owerri
    Port Harcourt
    Yaba/Yaba Lagos

Kinyarwanda
Rwanda
    Butare
    Kigali

Northern Sotho
South Africa
    Johannesburg
    Pretoria

Shona
South Africa
    Cape Town
Zimbabwe/Southern Rhodesia
    Gweru/Gwelo
    Harare/Salisbury

Southern Sotho
Lesotho
     Maseru
     Mazenod
     Morija
South Africa
     Johannesburg
     Pretoria

Swahili
Kenya
     Nairobi
Tanzania
     Arusha
     Morogoro
     Peramiho
     Tabora
Uganda
     Kampala

Swazi
South Africa
     Goodwood
     Pietermaritzburg
     Pretoria

Tsonga
Mozambique
     Maputo
South Africa
     Pretoria

Tswana
South Africa
     Makapanstad
     Pretoria
     Tlaseng Rustenburg

Venda
South Africa
     Johannesburg
     Pretoria

Wolof
Senegal
>Dakar

Xhosa
South Africa
>Johannesburg
>Umtata

Yoruba
Nigeria
>Ibadan
>Ikeja
>Ilesha
>Lagos

Zulu
South Africa
>Cape Town
>Johannesburg
>Pietermaritzburg
>Pretoria

A Look at Hebraica Cataloging
in the United States:
Access versus Cost

Heidi G. Lerner

SUMMARY. Many American academic and research libraries are cataloging Hebrew script materials into online catalogs. These are items that are currently being acquired, extant collections that are undergoing retrospective conversion, or uncataloged backlogs. Institutions need to decide whether to include vernacular Hebrew script in the catalog records or to provide records in romanization. This paper will look at the choices American institutions have made about using vernacular Hebrew script to catalog Hebraica, issues involved in these choices, such as evaluating the financial and technical resources that are available for cataloging Hebrew script materials, and the tradeoffs between benefits and their costs.

OVERVIEW

Many research and academic institutions in the United States have already developed or are currently developing substantial collections of

Heidi G. Lerner is Hebraica Cataloger, Stanford University Libraries, Stanford, CA.

The author would like to thank Joan Aliprand (Research Libraries Group), Wilma Cromwell (Stanford University), and Mia Rode (Stanford University), for providing invaluable insights, suggestions, and editorial comments on this paper.

[Haworth co-indexing entry note]: "A Look at Hebraica Cataloging in the United States: Access versus Cost." Lerner, Heidi G. Co-published simultaneously in *Cataloging & Classification Quarterly* (The Haworth Press, Inc.) Vol. 17, No. 1/2, 1993, pp. 115-131; and: *Languages of the World: Cataloging Issues and Problems* (ed: Martin D. Joachim) The Haworth Press, Inc., 1993, pp. 115-131. Multiple copies of this article/chapter may be purchased from The Haworth Document Delivery Center [1-800-3-HAWORTH; 9:00 a.m. - 5:00 p.m. (EST)].

Hebraica materials. These are materials in which the dominant portion of text, as well as the title page, are written in Hebrew script and can include Hebrew, Yiddish, Judezmo (or, as it is often called, Ladino), Judeo-Arabic, Judeo-Persian, etc. During the past thirty years, the descriptive cataloging of Hebraica materials has become increasingly standardized and more in line with general library practices. The majority of large Judaica institutions are now, along with major American universities and research institutions, contributing Hebraica cataloging records into one or more of the national bibliographic online utilities (RLIN or OCLC) as well as into their own online catalogs. This paper will examine various techniques that institutions are using in cataloging their Hebraica collections, focusing on the question of the use of vernacular Hebrew script in cataloging versus romanized only cataloging, ways of retrieving these materials, and the tradeoffs between benefits and their cost. The methods employed by various institutions will be summarized.[1]

HEBREW VERNACULAR SCRIPT

The Hebrew alphabet is made up of twenty-two single-case consonants, five of which change form when they appear at the end of a word, making a total of twenty-seven characters. Vowels and accent marks (vocalization) appear as signs above, below, and within the consonants; in addition, some consonants can take on a vowel value, an orthographic phenomenon known in Latin as *mater lectionis* (mother of reading). Most Hebrew materials are written without vocalization, requiring the reader to supply them mentally according to grammar and context. Variant orthographies are found on printed Hebrew materials, due in part to the fact that some other Hebraica languages such as Yiddish and Judezmo, which include words borrowed from other languages (German for Yiddish and Spanish for Judezmo), make use of the *mater lectionis* to represent vowels of the non-Hebrew language.[2] What are the implications for catalogers who are providing romanization for standard MARC formats? Hebraica catalogers must not only have a reading ability in Hebraica but also a thorough knowledge of grammatical principles and rules; incorrect romanization can prevent the reliable retrieval of items in an online environment.

HISTORY

Up until 1983 most Hebraica items in American libraries were cataloged for manual card catalogs using Hebrew typewriters or typesetters.

For materials cataloged by the Library of Congress, the romanization included in the record was very minimal: only the main entry, brief title, added entries, date of publication, collation, and some notes were romanized. Materials were either interfiled into the regular card catalogs or retained in separate Hebraica card catalogs. Some institutions also maintained Hebrew title indexes in Hebrew vernacular script–for example, the Harvard University Library Judaica Collection, Klau Library of the Hebrew Union College in Cincinnati, and New York Public Library (NYPL) catalogs.[3]

In 1974 the New York Public Library (one of the largest American repositories of Hebraica) selected Hebrew materials to be included as the first non-roman script collection in its automated book catalog *Dictionary Catalog of the Research Libraries*.[4] The automated catalog could not support non-roman scripts at this time so the library began use of the American National Standards Institute (ANSI) transliteration table for data entry and later for input of Hebraica records into the RLIN database. This allows in general for one-to-one substitution of the Hebrew characters as they appear in vernacular Hebrew script records. One of the major advantages of this scheme is that it is reversible, allowing a one-to-one character transcripton. Romanized script can then be easily converted to an online system that has the capability to utilize vernacular Hebrew script. Major drawbacks of the ANSI reversible romanization are that it is not frequently used and does not conform to the ALA/LC transliteration standard widely used by libraries in the U.S. and other countries. In 1988 the New York Public Library discontinued the use of ANSI reversible romanization although many of these records are still found in the RLIN database (see Figure 1).[5]

The ALA/LC transliteration tables for Hebraica have undergone several modifications during the past fifty years. Until 1948, it was based, with some modification, on the transliteration table found in the 1901 *Jewish Encyclopedia*. Changes were made in 1948 to reflect the pronunciation of Hebrew that became popular in Israel (Sephardic, as opposed to Ashkenazic, or, Eastern European pronunciation) and rules for Yiddish romanization became identical to those used by the Yiddish Scientific Institute (YIVO) in New York. In 1976, diacritics were added to several letters.[6]

In 1983, the Library of Congress began online MARC cataloging of materials written in non-roman script languages, necessitating the complete romanization of these language materials if they were to be cataloged in an online environment. The ALA/LC romanization tables became the standard for most American libraries contributing Hebraica records to a national online utility such as OCLC or RLIN.

FIGURE 1. Two different romanizations for the same title as found in RLIN

1) {H}ZWWALYN&R YZKWR BW/K / ({H}NYW-YARK : ZWWALYN&R LANDSMAN'SAP_T AY/N NYW-
   YARK,{R} 1982.)
   NYPX (c-9114 NN)

2) Z_VOLINER YIZKER BUKH / (Nyu-Yor_k : Z_voliner landsmanshaf_t in Nyu-Yor_k,
   I982.)
   MABX (c-9110 MWalB [HBR])   DCLC (c-9110 DLC)   FIUG (c-9665 FU)
   MIUG (c-9114 MiU)   NYCG (c-9110 NNC)   NYJH (c-9110 NNJ [HBR])

Note: No. 1 shows New York Public Library's (NYPX) use of ANSI romanization. No. 2 shows Brandeis University, Library of Congress, University of Michigan, Cornell University, and Jewish Theological Seminary's (MABX, DCLC, MIUG, NYCG, and NYJH) use of ALA/LC romanization. The four letter codes are RLIN identifiers.

In 1988, a new development in online cataloging of Hebraica emerged for American libraries, the availability of a Hebrew character set in the RLIN database which enables a cataloger to transcribe bibliographic data into the online record in vernacular Hebrew script as it appears on the piece in hand. Bibliographic information that can be transcribed includes the title statement (245 field), edition statement (250 field), imprint data (260 field), and series statement (440 field). This is bibliographic information that is cited in AACR2 rule 1.0E as requiring exact transcription whenever possible; catalogers also have the option of providing additional vernacular Hebrew script access to added entries, notes, subject headings, and series tracings. Vernacular fields appear as linked fields to the romanized data that are required by current MARC conventions.[7]

Although the ALA/LC transliteration scheme has become today's accepted standard in most American research institutions and large Judaica libraries, many other transliteration schemes are in use. Certainly on a larger global scale there is no uniformity in acceptance of a single transliteration scheme for Hebrew script into roman script. Even if a scheme were accepted, chances are very small that it would be applied consistently, and the difficulties of applying any romanization scheme result in errors and mistakes when converting the Hebrew script. A major difficulty also exists for catalogers who are cataloging materials in non-Hebrew languages written in Hebrew script such as Ladino, Judeo-Arabic, and Judeo-Persian, due to minimal guidelines provided by the Library of Congress: "The ALA/LC consonantal table . . . for Hebrew and Yiddish is applicable to all Hebraica languages. The vowels are supplied on a language-specific basis."[8] The vagaries of this statement are implicit, and catalogers are either expected to be very familiar with the non-Hebrew language or have access to someone who is.

HEBREW CATALOGING TECHNIQUES
IN AN ONLINE ENVIRONMENT

As institutions either acquire and catalog new Hebraica materials, catalog existing backlogs, or automate older card catalogs, decisions must be made as to whether vernacular Hebrew script access should be made available to technical staff processing these materials or patrons who may be searching for them. The decision to provide vernacular access traditionally depends on the system utilized by a cataloging agency, whether the cataloging agency feels that providing vernacular script access sufficiently benefits library staff and patrons, whether the added cost of providing vernacular Hebrew script access is affordable, and whether or not it represents a break with past cataloging practices requiring extensive recataloging of materials.

Of the two major national bibliographic utilities in use in the United States today (OCLC and RLIN), only RLIN offers a vernacular Hebrew script capability. Vernacular Hebrew script can be added to records cataloged originally or records derived from online copy. The vernacular Hebrew script is entered from right to left. RLIN has defined certain fields as core fields (245, 250, 260, 440) which are required to always be paired with romanized equivalents. These fields which are used by RLIN for clustering, "the gathering together of records for the same bibliographic edition of a work," include romanized core fields, enabling records that contain vernacular script to be clustered with non-vernacular records. Non-core fields may be entered either in roman script, in Hebrew vernacular script, or both (see Figures 2 and 3).[9]

At present, there are no U.S. standards for authority control for Hebrew and Yiddish names in Hebrew script. Stanford University enters a personal or corporate name in vernacular Hebrew script as it appears on the piece in hand. Brandeis University Hebraica librarians have always maintained an authority file for Hebraica names which they also consult in deciding how names should be entered in vernacular Hebrew script online.[10] The YIVO Institute for Jewish Research Library has maintained a multi-script authority file (Hebrew, roman and Cyrillic scripts) for Yiddish names since the early 1970s. The YIVO Institute Library, under the editorship of Zachary Baker and Bella Hass Weinberg, has recently published its catalog and authority file. This reference tool can assist catalogers who want to establish vernacular Hebrew script forms of Yiddish names, as well as to help catalogers "who seek the Library of Congress romanized counterpart of a Yiddish heading."[11]

Two different methods are used for adding the vernacular Hebrew script to main and/or added entries in Hebraica records that utilize the RLIN vernacular Hebrew script enhancement. Some libraries are allowing only non-roman script access points or subject headings to be paired in parallel fields when the romanized headings have been established systematically by romanizing personal names or corporate bodies according to the ALA/LC transliteration tables. If headings have not been established by following the ALA/LC tables, but rather according to popular usage, some libraries are adding the vernacular Hebrew script entries in local fields only (79x, 69x).[12] When the Hebrew vernacular access is paired in a local field, the implications are crucial for institutions deriving these records for copy: the local fields are not transferred in the copy cataloging

FIGURE 2. Vernacular Hebrew script records paired with romanized fields in an RLIN Hebrew record

1)

```
ID:DCLH91-B4528                    DCLH91-B4528
CC:9114  BLT:am      RTYP:c    ST:p   FRN:    MS:       EL:       AD:11-26-91
CP:is    L:heb       DCF:a     MOD:   SNR:    ATC:      UD:01-15-92
PC:s     PD:1990/    CSC:      BIO:0  FIC:0   CON:b
MMD:     OR:   POL:  GPC:f     CPI:0  FSI:0   ILC:af    II:1
010      91828166/HE INT:      REP:          COL:      EML:      GEN:      BSE:
020      9650505326        DM:     RR:
040      OCH≠cOCH≠dNN≠dDLC-R
043      a-is---
050   0  DS110.J3≠bE45 1990 <Hebr>
100   1  Elkayam, Mordekai,≠d1910-
100   1                                         אלקיים, מרדכי,
245  10  Yafo, Ne.veh-Tsede.k :≠breshitah shel Tel-Aviv : toldot ha-yishuv ha-Y
         ehudi be-Yafo me-reshit ha-me'ah ha-19 /≠cMordekhai El.kayam.
245  10  יפו, נוה-צדק : בראשיתה של תל-אביב : תולדות היישוב היהודי ביפו מראשית המאה ה-19 / מרדכי אלקיים.
260      [Tel Aviv] :≠bMi'srad ha-bi.ta.hon,≠c[1990]
260      [תל אביב] : משרד הבטחון, ‎c[1990]
300      317 p. :≠bill. ;≠c25 cm.
500      Title on verso of t.p.: Jaffa, Neve-Tzedek.
500      Includes bibliographical references and indexes.
651   0  Jaffa (Tel Aviv, Israel)≠xHistory≠y19th century.
651   4  Jews≠zPalestine≠xHistory≠y19th century.
650   0  .Hibbat Zion≠xHistory.
650   0  Palestine≠xHistory≠y1799-1917.
651   4  Jaffa, Neve-Tzedek.
740  01  .יפו
         אלקיים-ישראל,
```

121

FIGURE 3. RLIN cluster containing records that are romanized only and records that utilize the RLIN Hebrew script enhancement

```
Brenner, Joseph _Hayyim, 1881-1921.
  [Ba-_horef]
  Ba-_horef ; Mi-saviv la-ne_kudah / Y._H. Brener ; a_harit davar me-et Ari_el
  Hirshfeld. -- Tel-Aviv : Devir, [1988]
  343 p. ; 22 cm. -- (_Kolot)

Series: Kolot (Tel Aviv, Israel)
ISBN 9650102272
LCCN: 89208143/HE
L.C. CALL NO: PJ5053.B7.B3 1988 <Hebr>
ID: DCLH89-B1424             CC: 9118          DCF: a          [HBR]
- - - - - - - - - - - - - - - - - - - - - - - - - - - - - - - - - - -
DCLH (c-9118 DLC-R [HBR])    CLHH (c-9118 CLHU [HBR])   CSUG (a-9118 CSt)
CUBG (c-9665 CU)    FLUG (c-9665 FU)   GAEG (c-9665 GEU)
MABX (c-9118 MWalB [HBR])    MHAU (c-9662 MH)   MIUG (c-9118 MiU)
NJPG (c-9118 NjP)    NYBG (a-9118 NBiSU)   NYCX (c-9995 NIC)
NYHH (c-9118 NNHeb [HBR])    NYPX (c-9118 NN [HBR])   OHHH (c-9118 OCH [HBR])
PAUG (b-9118 PU)    RIBG (c-9118 RPB)
.?
```

Note: HBR indicates presence of vernacular Hebrew script.

process, forcing these fields to be added manually and increasing cataloging time.

PROS AND CONS
OF VERNACULAR HEBREW SCRIPT ACCESS

The Hebraica library community in the United States is divided in its opinion as to whether or not Hebrew vernacular script is an essential component in the cataloging record. Proponents of vernacular script access feel that:

- Romanized Hebraica records are prone to error and impede reliable searching; vernacular Hebrew script in the catalog record ensures more accurate and speedier access for library patrons and staff.
- Hebrew vernacular script access provides additional searching possibilities in an online environment.
- Romanized only Hebraica records require patrons to be familiar not only with the Hebraic language with which they are working but also the particular romanization scheme used by the cataloging agency.
- The potential exists that Israeli cataloging may one day be available to American libraries via networking capabilities or through a bibliographic database that has Hebrew vernacular script capabilities. (Israeli cataloging of Hebraica, apart from those institutions using LC subject headings, contains little or no roman script.)
- Hebraica items cataloged using a non-ALA/LC romanization scheme must be converted to the original Hebrew script and then re-transliterated into the ALA/LC romanization scheme before they can be searched.

Proponents of romanized access only feel that:

- The added costs of providing vernacular Hebrew script access outweigh the benefits: (a) adding vernacular Hebrew script fields increases cataloging time, and (b) since many Hebraica items in the national databases are already cataloged without vernacular Hebrew script fields, extra work would be required for copy catalogers to enhance these available source records with Hebrew script.
- Since some libraries have already cataloged and automated large Hebraica collections, providing additional vernacular Hebrew script would require either recataloging these collections or splitting the

mode of access to these materials (patrons expecting to search the entire Hebraica collection in the vernacular would not get reliable search results: items that had not been recataloged with vernacular Hebrew script would not be retrieved in a vernacular search).
- Transliteration difficulties are not insurmountable.
- Vernacular access through a national utility is not of use to local patrons because most local online catalogs in the U.S. do not currently support non-roman scripts.

SURVEY OF CURRENT PRACTICES

In March 1992, the Stanford University Catalog Department sent out an informal survey to twenty-three large academic and Judaica libraries in the United States to find out about their current cataloging practices.[13] Results of the survey reveal that these libraries catalog into:

1. RLIN and utilize its vernacular Hebrew script capability,
2. RLIN and do not utilize its vernacular Hebrew script capability,
3. OCLC which does not offer a vernacular Hebrew script capability,
4. Local online databases that do not support vernacular Hebrew script and then provide tapes or upload into RLIN or OCLC,
5. Local online databases that do support vernacular Hebrew script and then provide tapes or upload into RLIN or OCLC, or
6. OCLC and download into local systems which support non-roman scripts.

Respondents who currently are cataloging directly into RLIN and utilizing its vernacular Hebrew script capability (New York University School of Law, Yeshiva University, Yale University, Spertus College of Judaica, Brandeis University, New York Public Library, the University of Michigan, the University of Judaism in Los Angeles, and Hebrew Union College in Cincinnati) have all expressed a commitment to continue to provide vernacular Hebrew script access. These librarians found that keying in vernacular Hebrew script did not add much time to the cataloging process.

These institutions have varying standards for the amount of vernacular Hebrew script and how much romanization they provide. Some institutions provide vernacular Hebrew script access only for those core fields that have been defined by RLIN; others provide vernacular access for main and/or added entries, notes, and subject headings as well. Some institutions do not provide romanization for the statement of responsibility (subfield c of the 245 field) or beyond the title proper (subfield b of the 245). In 1990 the Cataloging Sub-Committee of the Jewish and Middle East Studies Program of the Research Libraries Group, chaired by Rosalie Katchen of Brandeis University Library, sent a proposal to the Library of Congress regarding this issue; LC's subsequent proposal states in part: "The Library of Congress is considering a change to its cataloging policy for monographic materials written in the Hebrew alphabet. The proposal has been made to give only the title proper (MARC tag 245, subfields a, n, p) in romanized form when the MARC record contains a complete title and statement of responsibility in the corresponding vernacular."[14] Proponents of this proposal feel that the amount of actual cataloging time would be decreased by as much as ten percent because of less data input and also because less romanization would be required. The costs of providing full romanization and vernacular access is not small. One impact of the application of this proposal is that patrons and library staff using roman script only systems cannot take full advantage of the expanded and flexible title word searching capability offered by RLIN.

Because most local online catalogs do not currently support non-roman scripts, Hebrew script access must be provided by other means. For example, University of Judaism and Hebrew Union College (HUC) in Cincinnati are producing Hebrew script cards using a program developed by HUC.[15]

Yale University, the University of Michigan, and Stanford University libraries are stripping out the vernacular Hebrew script fields when Hebraica records are transferred or passed into their local NOTIS-based systems. If in the future NOTIS is able to support Hebrew and other non-roman scripts, the RLIN records can be transferred into NOTIS, overlaying their earlier stripped counterparts. Because of technical considerations, NOTIS cannot store non-roman scripts. Until that time, RLIN can serve as a de facto local catalog for patrons and librarians; a search result may be refined to contain only the library's holdings.

Princeton University, The University of Pennsylvania, and Columbia University librarians report that they are cataloging into RLIN but are not utilizing the Hebrew vernacular script capability and do not know of any plans to do so in the future. While the staff there feel that vernacular access would be desirable, they find that, with a little bit of perseverance and creativity, they can overcome searching problems stemming from faulty or difficult transliterations. Librarians at Princeton University report that they might start to contribute Arabic records utilizing RLIN's vernacular Arabic script capability.[16]

Four of the respondents surveyed catalog their Hebraica into OCLC: the University of Florida, the University of Washington, the University of Arizona, and the University of Texas at Austin. OCLC does not provide the capability to display vernacular Hebrew script. These respondents also recognize the desirability of vernacular access but, like many of their RLIN colleagues, do not feel that transliteration problems are insurmountable.

Harvard University, the University of California at Los Angeles, the University of California at Berkeley, and Cornell University all catalog Hebraica into local OPACs which do not have Hebrew script capability. They then tape-load their records into OCLC or RLIN. These institutions have no immediate plans to catalog Hebraica with vernacular Hebrew script fields. "Harvard does not plan at present on changing its way of cataloging Hebraica (i.e., cataloging into HOLLIS [Harvard's local system] and then tape-loading to OCLC and RLIN) because this is the only way it is possible to meet its commitment to providing timely access for students and faculty to books added to its Hebraica Collection, which is the only fully automated Hebraica collection in the world. The librarians at Harvard feel that cataloging into RLIN, and utilizing its Hebrew script capability, would increase their cataloging time and decrease productivity."[17] Similarly, the Judaica bibliographers at UCLA and Cornell indicate a preference to continue producing romanized only records because it is felt that double inputting would not be productive and that fewer records would be added to the database. No scientific study has yet been done to determine how much added production time or cost is involved in enhancing records with vernacular Hebrew script and ultimately making these records available to patrons.

The libraries of the Annenberg Research Institute, the Jewish Theological Seminary, and Ohio State University have installed ALEPH (Automated Library Expandable Program), a fully integrated library management system that is capable of handling both roman and non-roman scripts. ALEPH was developed in Israel in the 1970s and currently supports Latin, Arabic, Cyrillic, and Hebrew scripts.[18]

Jewish Theological Seminary reports that it does its original Hebrew cataloging in ALEPH. RLIN records that are available are downloaded into ALEPH and enhanced with vernacular Hebrew script if it's lacking. Records are then loaded into the RLIN database from tape.

Annenberg Research Institute's library has been undergoing a retrospective conversion project with OCLC. If an item is not found in OCLC, RLIN is searched (Annenberg has found a 95 percent hit rate in OCLC). OCLC and RLIN Hebraica records are downloaded into ALEPH and are enhanced with vernacular Hebrew script titles only (for OCLC records and RLIN copy that is found without the vernacular Hebrew script enhancement). Original cataloging of Hebraica is done in RLIN, and then those records are passed into ALEPH. Annenberg Research Institute provides vernacular Hebrew script fields to the 245, 250, 260, and 4xx fields for records that are cataloged originally.

Ohio State University Libraries plan to include all their Hebrew, Yiddish, and Arabic script records in the ALEPH database to serve their local clients. Hebraica records are cataloged into OCLC and then downloaded into ALEPH. They currently have 22,000 titles in the database, including all new purchases from January 1, 1992, records for items from an existing backlog, and records that have been recataloged for entry into ALEPH. Ohio State University librarians are adding the 245 and 740 fields in vernacular Hebrew script. Authors are entered in the romanized form but have cross-references from the Hebrew form of the same name. Hebraica records also appear in the main public catalog, LCS (Library Computer System), without the vernacular Hebrew script titles.[19]

FUTURE DIRECTIONS

Librarians continue to think about the best ways to make materials accessible for patrons at minimal cost. New technologies are emerging and new ways of cataloging are being developed that may influence the romanization versus vernacular debate. These include:

A. The use of the Internet as a cataloging tool,
B. The exchange of Israeli and American cataloging,
C. Cooperative cataloging arrangements among American libraries, and
D. Multi-script capability on local American OPACs.

A. Internet

The Internet can be used to access other libraries' online catalogs nationally and internationally. ALEPH Hebrew script records from Israel's research institutions and National Library are available to American librarians who are connected to the Internet and have the correct hardware and software. ALEPH may contain bibliographic records for materials not cataloged in the U.S. or have more complete bibliographical information than records available online in the U.S. While ALEPH records cannot be used as source records for copy by American libraries, they can provide helpful bibliographic data.

B. Israeli Cataloging

Israeli libraries receive current Hebraica materials sooner than their U.S. counterparts and, it is assumed, are more up-to-date in the cataloging of these materials. Making these catalog records available to American libraries is an ideal way to decrease the amount of full original cataloging (anything that decreases the amount of keying is important to institutions trying to keep costs down) that these institutions have to do. These items cannot now be used directly, but if the technical aspects of such an arrangement could be worked out, then Israeli libraries could receive American cataloging data as well.[20]

C. Cooperative Cataloging

As institutions expand their Hebraica collections and acquire new materials and as libraries automate their catalogs, the need for resource sharing grows. Libraries need to provide, and patrons want, the most complete access to items possible–desires which may be thwarted by the expense involved in providing such access. However, cooperative arrangements may be one way out of this dilemma. Arrangements can be developed between institutions in which libraries will be responsible for the acquisition and cataloging of different bodies of materials. If libraries do not have to provide cataloging for vast quantities of material, they might be able to absorb more easily the costs involved in providing enhancements such as vernacular access. Such cooperative arrangements have had, however, a rocky history, and few have succeeded for long. Carefully articulated and realistic standards will be necessary if institutions are to buy into a cooperative response to cataloging Hebraica. Professional organizations such as the Association of Jewish Libraries could play an important role in both respects as well as a role in developing such reciprocal arrangements.[21]

D. Multi-Script Capabilities

Multi-script capabilities in local public systems are going to be a necessity as the international exchange of bibliographical data becomes more and more a reality. Innovative Interfaces, maker of INNOPAC and a major vendor of integrated library software to the Far East, has developed a CJK (Chinese, Japanese, Korean) capability for its online catalog product. A formal enhancement request was sent to the NOTIS Cataloging/Authorities Interest Group by Stanford University in June 1992, which recommended that NOTIS support and implement foreign character sets such as Hebrew, CJK, Cyrillic, and Arabic. ALEPH is the only online integrated library system in the U.S. that supports the Hebrew character set, and it has been successfully implemented by three institutions (see above). However, it is unlikely that most large research institutions which are utilizing systems such as NOTIS, GEAC, and INNOPAC will agree to maintain a separate public system for managing its Hebraica collections (Ohio State University Libraries is a notable exception). Hebraica librarians must work together to put pressure on the makers of these large library systems to develop a Hebrew script capability. As a first step towards creating a central agency to work with vendors, the Association of Jewish Libraries has recently established a Committee of Automation headed by Rick Burke, Librarian at the University of Judaism in Los Angeles. Looking to the future, companies such as Hewlett-Packard, Apple Computer, and Adobe Systems are developing tools to support non-roman scripts which ideally could be incorporated into library management systems.

CONCLUSION

Some librarians claim that too much time and cost are involved in enhancing romanized Hebraica records with vernacular Hebrew script. However, searching for an item using romanized Hebrew is very painful and time-consuming for anyone lacking a thorough knowledge of Hebrew and the multifarious transliteration schemes used to represent it. Similar problems occur with accessing other non-roman script language materials. The most effective way to retrieve Hebraica is in its true script.

As we acknowledge the changing economic climate in the United States, institutions, administrators, and librarians are naturally hesitant to implement changes that could increase monetary and time costs. However, as has been noted above, new developments in technology and sharing of resources can have an impact on the potential use of vernacular scripts in library systems. Technologies such as low-cost bit-mapped displays, and loadable fonts such as those produced by Adobe Systems are proliferating in applications used in the business and academic worlds. It is natural that library patrons and staff will expect to see such technologies applied where they can serve them as well. Hebraica librarians and their library colleagues and administrators must work as a coalition to jointly and most economically improve their systems and re-evaluate existing standards for cataloging of Hebraica.

NOTES

1. For a related article on automation of Hebrew and Arabic script materials, see: Elizabeth Vernon, "Hebrew and Arabic Script Materials in the Automated Library: The United States Scene," *Cataloging & Classification Quarterly* 14:1 (1991): 49-67.

2. Bella Hass Weinberg, "Hebraica Cataloging and Classification," in *Cataloging and Classification of Non-Western Material: Concerns, Issues, and Practices,* ed. Mohammed M. Aman (Phoenix: Oryx Press, 1980), 322-323.

3. Harvard University Library, *Catalogue of Hebrew Books* (Cambridge: Distributed by Harvard University Press, 1968), vols. 5-6, Suppl. (1972), vol. 3; Klau Library, Hebrew Union College, *Dictionary Catalog of the Klau Library* (Boston, G.K. Hall, 1964), vols. 29-32; New York Public Library. Research Libraries, *Hebrew Character Title Catalog of the Jewish Collection* (Boston: G.K. Hall, 1961).

4. Michael Malinconico, "Vernacular Scripts in the NYPL Automated Bibliographic Control System," *Journal of Library Automation* 10:3 (September 1977): 205-225.

5. Research Libraries Group (RLG) is in the process of adding Hebrew script to NYPL's reversibly romanized records. The romanized fields in the records will continue to be reversibly romanized, but the restored Hebrew script will be invaluable to those libraries which utilize the vernacular Hebrew script capability in RLIN for copy cataloging. Joan Aliprand, Library Systems Analyst Program Officer, Research Libraries Group, e-mail correspondence with author, Sept. 30, 1992.

6. For a more complete overview of the history and the implementation of ALA/LC romanization practices, see: Paul Maher, *Hebraica Cataloging: A Guide to ALA/LC Romanization and Descriptive Cataloging* (Washington, D.C.: Cataloging Distribution Service, Library of Congress, 1987).

7. For a fuller profile of the implementation and use of the vernacular Hebrew script enhancement on RLIN, see: Joan M. Aliprand, "Hebrew on RLIN," *Judaica Librarianship* 3:1-2 (1986-1987): 5-16; "Hebraica on RLIN: An Update," *Judaica Librarianship* 5:1 (1989-1990): 12-20.

8. Maher, *Hebraica Cataloging*, 8.

9. Aliprand, "Hebrew on RLIN," 9-10.

10. Rosalie Katchen, "Hebrew Online: Current Issues and Future Concerns: A View from the Field," *Judaica Librarianship* 5:1 (1989-1990): 22-25.

11. Yivo Institute for Jewish Research. Library, *Der Yidisher Katalog un Oytorintet-Karotek fun der YIVO Bibliotek,* ed. Zachary Baker and Bella Hass Weinberg (Boston, Mass.: G.K. Hall, 1990), vol. 5.

12. For a fuller discussion on the relationship of roman and non-roman fields, see: Joan Aliprand, "Linkage in USMARC Bibliographic Records," *Cataloging & Classification Quarterly* 16:1 (1993): 5-37.

13. I would like to extend my appreciation to those librarians who responded to the survey that I sent to them in March 1992. My sincerest apologies to those librarians whom I was unable to reach to get their permission to publish their responses. Any information that may be misrepresentative or faulty is my responsibility.

14. "Hebrew Cataloging Proposal," *Cataloging Service Bulletin* 49 (Summer 1990): 45.

15. David Gilner, Ellen Siegel Kovacic, and Herbert C. Zafren, "Hebrew Cataloging at Hebrew Union College on an Apple II+," *Judaica Librarianship* 1:1 (1983): 4-8.

16. Rachel Simon, Hebraica Cataloger, Princeton University Library, Princeton, N.J., e-mail correspondence with author, Sept. 24, 1992.

17. Charles Berlin, Head, Judaica Division, Harvard College Library, Cambridge, Mass., e-mail correspondence with author, Sept. 25, 1992.

18. For a history and description of ALEPH, see: Susan S. Lazinger, "ALEPH: Israel's Research Library Network: Background, Evolution, and Implications for Networking in a Small Country," *Information Technology and Libraries* 10:4 (December 1991): 275-291.

19. Joseph Galron, Hebraica Cataloger, Ohio State University Libraries, Columbus, Ohio, e-mail correspondence with author, Sept. 23-25, 1992.

20. For fuller discussions on the exchange of Israeli and American cataloging data, see: Elhanan Adler, "Hebrew Cataloging and the Computer: The View from Israel," *Information Technology and Libraries* 1:3 (September 1982): 238-245; Elhanan Adler, "The Use of Israeli Machine-Readable Cataloging by American Libraries: A Proposal," *Judaica Librarianship* 4:1 (1987-1988): 23-26; Joan M. Aliprand and John A. Eiltz, a response to the previous article in "Commentaries (Letters from Our Readers)," *Judaica Librarianship* 4:2 (1988-1989): 138-139.

21. For a discussion of shared cataloging among Judaica libraries, see: Bella Hass Weinberg, "From Copy Cataloging to Derived Bibliographic Records: Cataloging and Its Automation in American Judaica Research Libraries from the Sixties through the Eighties," *Judaica Librarianship* 4:2 (1988-1989): 120.

Cataloging of Middle Eastern Materials (Arabic, Persian, and Turkish)

Edward A. Jajko

SUMMARY. Cataloging of materials in Arabic, Turkish, Persian, and related languages presents numerous special difficulties. The author discusses in detail problems presented by the languages and scripts and their romanizations. He also deals with different calendar systems used in the Middle East and with representative problems in Library of Congress classification of Middle Eastern materials. The Middle East cataloger must be aware of and deal with these and other problems on a daily basis. Library administrators, heads of technical services and catalog departments, and other catalogers also need to be aware of the particular difficulties that Middle East catalogers face.

In this paper, I wish to discuss some of the problems that face the cataloger of Middle East materials, here defined as books, serials, etc., in Arabic, Persian, Turkish, and related languages. The topics discussed below are items which the cataloger must know or be aware of, or difficulties which the cataloger may encounter. I exclude discussion of the minutiae of computer-based cataloging, as well as the plethora of details relating to changes in rules, subject headings, and classification with which today's catalogers are expected to keep up. Rather, the following is a discussion

Edward A. Jajko is Deputy Curator, Africa-Middle East Collection, Hoover Institution on War, Revolution and Peace, Stanford University, Stanford, CA 94305-6016. Fax: 415-723-1687. E-mail: JAJKO@HOOVER.BITNET or JAJKO@ HOOVER.STANFORD.EDU.

[Haworth co-indexing entry note]: "Cataloging of Middle Eastern Materials (Arabic, Persian, and Turkish." Jajko, Edward A. Co-published simultaneously in *Cataloging & Classification Quarterly* (The Haworth Press, Inc.) Vol. 17, No. 1/2, 1993, pp. 133-147; and: *Languages of the World: Cataloging Issues and Problems* (ed: Martin D. Joachim) The Haworth Press, Inc., 1993, pp. 133-147. Multiple copies of this article/chapter may be purchased from The Haworth Document Delivery Center [1-800-3-HAWORTH; 9:00 a.m. - 5:00 p.m. (EST)].

133

based on general principles, of things that make cataloging of Middle East materials problematic and different from any other kind of cataloging. Because there are so many, and space is limited, I have chosen to concentrate on only a few.

My selection is subjective and by no means inclusive. Other catalogers might come up with rather different lists. This one is based on more than twenty-two years' experience in cataloging materials in more than thirty languages, with a concentration in Arabic, Persian, Turkish, Hebrew, and Yiddish, and training and supervising some fourteen professional and nonprofessional assistants in bibliographic searching, copy cataloging, and original cataloging of materials in Arabic, Persian, Turkish, Hebrew, Yiddish, and other languages.

Regrettably, there is no handy guide to Middle East cataloging. Each cataloger builds up a fund of information over the years, but there is no single printed source of information that catalogers can refer to. Members of the Middle East Librarians Association and the Library of Congress have recently begun to consider publication of a guide to Middle East cataloging.

LANGUAGES, SCRIPTS, AND ROMANIZATIONS

It is not too obvious and elementary to start by saying that the Middle East cataloger must know the languages of the Middle East. The librarian whose institution collects in all the major languages of the Middle East faces a serious challenge right from the beginning. Those major languages–Arabic, Persian, and Turkish–are totally unrelated linguistically although very closely linked culturally and historically. Arabic is Semitic, Turkish is Turkic or Ural-Altaic, Persian is Indo-European. A considerable amount of Arabic vocabulary is used by Persian and by earlier forms of modern-day Anatolian Turkish (i.e., Ottoman and Early Republican roman-alphabet Turkish), but that vocabulary often has meanings different from the Arabic originals and may require romanizations totally different from the Arabic. Because the structures of the languages are entirely different and the three languages conceptualize and handle information in ways radically different from each other and from English, it can be a considerable feat to shift mental gears and go from one language to another. It can even be difficult sometimes for the cataloger to figure out what is actually the language of the title page (or the title, even if all else is known), which can seriously affect how one romanizes it (and, for those libraries that follow LC on Ottoman romanization, whether one uses the original script at all).

LC/ALA have established romanization systems for a number of languages that are more or less letter-for-letter systems. Examples of these are the systems for languages written in the Cyrillic, Greek, or Armenian alphabets, the Amharic syllabary, and Devanagari letters or variations thereof. In theory, someone who does not read these languages at all should be able to take a title page that is completely in the original alphabet or script, and, applying the rules of the appropriate LC/ALA romanization tables, should be able to generate an accurate romanization of the text in hand.

However, this does not work for any language written in the Arabic alphabet, whether Arabic, Persian, or Turkic (nor indeed for Hebrew-alphabet Hebrew, which is treated in another article in this volume). The first requirement for romanizing text written in the Arabic alphabet is a knowledge of the language, not an ability to compare the letters with the romanization tables. This is because the Arabic alphabet is made up of thirty-six consonants only.[1] The three short vowels and the long vowels of some words of Arabic (and some four vowels of Persian and up to eight vowels of Turkish) are not expressed in the alphabet. Reading Arabic, the reader must supply the short vowels (and those long vowels that are not marked by the corresponding consonant/semi-vowel) from context and so determine the meaning of the text.

Incorrect vocalization can affect the meaning of the text, sometimes drastically. From the librarian's point of view, incorrect vocalization affects not only the meaning of the text but also the filing of the entry and its retrievability. By way of example, in Arabic the letters *slm* can be read in many ways: as *salm*, a masculine noun meaning "peace"; as *silm*, a noun both masculine and feminine meaning "peace; the religion of Islam"; as *sullam*, a masculine noun meaning "ladder; (flight of) stairs, staircase; stair, step, running board; (*mus.*) scale; means, instrument, tool"; as the verb *salima*, meaning "to be safe and sound, unharmed, unimpaired, intact, safe, secure; to be certain, established, clearly proven (fact); to be free; to escape"; or as the second form of the same verb, *sallama*, meaning "to preserve, keep from injury, protect from harm, save; to hand over intact; to hand over, turn over, surrender; to deliver; to submit; to greet, salute; to grant salvation (God to the Prophet); to admit, concede"; etc.[2] The Arabic language has an infinity of other homographic combinations of letters that have more than one meaning, depending on their vocalization or reading. Both meaning and vocalization must be determined from context and knowledge of the language.

Arabic, Persian, and Ottoman Turkish are all written in the Arabic alphabet. The cataloger must know how to read the standard forms of that alphabet as found in printed text. The cataloger must also be able to read the Arabic alphabet in its various calligraphic forms, which are used on title pages as a way of grouping words and phrases and for esthetics. Middle East catalogers must, from time to time, resort to the technique that all students of the Arab East have to use and trace the letters with a pencil or their fingers in an attempt to figure out what they are and to account for all the diacritical marks that are parts of many letters but can be offset by calligraphers for the sake of balance, style, and look. Numerous book covers and title pages in the Arabic alphabet have calligraphy as intricate, challenging, and beautiful as that found on the most exquisitely carved and inlaid mosques.

Within the Arab world, local usages can change the values of written letters. The Maghreb has its own way of writing the letters *F* and *Q* that differs from standard usage and can confuse the unwary. The Maghreb also has a non-standard letter representing *G* which in the rest of the Arab world may be used to represent *V.* (Neither sound exists in classical Arabic.) In most of the Arab world, the letter *Jīm* represents the sound *J*, as in *Jake*. In some parts of the Levant, the letter is pronounced *Zh*, like the French *J*. In Egypt, which probably publishes more Arabic books than any other country, the standard pronunciation of this letter is *G* (as in the first name of the late president Gamal Abdel Nasser, which is pronounced *Jamāl* in the rest of the Arab World). The Egyptian writer and reader automatically read this letter as *G*. The Library of Congress reads it as *J* following classical Arabic. When an Egyptian title page includes a letter based on the same letter form, which an Egyptian would recognize as *J*, the Library of Congress romanizes it as *Zh* and sometimes *Ch*.

Persian adds modified Arabic letters for sounds not existing in Arabic. Persian letter forms are often quite different from their Arabic counterparts and can be difficult to read for someone accustomed primarily to Arabic. Persian has an added complication in that not only does the writing not express the vowels of most words, but it also does not always express a major grammatical feature of the language, the *ezāfet*.[3] *Ezāfet* is a connecting vowel, expressed in Library of Congress romanization as *-i*, that links words to indicate possession or adjectival or other modification. Library of Congress romanization requires that the *ezāfet* be added to the text, except for proper (personal) names. But it takes a moderately good knowledge of Persian, or of Ottoman Turkish, which borrowed the *ezāfet* from Persian, to know when to put the *ezāfet* in and when to leave it out. One clearly has to understand the text in order to romanize it properly.

Persian romanization is highly problematic for another reason. The Library of Congress has chosen to romanize Persian as if it were Arabic, with the Arabic vowels *a, i, u, ā, ī, ū*. But Persian has its own rather different vowels–*a, ā, i, e, o, u*. An Iranian would tend to pronounce the name of the Muslim Students Following the Line of the Imam as *Dānesh-juyāne Mosalmāne Peyrowe Khatte Emām*. LC's romanization does not allow for a form like *peyrow*. Instead, LC's treatment of this purely Persian word requires that it be romanized as if it were Arabic, forcing *payraw* or *payru*. Of these two, *payraw* is marginally better, though inaccurate, and that is the form that is used for the LC romanization *Dānishjūyān-i Musal-mān-i Payraw-i Khaṭṭ-i Imām*. LC's romanization of Persian does genuine damage in its transliteration of the source text in that it *requires* incorrect and inaccurate vocalizations. This romanization system is a perennial source of complaint among librarians of Iranian origin, Iranian readers, and scholars of Persian.

The romanization of Ottoman and other Turkic languages written in Arabic script is to romanization as reading *Finnegans Wake* is to English literature. Reading *Finnegans Wake*, does one read the words as if they were in their original form, or does one try to read and grasp the multitude of puns and allusions all at once, or does one read once for one batch of puns, then reread as many times as necessary in order to sort out all of the remaining puns, one by one? The Arabic alphabet is totally unsuited to the representation of Turkish, yet the Ottomans used it for centuries. If one knows the language and the orthography, one can read it without great difficulty. The problem comes in trying to romanize it. LC/ALA romaniza-tions seek a middle ground between the two poles of representation of the sound of the target language and literal one-for-one representation of its written letters. In Ottoman Turkish, as in Arabic and Persian, the written text does not express everything that is said, since it does not include certain vowels. The Arabic consonantal alphabet is well-suited for writing Arabic but not for Turkish. In Ottoman, as in other Arabic-alphabet Turkic languages, some Arabic consonants are used to express more than one Turkish sound or have variable Turkish values. When romanizing Otto-man Turkish (or any other Turkic language written in the Arabic script), one has numerous options:

1. Romanize the written text, letter for letter, without adding unex-pressed vowels;
2. Romanize the written text, letter for letter, adding Turkish vowels not expressed in the text;
3. Romanize the written text, letter for letter, adding vowels based on another language, like Arabic;
4. Romanize the written text as if it were Arabic (or Persian or other language);

5. Use Turkish vowels, adding diacritical marks to indicate vowels expressed by letters in the Arabic-alphabet source text; use modern Turkish consonants, adding markers to indicate Arabic consonants in the source text that have no value or a modified value in Turkish;
6. Use Turkish vowels, adding diacritical marks to indicate vowels expressed by letters in the Arabic-alphabet source text; use consonants from an accepted romanization system for Arabic;
7. Use modern Turkish equivalents for consonants, Turkish vowels for Turkish words, Arabic vowels for Arabic words;
8. Use modern Turkish equivalents for all words that have them and an artificial systematic romanization for those words that cannot be found in standard Turkish dictionaries and encyclopedias.

LC has chosen option 8. All are possible, and there are other combinations or systems not listed here that have been or are currently used. Options 1 through 3, for example, each have two versions: (1) romanize the written text as is, letter for letter, and (2) romanize the written text but use the appropriate roman letter when the value of the Ottoman Turkish Arabic-alphabet letter changes. None of these options is 100% satisfactory. If romanization is absolutely necessary, however, a strict letter-for-letter substitution, without adding vowels, is probably best although very difficult to read.

Systematic romanization of languages written in the Arabic alphabet–and in the Hebrew alphabet, Chinese characters, Egyptian hieroglyphics, Mayan glyphs, etc.–means forcing something into a mold that was not designed to fit it. Something of the original is bound to be lost or distorted in the attempt to satisfy the requirements of the new form. Arab, Persian, and Turkic names can be seriously distorted when forced into LC romanization. The librarian gets used to this and tries to develop a cross-referencing structure that will help the reader find the desired material. Inevitably there are those readers for whom it is next to impossible to find the Arab or Persian names they seek in a roman alphabet catalog because they do not understand the romanization system in use, or cannot comprehend or read the romanized entries that may appear on a video screen or in a card catalog, or because the romanization system violates the rules of their native languages.

The Turkic and Persic languages of Central Asia are beyond the scope of this article. I do want to mention, however, that while there are highly developed LC romanization tables for these languages when printed in the Cyrillic alphabet, corresponding tables for their Arabic alphabet avatars are not to be found. The Library of Congress is of no help except to say that the Cyrillic tables cannot be applied on the principle that it is *script* that is romanized, not *language*. The Middle East cataloger who must handle the Persian and Turkic languages of Central Asia in Arabic script is in a bind: create a home-made romanization that is bound to differ from whatever LC may devise, barring miracles; catalog from a Russian title page only, if available, a totally unacceptable compromise; or push those titles a little further into the backlog.[4]

CALENDARS AND DATING

The Middle East cataloger must be able to work with at least four different dating or calendar systems currently or previously used in the Middle East and their several variants. The systems the cataloger *must* know are:

- Gregorian (Christian or Western) calendar
- Muslim calendar
- Iranian calendar
- Turkish civil calendar[5]

Gregorian Calendar

The Gregorian calendar, which we use to reckon our dates, is not problematic. Rather, what is difficult is trying to remember the names of the months. Arabs have at least three ways of expressing the months of the Gregorian calendar. In Syria, Lebanon, and elsewhere, they use Arabic forms of the ancient Semitic names of the months.[6] In Egypt and other Arab countries, the Semitic names have been replaced by variants of the familiar Roman names.[7] In the Maghreb, the Roman names appear in variants of their French forms.[8] In non-Semitic Turkey, five months have their ancient Semitic names, three have variants of the Roman names, and four have Turkish names.[9]

Muslin Calendar

The Muslim year, known as *A.H.* for *Anno Hegirae*, i.e., year of the Hegira or Hijrah, is a purely lunar calendar, eleven days shorter than the Gregorian calendar. There is no intercalation or adjustment to align the calendar with the period of the earth's rotation around the sun. The months of this calendar are as follows (figures after the names are the number of days in each month):

Muḥarram	30
Ṣafar	29
Rabīᶜ al-Awwal	30
Rabīᶜ al-Thānī	30
Jumādá al-Ūlá	30
Jumādá al-Thāniyah	29
Rajab	30
Shaᶜbān	29
Ramaḍān	30
Shawwāl	29
Dhū al-Qaᶜdah	30
Dhū al-Ḥijjah	29

The months of the Muslim or Hijrah year do not correspond with those of any other calendar. March 1993, for example, is equivalent to the last 22 days of the month of Ramaḍān and the first eight days of the Shawwāl of the Muslim year 1413. The Muslim year 1414 (beginning on 1 Muḥarram) starts at sundown on 21 June 1993.

Conversion of Muslim dates to Gregorian, or Gregorian to Muslim, is a complicated business. It would be nice if some enterprising company would produce a little pocket calculator that could do the conversions. Lacking that, the cataloger must use one of the several books of tables and formulas that are available. The best of these is Freeman-Grenville.[10] This slim volume is very difficult to use if one has to convert an exact date. Catalogers generally need to convert years, which is relatively easy to do and can be learned in a few minutes. It is possible, however, that if one has the exact date of publication, or even the month of publication, according to the Muslim calendar, one might be faced with the difficult task of converting to an exact Gregorian date in order to determine in which of two years A.D. a book may have been published.

Iranian Calendar

Iran has its own calendar, which begins on 21 March. It is roughly equivalent to the zodiac calendar, and in fact in Afghanistan (as in some earlier Iranian usage), the months still have the names of the signs of the zodiac.[11] The Iranians call theirs the *solar hijri* year. One derives the Iranian year from the current Gregorian year by subtracting 621 or 622 (depending on the month). Conversely, one derives the Gregorian year from the Iranian year by adding 621 or 622 (again depending on the month). The cataloger who has an Iranian imprint date of, say, 1348, but does not know the actual month of publication, has to express the year of imprint as 1348 [1969 or 1970]. If the cataloger knows that the book was published in the month of Farvardin of the Iranian year 1348, then the imprint date is 1348 [1969]. If the cataloger knows that the book was published in Bahman 1348, then the imprint date is 1348 [1970]. If the book was published in the month of Dayy 1348 (exact day unknown), then the imprint date is 1348 [1969 or 1970], since Dayy begins in December and continues through the first three weeks of January.

During the time of the late Shah, the Iranian calendar was changed, to base it "on the supposed year of accession of the first Achaemenid king, Cyrus the Great (559 B.C.); thus, 21 March 1976 became the first day . . . of the year 2535 in the Sāhanšāhī era. The month names of the Persian solar Hejrī calendar were retained without change. Official documents and publications were dated according to the new calendar. This caused much confusion and created widespread discontent, particularly among the clergy. Eventually, on 5 Sahrivar 1357 S./27 August 1978, the government, in the face of the coming revolution, reverted to the solar Hejri calendar."[12]

Turkish Fiscal Calendar

The Ottoman Turks, faced with the difficulty of administering a vast and diverse empire using the Muslim lunar calendar, devised the *Mali* or "fiscal" calendar. Eventually, all official publications were issued with the *Mali* date only. This is of significance to catalogers who are processing late Ottoman publications, which bear a date that looks suspiciously like a year in the Hijrah calendar. Many catalogers have inadvertently assigned the wrong equivalents in Gregorian dates, forgetting that they are transposing from *Mali* rather than Hijrah years. The only source I know of for tables for the transposition of *Mali* dates is the section entitled "Mali yılların hangi Milâdî ve Hicrî-kamerî yıllara rastladığını gösterir Cetvel" in Unat's *Hicrî tarihleri Miladi tarihe çevirme kılavuzu.*[13]

The vagueness the reader may have noticed in the preceding paragraph about the beginning year of the *Mali* calendar is intentional. One general source[14] simply dates it to the reign of Mahmud I, 1730-1754. Another says that it "was introduced . . . in A.D. 1789."[15] Unat[16] himself begins his Mali table with the year 1086, equivalent to 1676 A.D. What is important for the Middle East cataloger is to be aware that what looks like a

Hijrah year imprint date may actually be a *Mali* date and to remember to turn to Unat for help.

CLASSIFICATION

I shall discuss only a few of the many areas of the LC classification schedules that are inadequate for Middle East cataloging. They are:

1. History of Palestinian Arabs
2. Persian and Turkish literature
3. Islamic law.

History of Palestinian Arabs

Materials on the history of Arab Palestine and the Palestinian Arabs are classified in DS101-151, which is headed **ISRAEL (PALESTINE). THE JEWS.** While there are a couple of numbers within this area, DS119.7-119.75, that accommodate some of these materials, the thrust of DS101-151 is the history of the Jews. DS101-151 otherwise does not work for materials dealing purely with the Palestinians. Art imitating life, the Palestinians and the Jews just don't fit in the same area.

Persian and Turkish Literature

In the 1970s, the Library of Congress produced an excellent expansion of the tables for modern Arabic literature, 1801- (PJ7800-7876). The expansion was necessary because so many Arabs share the same or similar names. Without the expansion, exquisitely fine cuttering involving many, many numbers would have been required to arrange authors in the shelf list. However, no expansions were created for modern Persian literature and all of Ottoman and Modern Turkish literature, each of which continues to use one main class number (PK6561 for Persian, PL248 for Turkish), followed by an author cutter based on the first letter of the author's entry name.[17] The sharing of names is greater in Persian than in Turkish, but it would have been of great help to catalogers had LC expanded the modern literature classes for both these languages. Modern literature is, after all, open-ended, and the number of individual author cutters to be added after PK6561 and PL248 will grow constantly, forcing catalogers to create ever finer, hence ever longer, author cutter numbers to keep authors separate and in alphabetical order. Catalogers who have to incorporate LC cutters into their shelf lists "as is" will face great problems when classifying literary authors not previously handled by LC.

Islamic Law

At long last, new LC classification schedules are available for the civil law of the Middle East.[18] The schedules are difficult for a non-specialist to use, but with logic and application, an experienced cataloger can figure out how to build the necessary numbers. Many titles that have long mouldered in backlogs will now see the light of day.

There is a vast body of publication in the field of Islamic law, one of the main pillars of the theoretical and practical application of Islamic principles. This immense and extremely important literature, existing in all the major languages of the Middle East, most of the languages of scholarly publication of Western and Eastern Europe, and other languages as well, remains without an LC classification. This situation exists despite the fact that a comprehensive collection on Islamic law would contain many thousands of books, dealing with principles, sources, codes, commentaries and supercommentaries, Shiite law, Sunni law, attempts to reconcile differences among the canonical Sunni schools, etc. Catalogers, who must classify materials in Islamic law whether an accepted classification system exists or not, have had to jerry-build home-made classifications. Some libraries use the parenthesized section of BP, BP140-157. Others use K.Author cutter, KBL.Author cutter, or other letters from class K followed by an author/main entry cutter. The Hoover Institution generally uses BP140-157 for Islamic law.[19]

BIBLIOGRAPHER? CATALOGER? BIBLIOGRAPHER-CATALOGER?

Finally, a quite common problem among Middle East specialist librarians is one of identity. Middle East librarianship seems to be one of the last of the areas of specialized librarianship still subject to the unitive theory of management—"One person can do it all." No self-respecting research library in this country would expect its bibliographer of American or English literature, say, or its curator of French, to personally catalog the books he or she acquires. But in far too many institutions, the belief seems to persist that something about Middle Eastern materials makes it suitable to render their selection, acquisition, and cataloging part-time operations. This can create endless problems for the Middle East librarian who must serve more than one master, and it is a disservice to librarianship and to the readers. That many Middle East librarians work as part-time bibliographers and part-time catalogers is something of a tribute to their dedication and a sign of sad economic reality. Those librarians, and the field they specialize in, deserve better from the institutions they work for and from their administrators.

NOTES

1. Three letters, *alif, wāw,* and *yā'*, can also serve as indicators of long vowels and as supporters of the marker for glottal stop. *Alif* and *yā'* also function as supporters for *tanwīn,* and *alif* and *wāw* are used as unpronounced grammatical markers or to distinguish between allophonic homographs.

2. All definitions from Hans Wehr, *A Dictionary of Modern Written Arabic (Arabic-English),* ed. J. Milton Cowan, 4. ed., considerably enlarged and amended by the author (Wiesbaden: Otto Harrassowitz, 1979), 495-496.

3. From Arabic *iḍāfah,* meaning "addition." The spelling in the text reflects the Persian pronunciation; in correct Library of Congress romanization it is spelled *iẓāfat.*

4. For an informed, interesting, and thorough study of romanization and its problems, see: Hans H. Wellisch, *The Conversion of Scripts–Its Nature, History, and Utilization* (New York: John Wiley & Sons, 1978).

5. Three other calendars of less immediate significance to Middle East cataloging, but ones that the cataloger should at least be aware of, are the Coptic, Jewish, and Julian calendars. For further information on calendars, see: Jere L. Bacharach, *A Near East Studies Handbook* (Seattle: University of Washington Press, 1974) and later editions. Bacharach's book is a handy quick reference that contains a wealth of information. Also: S. H. Taqizadeh, "Various Eras and Calendars Used in the Countries of Islam," *Bulletin of the School of Oriental and African Studies* 9:4 (1939): 903-922; 10:1 (1939): 107-132.

6. January	Kānūn al-Thānī
February	Shubāṭ
March	Ādhār
April	Nīsān
May	Īyār, sometimes Ayyār
June	Hazīran
July	Tammūz
August	Āb
September	Aylūl
October	Tishrīn al-Awwal
November	Tishrīn al-Thānī
December	Kānūn al-Awwal

December is "First Kānūn" and January is "Second Kānūn," reflecting times when the new year began in spring or fall.

7. January   Yanāyir
   February   Fibrāyir
   March   Māris
   April   Abrīl
   May   Māyū
   June   Yūniyū or Yūniyah
   July   Yūliyū or Yūliyah
   August   Aghusṭus
   September   Sibtimbar or Sibtimbir
   October   Uktūbar or Uktūbir
   November   Nūfimbar or Nūfimbir
   December   Dīsimbar or Dīsimbir

8. The Algerian and Tunisian forms (for which I am indebted to Dr. Tarek Echekki, a Tunisian graduate student at Stanford) are as follows:

   January   Jānfī (pronounced Zhanvi)
   February   Fīfrī (pronounced Fivri)
   March   Māris
   April   Afrīl (pronounced Avril)
   May   Māy
   June   Juwān (pronounced Zhwan)
   July   Juwīliyah (pronounced Zhwīliyah)
   August   Ūt
   September   Sibtambar
   October   Uktūbar (pronounced Uktobar)
   November   Nūfambar (pronounced Novambar)
   December   Dīsambar

Morocco has different forms (I am grateful to Hédi BenAicha of the Princeton University Library for these names and their romanization):

   January   Yanāyir
   February   Fabrāyir
   March   Māris
   April   Abrīl
   May   Māy
   June   Yūnyūh
   July   Yūlyūz
   August   Ghūsht
   September   Shitanbar
   October   Uktūbar
   November   Nwinanbar
   December   Dījanbar

9. January   Ocak
   February   Şubat

March	Mart
April	Nisan
May	Mayıs
June	Haziran
July	Temmuz
August	Ağustos
September	Eylül
October	Ekim
November	Kasım
December	Aralık

10. G.S.P. Freeman-Grenville, *The Muslim and Christian Calendars: Being Tables for the Conversion of Muslim and Christian Dates from the Hijra to the Year A.D. 2000*, 2nd ed. (London: Rex Collings Ltd., 1977); 1st ed., 1963. One hopes to see a new edition of Freeman-Grenville that will carry us beyond 2000 A.D.

11. Names of the months in Persian and their Western equivalents are:

Farvardīn	March/April
Urdībihisht	April/May
Khurdād	May/June
Tīr	June/July
Mrudād	July/August
Shahrīvar	August/September
Mihr	September/october
Ābān	October/November
Azār	November/December
Dayy	December/January
Bahman	January/February
Asfand	February/March

The Kurds also use this calendar, but give their months entirely different names. March 21, 1993, is Iranian *Nawrūz*, New Year's Day, the first day of Farvardin, 1372.

12. "Calendar," *Encyclopaedia Iranica*, ed. Ehsan Yarshater (London; Boston: Routledge & Kegan Paul, 1982-); 4:627. I am indebted to Dr. Hamid Mahamedi, Islamica Bibliographer of the University of California, Berkeley, for this reference.

13. Faik Reşit Unat, *Hicrî tarihleri Milâdî tarihe çevirme kılavuzu* (Ankara: Maarif Matbaası, 1943).

14. "Takvim," *Büyük Lugat ve Ansiklopedi* (Cağaloğlu, İstanbul: Meydan Yayınevi, 1985-); 11:857. This publication is also known by its cover title, *Meydan-Larousse*.

15. *Handbook of Oriental History*, by members of the Department of Oriental History, School of Oriental and African Studies, University of London, ed. C.H. Philips (London: Offices of the Royal Historical Society, 1951). The inscrutably

orientalist three lines on p. 32 of this rather quaint book that cover the Ottoman fiscal calendar are worth quoting in full: "The Turkish Financial Year (Maliye). An adaptation of earlier 'fiscal' calendars, combining the *Hijrī* era with a solar year, was introduced into the Ottoman revenue administration in A.D. 1789. This was a Julian year with most of the Syrian month names used with a *Hijrī* era and a system of 'sliding' at intervals to bring the two eras into line."

16. Unat, 94.

17. Although the Library of Congress has assigned "New Persian" literature prior to 1870 a tremendous range of numbers, PK6450.9-6559, "New Persian" is the form of the language that developed after the Islamic conquest and the admixture of Arabic.

18. Turkey (KKX) is covered in *Law of Europe: Classification: Class KJ-KKZ* (Washington: Library Of Congress, 1988). The other states of the Middle East are covered in *Law of Asia and Eurasia, Africa, Pacific Area, and Antarctica, KL-KWX:* (Washington: Library of Congress, 1993). The breakdown is as follows: KMC-KMY, the Arab countries, Iran, and Israel; KNF, Afghanistan; KQG, Algeria; KRM, Egypt; KSP, Libya; KSW, Morocco; KTQ, Sudan; KTV, Tunisia.

19. For civil law of the Middle East, the Hoover Institution now uses KKX and the classes listed in the previous note. Previously, the Hoover classed civil legal materials in the LC classes in which they would have been entered had they not been on law; for example, family law in HQ, constitutional law in JQ-JS, law relating to economics, business, etc., in the appropriate section in H, military law in U or V, etc.

Central Asian Cataloging:
Problems and Prospects

Michael Walter

SUMMARY. Languages of Central Asia present unique problems in cataloging. Reference works are often scarce, unobtainable, or non-existent, especially for Tibetan and Mongolian materials. Single-cutter numbers for languages result in shelflisting problems in some Central Asian languages. LC subject headings for Central Asian materials are generally adequate except for Tibetan. The breakup of the Soviet Union may result in literatures of the former republics, etc., adopting new scripts. Included is an appendix of some sources for literary works and authors in Central Asian languages.

It seems frequently the case that difficult points in a project, the challenges in a career, or the feeling of "crossing over the pass" (which is a powerful symbol for Tibetans, for obvious reasons) make any effort seem worthwhile. This feeling expresses what I have enjoyed about cataloging Central Asian materials, as problems in their cataloging have often provided me opportunities for improvisation, as well as giving me an attitude of taking nothing for granted while working with these materials.

I have been cataloging materials in Indian languages (Sanskrit, Hindi, Gujarati, Bengali); Tibetan; Mongolian, including Buriat and Kalmyk (in

Michael Walter is Assistant Professor, Department of Central Eurasian Studies (formerly Department of Uralic and Altaic Studies), Indiana University, and former South and Central Asian Cataloger, Indiana University Libraries, Bloomington, IN 47405 (e-mail: walterm@ucs.indiana.edu).

[Haworth co-indexing entry note]: "Central Asian Cataloging: Problems and Prospects." Walter, Michael. Co-published simultaneously in *Cataloging & Classification Quarterly* (The Haworth Press, Inc.) Vol. 17, No. 1/2, 1993, pp. 149-157; and: *Languages of the World: Cataloging Issues and Problems* (ed: Martin D. Joachim) The Haworth Press, Inc., 1993, pp. 149-157. Multiple copies of this article/chapter may be purchased from The Haworth Document Delivery Center [1-800-3-HAWORTH; 9:00 a.m. - 5:00 p.m. (EST)].

Mongolian and Cyrillic scripts); Turkic languages (e.g., Altai, Azerbaijani, Bashkir, Chuvash, Kazakh, Kirghiz, Tatar, Turkish, Turkmen, Uyghur, Uzbek, Yakut); Tajik; and the Tungus languages, especially Manchu, as well as Arabic and Russian, when needed, in the Indiana University Libraries for a number of years now.

There are several universals which provide many of the challenges faced on nearly a daily basis in this work. Reference works are often either scarce or unobtainable if they ever existed at all. In Tibetan, for example, only the best-known figures in that culture are found in secondary works, not to mention primary sources. Biographies in Tibetan will thus continue to be invaluable resources but are really not well represented in PL480 Tibetan collections such as Indiana University's (a catalog of which I am preparing for publication at the present time). Because many Tibetan monks and yogis who composed works wrote under a variety of names, due to numerous initiations into different traditions of practice, the value of a reference source centering on just one figure of interest at the moment is magnified. Among primary sources, our court of first resort is Ketsun Sangpo's *Biographical Dictionary of Tibet and Tibetan Buddhism*. If one knows to which tradition authors belonged and the authors are well-known, the chances are favorable that they can be found in this source. If they are not found here, a second stop could be the collected biographies of that tradition. Very few secondary works in Tibetan scholarship are useful here.

Closely related to the general problem of lack of bibliographical sources is the game of pinning the author to the work. If a work is by an author with a commonly occurring initiatic name, correctly identifying that author may be difficult. Traditional Tibetan sources are interested in describing a person's place in a spiritual lineage of practices; associating a writer with what he/she wrote, in terms of a total oeuvre, is virtually unknown. Printed catalogs of text collections then become a vital source. Particularly recommended here are E. Gene Smith's *University of Washington Tibetan Catalogue, Part I*, and the now nine-volume *Tibetische Handschriften und Blockdrucke*, begun by Manfred Taube and continued by others, part of the huge Verzeichnis der orientalischen Handschriften in Deutschland series.

In both Inner and Outer Mongolian materials, the situation is different but not better. With virtually no vernacular reference works on Mongolian literary and scholarly writers, many names are established only with the surname and first initial, as they appear on Mongolian title pages. We do get some useful references and birth/death dates from the few Russian-language bibliographies and critical works on Buriat and Khalkha authors, but even such a simple thing as the full form of the name in the vernacular will usually elude us.

The cataloger's luck improves when he or she works with Central Asian Turkic languages. Especially recently, with the central authority of the Soviet Union absent, more and more vernacular sources are being published and reaching the West (which two points are not really the same thing; publishing in these languages never ceased; their distribution was, however, hampered by the Soviets). To an extent not seen elsewhere in the old Soviet Union (e.g., Siberia) or outside of it (e.g., Mongolia), the Turkic and Tajik peoples have been actively presenting their literary histories, both for internal and external consumption. Several problem areas remain, however; North American libraries need more sources on the bibliography of Turkmen and Siberian Turkic languages, for example. (Please note the appended list of resources which I have found particularly useful in tracing literary works and their authors in some of the Central Asian languages in which I catalog.)

Problems also arise in shelflisting in some Central Asian Turkic languages. The Library of Congress classification system uses a single-cutter number for many of these languages, obviously based on an initially small amount of material in LC and the impression that publishing activity in these republics and ASSRs would be limited. Unfortunately, that is not the case now with Kazakh, Kirghiz, and Tatar languages (LC recently moved Uzbek to a two-cutter environment), shelflisted using Table XVI of LC's *Language and Literature Tables*. Practically, this means a very small range to fit in the works of all authors of fiction, poetry, etc. For example, the numerous works of the Kirghiz author Chingis Aitmatov were taking up a large range of available cutters in *A* (from about A26 through A49) in the Indiana University Libraries until recently; now all works fall within PL65.K59A29. While we now have more room for individual author cutters, a translation may extend the complete number out many digits (e.g., PL65.K59A29687913) to preserve shelflist consistency and to avoid taking up a wide range of available space for other authors whose names begin with *A*.

A related problem in the cataloging of Turkic and Mongolian, especially materials from the Mongolian People's Republic, is the application of uniform titles to literary works. In the wake of over seventy years of Sovietization, the works of many writers were rendered into Russian to enhance their accessibility throughout that vast country. A coherent shelflist and ready access to various versions of the same work are especially important in a research library, and knowing the title of a work in the vernacular is vital to achieve this goal. Formerly, the greatest source for

Soviet literary biobibliography was the more or less official bibliographies published for the accepted writers within each republic (several of which are found in the attached list of sources). However, they usually give the titles only in Russian, as well as the authors' names in their Russified forms, so are useless in establishing vernacular forms of names.

An aspect of uniform title application not considered in *AACR2* and LC's interpretations is the relationship of titles in different scripts but in the same language. An example is Uzbek, the modern reflex of the Arabic-script Turkic language called Chaghatai. There is currently no provision for applying uniform titles to works composed centuries before, now being edited and transcribed into Cyrillic-script Uzbek. Such uniform titles are necessary and would be helpful to students of many other Turkic languages also originally written in Arabic script (e.g., Tatar, Kazakh, Kirghiz, Azerbaijani, Turkmen) whose works are being offered anew. Transliterations of titles in different scripts can be widely divergent. An example is a work, composed by a seventeenth-century poet, which was published in Cyrillic-script Uzbek as *Sabotul ozhizin*. Its title in Uzbek in Arabic script, also published recently, is romanized as *Thabāt al-'ājizīn*. Even a specialist, who knows well these and other correspondences, should not have to look under both forms to find all the available editions of this work.

Subject analysis has been, for the most part, the least of the problems facing cataloging of works from Central Asia. An exception, however, is Tibetan material. Whereas the majority of monographs received from Central Asia in the Indiana University Libraries is fiction, literary criticism, or materials in modern social sciences, in Tibetan we meet with a vast amount of Buddhist literature: sacred works (translations from Indic sources), commentaries on them, philosophical discourses, local ritual materials, works on Tantric yogic practice, etc. When I began working with this material, I frequently created subject headings as there was little I could find in *Library of Congress Subject Headings (LCSH)* that I felt was appropriate. This situation has improved somewhat over the years, but I feel that there is yet much to be done to improve the specificity of, and remove ethnocentric notions from, headings therein.

An example of inconsistency is the subject heading **TĀRĀ (GOD-DESS)** rather than **TĀRĀ (BUDDHIST DEITY)**, which would bring this heading in line with other usages in the 16th edition of *LCSH* such as **MAÑJUSRĪ (BUDDHIST DEITY)**. One example of lack of specificity is that LC has not established a subject heading **SĀDHANA** (or something to that effect), even though the vast amount of Tantric literature in Tibetan and Sanskrit is concerned with aspects of this spiritual process. Consistency is sometimes needed as well; **MAHĀMUDRĀ (TANTRIC RITE)** seems a strange subject heading because it is an entire meditational tradition, analogous to **RDZOGS CHEN,** which is also not dealt with precisely in the 16th; it leaves the impression that all writings, practitioners, etc., of this tradition have been only Bon-po or Rñiñ-ma-pa adherents.

The greatest challenge that I see on the horizon, with the breakup of the Soviet Union, is the potential switchover of nearly all literatures of the Turkic, Buriat Mongolian, and other republics and ASSRs to scripts of their choice. The Indiana University Libraries have already received materials in such languages as Kazakh, Uzbek, and Azerbaijani, which are partially or completely in Arabic script. That the situation is fluid and may remain so for quite some time is indicated by the fact that, despite having received such materials, predominant Azeri opinion supposedly favors a romanized alphabet, in keeping with the proximity of Azerbaijan to Turkey. The appropriate offices at the Library of Congress are working to anticipate and deal with these changes, but a difficult interim period is certainly ahead for us. As a sort of postscript–or prescript?–to this topic, I should add that we have also received materials from Central Asia which are so old that they contain letters not found in any of the available tables in *ALA-LC Romanization Tables: Transliteration Schemes for Non-Roman Scripts.*

The situations for Mongolian and Manchu are different but also present a few problems. In 1984 LC published a romanization table for Mongolian, but it lacks equivalents for several letters in use in Inner Mongolia (China). The Library of Congress also decided some time ago, on the basis of its apparently small Manchu collection, not to proceed with a romanization table for this language. We were thus forced to improvise a table when we cataloged a large set of microfilms consisting of dictionaries, grammars, and other works in that language. Several other Manchu works cataloged at Indiana have been handled in the same way. We have followed, more or less strictly, the romanizations used in Jerry Norman's *A Concise Manchu-English Lexicon,* which is not lexicographically extensive but whose romanization values are well thought out.

Online utilities such as OCLC provide access to works in particular languages through language codes in the fixed fields of bibliographic records. Such access is an efficient way to locate holdings for materials in languages such as we have been discussing, especially since many North American libraries would have none or very few of these materials. It is thus a desideratum that LC's Network Development and MARC Standards Office expand its code list to include such languages as Yakut, Manchu, Buriat and Kalmyk Mongolian, and Tungus languages now beginning to be written in Siberia.

APPENDIX

SOME SOURCES FOR LITERARY WORKS AND AUTHORS IN CENTRAL ASIAN LANGUAGES

This list is not intended to be exhaustive or critical. It contains what I feel are some of the best sources available in the Indiana University Libraries. Some of the criteria that I have used in making these choices are the inclusion of names and titles in the vernacular and provision of accompanying biographical data which can help in cases of doubt about an author's identity.

ALTAI

Chañgkyr ăyldys. Tuulu Altaĭ: Altaĭdyñg bichikter chygarar izdatel'stvozynyñg, Tuulu Altaĭdagy Bŏlŭgi, 1984.
Dyldys. Tuulu Altaĭ: Altaĭdyñg bichikter chygarar izdatel'stvozynyñg, Tuulu Altaĭdagy Bŏlŭgi, 1984.
Katash, S. S. and Z. I. Tabakova. *Altaĭ literatura.* Tuulu Altaĭ: Altaĭdyng bichikter chygarar izdatel'stvozynyñg, Tuulu Altaĭdagy Bŏlŭgi, 1987.

AZERBAIJANI

Akhundov, N. *Azărbaĭjan sovet ădăbiiiaty kharijdă.* Baky: Ĭazychy, 1987.
Azărbaĭjan şovet ădăbjiiaty tarikhi. 2 vols. Baky: Azărbaĭjan SSR Elmlăr Akademiiasy năshriiiaty, 1967.
Azărbaĭjan sovet iazychylary. Baky: Azărbaĭjan dŏvlăt năshriiiaty, 1958.

BASHKIR

Istoriĭa bashkirskoĭ sovetskoĭ literatury. Moskva: Nauka, 1977.
Kŏmesh arba, kŏmesh at. Kazan: Tatarstan kitap nashriiaty, 1989. This work is in Tatar.

BURIAT MONGOLIAN

Buriaad shŭlĕgeĭ baglaa, 1963-1983. Ulaan-Ŭde: Buriaadaĭ nomoĭ khĕblĕl, 1983.
Tŭrĕlkhi literatura. Ulan-Ŭde: Buriaadaĭ nomoĭ khĕblĕl, 1988.

CHUVASH

Antologiia chuvashskoĭ sovremennoĭ prozy. Cheboksary: Chuvashskoe knizhnoe izdatel'stvo, 1986.
Chavash literaturi. Shupashkar: Chavash ASSR gosudarstvo izdatel'stvi, 1957.
ĬUr'ev, M., and Zoĭa Romanova. *Pisateli sovetskoĭ chuvashii.* Cheboksary: Chuvashskoe knizhnoe izdatel'stvo, 1988.

KARAKALPAK

Istoriia karakalpakskoĭ sovetskoĭ literatury. Tashkent: Izdatel'stvo "Fan" Uzbekskoĭ SSR, 1981.
Nurmukhamedov, M. K. *Karakalpakskaia sovetskaia proza.* Tashkent: Izdatel'stvo "Fan" Uzbekskoĭ SSR, 1968.
Watan ădebiiăty. Nŏkis: "Qaraqalpaqstan," 1989.

KAZAKH

Istoriia kazakhskoĭ literatury. 3 vols. Alma-Ata: Izdatel'stvo Nauka Kazakhskoĭ SSR, 1968-1971.
Pisateli Kazakhstana. Alma-Ata: Zhazushy, 1982.
Qazaq ădebietĭnĭñg tarikhy. 6 vols. Almaty: Qazaq SSR Ghylym Adademiiasy, 1961-1964.
Qazaq sovet ènt̄siklopediiasy. Almaty: Qazaq SSR Ghylym Akademiiasy, 1972.

KHALKHA MONGOLIAN
(Language of the Mongolian People's Republic)

Gerasimovich, L. K. *Literatura Mongol'skoĭ Narodnoĭ Respubliki, 1921-1964 godov.* Leningrad: Izdatel'stvo Leningradskogo universiteta, 1965.
Poėziia narodnoĭ Mongolii. 2 vols. Moskva: Khudozhestvennaia literatura, 1985.

KIRGHIZ

Kyrgyz sovet adabiiatynyn tarikhi. 2 vols. Frunze: Ilim, 1987-
Kyrgyz sovet ènt̄siklopediiasy. Frunze: Kyrgyz SSR Ilimder Akademiiasy, 1976.
Pisateli sovetskogo kirgizstana. Frunze: Adabiiat, 1989.

TATAR

Fătkhi, A. S. *Tatar ădiplăre hăm galimnăreneŋ kul''īazmalary.* Kazan: Kazan universitety năshriĭaty, 1986.

Gosman, Kh. *Egermenche ellarda Tatar poėziĭase.* Kazan: Kazan universitety năshriĭaty, 1964.

Tatar ădăbiĭaty tarikhi. 6 vols. Kazan: Tatarstan kitap năshriĭaty, 1984-1989.

TURKMEN

Ocherk istorii turkmenskoĭ sovetskoĭ literatury. Moskva: Nauka, 1980.

Türkmen sovet ėntsiklopediĭasy. Ashgabat: Türkmenistan SSR Ylymder Akademiĭasy, 1974.

TUVIN

Dorzhu, Ch. M., and M. D. Dorzhu. *Tyva uruglar ehogaaly.* Kyzyl: Tyvanyŋ nom ündürere cheri, 1987.

Kalzan, A. K. *Tyva literatura.* Kyzyl: Tyvanyŋ nom ündürer cheri, 1987.

Kiunzegesh, ĬU. Sh. *Tyva chogaal.* Kyzyl: Tyvanyŋ nom ündürer cheri, 1987.

UYGHUR
(Covers only literature produced by Uyghurs in Kazakhstan)

Uĭghur sovet ădăbiĭati. Almuta: Mektep, 1987.

Uĭghur sovet ădăbiĭatiniŋ tarikhi. Almuta: Qazaqstan SSR "Nauka" năshriĭati, 1986.

UZBEK

Abdullaev, V. A. *Ŭzbek adabiëti tarikhi.* 5 vols. Toshkent: Ŭqituvchi, 1980-1985?

Akademiĭa nauk Uzbekskoĭ SSR. Tashkent: Izdatel'stvo "Fan" Uzbekskoĭ SSR, 1983.

Istoriĭa uzbekskoĭ literatury. 2 vols. Tashkent: Izdatel'stvo "Fan" Uzbekskoĭ SSR, 1987-1989.

Pisateli sovetskogo uzbekistana. Tashkent: Gosudarstvennoe izdatel'stvo khudozhestvennoĭ literatury UzSSR, 1959.

Ŭzbek sovet ėntsiklopediĭasi. Toshkent: Ŭzbekiston Fanlar Akademiĭasi, 1971.

YAKUT

Novye gorizonty i͡akutskoĭ literatury. I͡Akutsk: I͡Akutskoe knizhnoe izdatel'stvo, 1976.
Ocherk istorii͡a i͡akutskoĭ sovetskoĭ literatury. Moskva: Izdatel'stvo "Nauka," 1970.

Languages of India:
Cataloging Issues

Usha Bhasker

SUMMARY. Issues confronting the cataloger of materials from India include problems relating to numerous languages with diverse scripts, confusion with variant name entries and how the name authority file handles this problem, some subjects pertaining to India and the people of India, and how the use of obsolete terms such as East Indies is an ongoing reference-service problem. Appendices list some of the most common problematic names and propose changes in some subject headings.

INTRODUCTION

The scope of this article will be limited to the languages of India rather than the languages of South Asia of which India is a part. South Asia is the geographic entity sometimes referred to as the Indian Sub-Continent and encompasses the following countries: India, Sri Lanka, Nepal, Bhutan, Bangladesh, Pakistan, and Afghanistan. Two major Indian language groups will be discussed here: (1) the Indo-Aryan, consisting of Assamese, Bengali, Gujarati, Hindi, Kashmiri, Marathi, Oriya, Panjabi, Rajasthani, Sanskrit, and Sindhi; and (2) the Dravidian, which includes Kannada, Malayalam, Tamil, and Telugu.[1]

This diversity of languages is visually reflected in the equal variety of

Usha Bhasker is Head, South Asia Section, in the Oriental Division, New York Public Library.

[Haworth co-indexing entry note]: "Languages of India: Cataloging Issues." Bhasker, Usha. Co-published simultaneously in *Cataloging & Classification Quarterly* (The Haworth Press, Inc.) Vol. 17, No. 1/2, 1993, pp. 159-168; and: *Languages of the World: Cataloging Issues and Problems* (ed: Martin D. Joachim) The Haworth Press, Inc., 1993, pp. 159-168. Multiple copies of this article/chapter may be purchased from The Haworth Document Delivery Center [1-800-3-HAWORTH; 9:00 a.m. - 5:00 p.m. (EST)].

scripts in which they are written although similarities exist among some languages. The dominant script in the North of India is the Devanagari, or Nagari for short. Hindi, Marathi, Rajasthani, and Sanskrit are written in this script. Various modified Nagari scripts are employed for Assamese, Bengali, Gujarati, and Oriya. Panjabi is written in the Gurmukhi script. Sindhi, being a combination of Hindi-Urdu, sometimes uses Nagari and sometimes Arabic script. Kashmiri is written in the Perso-Arabic script. Among the Dravidian group in the South of India, Tamil and Malayalam have similar-looking scripts and vocabularies. Likewise Kannada and Telugu can be paired off for script and vocabulary.

STAFF EXPERTISE

Assembling a staff which can handle the cataloging of the large number of items being published in these languages is a complicated problem.[2] Knowledge of two or more Indian languages is the standard requirement for recruiting catalogers. It is highly unlikely that people can be found who individually know a large number of the languages of this area and who are also trained catalogers. The solution then is to hire full or part-time people who have the language abilities needed and then to train them in descriptive and subject cataloging. In academic libraries, students are recruited part-time to catalog in the languages they are studying. Both the training and the quality control of production are problematic because supervisors and revisers do not know all of the languages involved. Also it is not uncommon to have Sanskrit texts on a wide range of subjects being published in other scripts–for instance, a book on Mundakopanishad written in Malayalam script. The Sanskrit cataloger may not know this script and will need to depend heavily on the transliteration tables. Likewise the Tamil sacred text *Tiruppavai* written in Telugu script will be difficult to catalog unless the cataloger has expertise in both languages.

TRANSLITERATION

"The Indian system of writing is in principle strictly alphabetical, and phonetic; but in its application, it is syllabic. The vowels, when they come after a consonant, are just contracted into small signs which are tagged on to the preceding consonants; and two or more consonants coming together without a vowel in between are combined into complicated ligatures, in most of the alphabets now current, in which the component consonants frequently occur as fragments of the original letters. These ligatures and other modifications bring up the total number of separate types to print the Nagari to some 450 or more separate type items, although the simple vowels and consonants in isolation number only 48."[3]

The structure of the Dravidian alphabet is slightly different from the Nagari. Tamil has thirteen vowels and eighteen consonants; Malayalam, eighteen vowels and thirty-six consonants; Telugu, eighteen vowels and thirty-five consonants; and Kannada, eighteen vowels and thirty-four consonants.

The Library of Congress' transliteration tables list twenty-one scripts of India including Arabic, Tibetan, and Urdu.[4] When one considers the difficulties involved in transcribing the phonetically-rich languages into the English alphabet, the tables are by and large precise, thorough, and accurate. Consonant-conjuncts are phonetically rendered with no ambiguity (e.g., *jna*, *kta*, *ddha*). Heavy use of diacritics are necessary due to the abundance of retroflex sounds and long vowel sounds (e.g., *Śrī Veṅkaṭēśamāhātmyamu* (Telugu), *Aṣṭādhyāyī* (Sanskrit), *Vāḷkkaiyiṉ viḷaiyāṭṭu* (Tamil). Diacritics slow down the inputting of catalog records into RLIN and OCLC. In the case of derived records, transliterated portions (especially fields 1XX, 245, 260, and 7XX) must be carefully reviewed for accuracy.

In the ALA/LC transliteration tables, minor inaccuracies occur in the diacritics of certain languages. In Marathi the diacritic for the nasal sound which occurs with a consonant is not correct. The tilde is used instead of anusvara (*Sãskṛti* instead of *Saṃskṛti*). The use of double diacritics is also incorrect (e.g., *Belagāva* should be *Beḷagāṃva*; *mīmãsā* should be *mīmāṃsā*). The letter *e* in the word *Êsosiesana* (which means *association* in English) should be the letter *a*.

Some Sanskritized letters in Tamil do not appear in the tables. Other limitations in this language have to do with the language itself in that all phonetics are not covered by the consonants of the alphabet.[5] Each of the following, *ka/ga* sound, *ta/da* sound, *tha/dha* sound, and the *pa/ba* sound, is represented by a single letter which creates public access problems. The westernized form *Ganesan* is rendered in Tamil transliteration as *Kanesan*, *Bhagavad-gita* as *Pakavat-kita*.

Certain sounds such as the *sh* sound and the *ch* sound, common to all the languages, are transliterated as *.s* and *c* respectively, and the vowel *i* is suppressed in some cases, creating public-service problems when searching author elements such as Krishna (Krsna), Premchand (Premacanda), or uniform title *Rig Veda* (*Ṛg Veda*). Other examples are *Chandrashekhara Shastri* (*Candrasekharasastri*); *Krishna Raya Chaudhari* (*Krsnaraya*

Caudari); *Dolagovinda Shastri* (*Dolagobinda Sastri*); *Mudumba Krish-namacharyulu* (*Mudumba Krsnamacaryulu*).

Another problem for catalogers is the choice between the westernized forms of names or the systematically transliterated versions: Dorai Ranga-swamy/Turai Arankacami (Tamil); Tagore/Thakur (Bengali); Sivagna-nam, M. P./Civananam, Ma. Po. (Tamil); Swaminatha Iyer, U. W./Camina-tayyar, U. Ve. (Tamil); Subrahmanya, S. P./Cuppiramaniyam, Sa. Po. (Tamil); Kailash Prakash/Kailasa Prakasa (Hindi); Gopinath Mahanty/Go-pinatha Mahanti (Oriya); Swinder Singh Uppal/Sawindara Singha Uppala (Panjabi); Marupooru Kothandarama Reddi/Marupuru Kodandaramareddi (Telugu); Nalini Devi Barua/Nalinidewi Baruwa (Assamese); S. K. Rama-chandra Rao/Es. Ke. Ramacandra Rav (Kannada); Thakazhi Sivasankara Pil-lai/Takali Sivasankarapilla (Malayalam); Jogesh Das/Yogesa Dasa (Assamese); M. F. Thomas/Em. Eph. Tomas (Malayalam); N. Tapaswee Kumar/Nam. Tapasvikumar (Kannada); Petlikar/Petalikara(Gujarati); and Deshpande/Desapande (Marathi).

NAME AUTHORITIES

The most time-consuming of all cataloging steps is the establishing of personal names. For well-known headings such as Sankaracarya, Ramanu-ja, and Kalidasa, it is a simple matter of following the established form in the name authority file (NAF). Sometimes even single element names pose the problem of polyonymy. Kautilya and Chanakya and Bhatrihari and Bhattaswami are examples of early names, and a twentieth century name Yuvacarya Mahaprajna is established in the NAF as **Nathamal**, $c **Muni**.

In classical Sanskrit, more than one author using the same name, such as Harsa, Jayadeva, and Jagannatha, are the bane of catalogers who have to do extensive research to come up with the correct entry, be it Jayadeva, 12th cent., or Jayadeva, 13th cent; Jagannatha, of Kavalavamsa, 18th cent., or Jagannatha Dasa, 1487-1547. The entry for Harsavardhana, King of Thanesar and Kanauj, fl. 606-647, contains a total of fourteen cross references.

Modern names in all the Indian languages pose a bewildering array of practices. In addition to one or more writers using the same name, there is often confusion with dates, with the same author using variant spellings in English language publications, and with two elements of a name some-times being combined, sometimes split.

Each language has its own unique system of prioritizing the important elements of a person's name. Honorifics are mentioned in *AACR2*

(22.25A1), but not all languages and practices are covered. In the name P. Govindarajulu Garu, the element *Garu* in Telugu is sometimes an enclictic and sometimes a suffix. In the name Selvi Vijayarathnam (Tamil) the element *Selvi* could be a prefix meaning *Miss*, or it could be a given name together with the given name Vijayarathnam.

Much has been written about this on-going concern with Indian name headings,[6] and the consensus is that uniformity of rules is impossible and that catalogers must of necessity maintain elaborate tables of names for each language, with separate charts for early, medieval, and modern names. Appendix A gives a few examples of Indian names with their variants but is by no means an exhaustive list.

SUBJECT HEADINGS

For Indians as a group originating from the subcontinent, the LC subject heading is **EAST INDIANS**. However, the latest U.S. census uses the term **ASIAN INDIANS** to describe this group. We need to come to grips with this major universe of subjects dealing with Indians from India and the Indians of North America, South America, West Indies, etc. Finding a logical solution will greatly aid reference librarians in assisting readers of these topics, in addition to satisfying both the ethnic groups that are generally unhappy with the status quo.

LC's scope note under **EAST INDIANS** states: "Here are entered works on the inhabitants of India in general. Works on the aboriginal peoples of the Western Hemisphere, including Eskimos, are entered under Indians." The entry for **EAST INDIES** has the following scope note: "Here are entered works dealing generally with South and Southeast Asia, including the Malay Archipelago, Indochina, and India. Works on specific regions within that area are entered under the headings for the specific regions." If we were to proceed on the logical assumption that East Indians originate from the East Indies (as for instance West Indians from the West Indies), then the headings **EAST INDIANS** and **EAST INDIES** do not match. A strong case can be made to limit the geographic scope note on **EAST INDIES** to denote Indonesia and other parts of Southeast Asia since Indonesia was formerly known as the Netherlands Indies.

A stronger case can be made to do away with the term **EAST INDIANS** and other subjects using the term **EAST INDIAN**, such as **COR-PORATIONS, EAST INDIAN;** **JEWS, EAST INDIAN;** and **EAST INDIAN AMERICANS IN BUSINESS**. The absurdity of the semantics involved can be seen in the heading **EAST INDIANS IN THE WEST INDIES** to describe Asian Indians who settled in the West Indies.

While subject headings can be reviewed and changed to achieve greater access on the bibliographic utilities for the terms **INDIAN** versus **AMERICAN INDIAN**, the same cannot be said about searching titles of monographs and serials which begin with the word **Indian**! Murari Lal Nagar, in his recent bibliography of Indian periodicals published in India, lists approximately 624 periodical titles in English beginning with the word **Indian**.[7] Unfortunately this is one headache with no solution for reference and acquisitions librarians.

The culinary arts of India are accessed by the subjects **COOKERY, HINDU** (giving an inappropriate religious connotation) and **COOKERY, INDIC**. Most popularly used terms, however, are **INDIAN CUISINE, INDIAN RESTAURANTS**, etc. A search in RLIN for the heading **COOKERY, INDIAN#** yielded a result of 110 clusters, but only sixteen of the titles were books on the cookery of India, and the rest dealt with the cookery of Native Americans. Clearly these sixteen are catalogers' errors and thus highlight the need to change these headings. Perhaps **COOKERY–INDIA** or **COOKERY, ASIAN INDIAN** would be more to the point.

Another heading that is not altogether precise in meaning is **INDIC LITERATURE** along with related terms **INDIC DRAMA, INDIC FICTION**, and **INDIC POETRY**. INDIC is being used in these headings to mean "of or pertaining to all of India," which is acceptable in general subject headings such as **FOLK DANCING, INDIC** or **MYTHOLOGY, INDIC**. The confusion arises, however, with the term **INDIC** being used with literature per se since the term **INDIC LANGUAGES** refers to the group of languages known as Indo-Aryan languages or Indo-European branch and thus linguistically forms an entity separate from the Dravidian group of languages. It makes sense, therefore, to list the literatures of India also under the same two broad groups: **INDO-ARYAN LITERATURE** and **DRAVIDIAN LITERATURE**, with narrower term (NT) references to the specific literatures of Hindi, Assamese, Tamil, etc.

There is no easy solution, however, for the other general terms, **INDIC DRAMA, INDIC FICTION**, and **INDIC POETRY**. Perhaps the adjective **ASIAN INDIAN** could be used for these subjects, with a scope note indicating inclusion of **DRAVIDIAN DRAMA, DRAVIDIAN FICTION, DRAVIDIAN POETRY**, etc. These last three would also have to be set up as narrower terms.

With literary works written in English by Indian authors, one encounters a whole array of subjects that need rethinking.[8] **INDIC LITERATURE (ENGLISH)** and the narrower terms **CHILDREN'S LITERATURE, INDIC (ENGLISH), INDIC DRAMA (ENGLISH), INDIC FICTION (ENGLISH), INDIC POETRY (ENGLISH)**, and **INDIC**

PROSE LITERATURE (ENGLISH) can all be better expressed by the term INDO-ENGLISH, which is widely used in India and by Indian writers worldwide. Thus an awkward heading such as SPEECHES, ADDRESSES, ETC., INDIC (ENGLISH) can be written as SPEECHES, ADDRESSES, ETC., INDO-ENGLISH. Appendix B is a list of existing subject headings with proposed changes.

PROPOSED NEW HEADINGS

There are some cultural and ethnic concepts unique to India for which no really appropriate topical heading has yet been established:

1. Harikatha

This popular rendering (in Telugu, Kannada, and Tamil) of Vaishnavaite mythology in a combination of devotional songs and prose narration is a tradition that is historic and contemporary.

2. Kuchipudi

In the dance genre, this could be described as dance-drama with many performers enacting and dancing to some mythological theme. It differs from **Bharata natyam**, which is usually pure dance with a solo performance.

3. Janaka
Melakarta

These two terms should be established as separate subjects and entered as NT's under the now existing heading **RAGAS**.

4. Sanskrit poetics
> **NT Alamkara**
> **Dhvani (Poetics)**
> **Kavya (Epic poetry)**
> **Rasas**

There is a vast body of literature dealing with Sanskrit poetics which is now accessed by the general term **POETICS**. The NT's **RASAS** and **DHVANI (POETICS)** already exist in *LCSH*.

5. Javali
Krti
Tillana
Varna

These should be established as new headings and listed as narrower terms for the existing heading **MUSIC, KARNATIC,** which is too broad.

CONCLUSION

The main thrust of this article has been to highlight some of the complex issues associated with multiscript languages and the near impossible task of uniformity in establishing personal names. These problems and difficulties point to the ongoing need for staff expertise in the languages and literatures of India. Some of the confusion in subject headings would be greatly alleviated if LC would adopt the proposed additions and changes discussed below in Appendix B.

NOTES

1. All languages mentioned here plus English and Urdu are the seventeen official languages of the Indian Constitution. Most of these languages correspond to the state languages of the various states of the Indian Union, Hindi being the language of the states of Bihar, Haryana, Himachal Pradesh, Madhya Pradesh, Rajasthan, and Uttar Pradesh.

2. Figures issued for titles cataloged by the Library of Congress Office in New Delhi for FY 1991 are: Assamese, 31; Bengali, 694; English, 3849; Gujarati, 170; Hindi, 1106, Kannada, 349; Kashmiri, 1; Malayalam, 282; Marathi, 262; Oriya, 98; Panjabi, 262; Rajasthani, 33; Sanskrit, 512; Sindhi, 23; Tamil, 538; and Telugu, 550.

3. Suniti Kumar Chatterji, *Languages and Literatures of Modern India* (Calcutta: Prakash Bhavan, 1963), 67.

4. *ALA-LC Romanization Tables: Transliteration Schemes for Non-Roman Scripts* (Washington, D.C.: Cataloging Distribution Service, Library of Congress, 1991).

5. For a comparison of the Tamil alphabet with the other Dravidian scripts, see: V. Kannaiyan, *Scripts in and around India* (Madras: Available with the Superintendent, Govt. Museum, 1960).

6. See, for example: Prithvi N. Kaula, "India's Contribution to Cataloging and Classification," in Mohammed M. Aman, ed., *Cataloging and Classification of Non-Western Material: Concerns, Issues, and Practices* (Phoenix, AZ: Oryx Press, 1980), 235-252.

7. Murari Lal Nagar, *TULIP: The Universal List of Indian Periodicals*, 10 vols. (Columbia, Mo.: International Library Center, 1986-1991).

8. India ranks third after the United States and the United Kingdom in the world's output of books and periodicals in English.

APPENDIX A

A SAMPLING OF INDIAN NAMES WITH THEIR VARIANTS

This list of twenty names illustrates two levels of problems:

a. Westernization: In this category we find variants such as **Banerji, Banerjee,** and **Banerjea.** Transliterated variants for this Bengali name would be **Bandopadhyay, Vandyopadhyaya,** etc.

b. Transliteration: There are variants in the way authors spell their names in a given language–e.g., in Tamil, **Cuppiramaniyan, Cupramanyam.** Westernized variants of this name would be **Subrahmanyam, Subramanian,** etc.

1. **Ayyar:** Aiyar, Aiyer, Ayer, Ayar, Iyer.
2. **Banerji:** Bandopadhyay, Bandopadhyaya, Bandyopadhyay, Bandyopadhyaya, Banerjea, Banerjee, Vandopadhyay, Vandopadhyaya, Vandyopadhyay, Vandyopadhyaya.
3. **Dikshit:** Dikshita, Diksit, Diksita, Dixit.
4. **Ghosh:** Ghosa, Ghose, Ghosha.
5. **Goswami:** Goswamy, Gosbami, Gosvami.
6. **Haq:** Haka, Haque, Hoque, Huq.
7. **Husain:** Hosena, Hussain, Hussein.
8. **Jain:** Jaina.
9. **Krishnamurthy:** Krishna Murthy, Krishnamoorthy, Krishnamurti, Krsnamurti, Krishnamurthi.
10. **Majumdar:** Majumadara, Majumder, Mazumdar, Mojumder.
11. **Mukherjee:** Mookerjee, Mookerji, Mookherjee, Mukarji, Mukerjee, Mukerji, Mukherji, Mukhopadhyay, Mukhopadhyaya.
12. **Murthy:** Moorthi, Moorthy, Moorti, Murti, Murty.
13. **Naik:** Nayak, Nayaka.
14. **Parikh:** Pareek, Parekh, Parikha.
15. **Patwardhan:** Paravardhana, Patvardhan.
16. **Raychaudhuri:** Ray Chaudhuri, Ray Choudhury, Rayachaudhuri, Rayacaudhuri, Roychoudhury, Roychowdhury, Roychoudhary, Roy Choudhury.
17. **Sastri:** Sastry, Shastri, Shastry.
18. **Singh:** Simha, Singha, Sinh, Sinha.
19. **Subrahmanyam:** Cuppiramaniyam, Cuppiramaniyan, Cupramanyam, Cupramanyan, Subrahmaniam, Subrahmanian, Subramaniam, Subramanian, Subramoniam.
20. **Tiwari:** Tevary, Tewari, Tewary, Tivari.

APPENDIX B

SUMMARY OF PROPOSED CHANGES
IN SUBJECT HEADINGS

This preliminary checklist is a summary of recommendations. It is beyond the scope of this article to specify all related terms, narrower terms, and cross references.

EXISTING HEADING	PROPOSED CHANGE
East Indians	Asian Indians
Indians of North America	Native Americans (North America)
Indians of South America	Native Americans (South America)
Cookery, Indian	Cookery, Native American
Cookery, Hindu	Cookery, Asian Indian
Indic literature (English)	Indo-English literature
	NT Indo-English drama
	Indo-English fiction
	Indo-English poetry

EXISTING CROSS REFERENCES	PROPOSED NEW HEADING(S)
Indian literature (American Indian)	Native American literature
Indian literature (East Indian)	Indo-Aryan literature
	Dravidian literature

These two headings are proposed instead of the existing **INDIC LIT-ERATURE**. Literatures of individual languages and dialects should appear as they do now as **NT**'s except that the literatures of the Dravidian group such as **Konkani** or **Moplah** will appear as **NT**'s under **DRAVIDIAN LITERATURE**.

Is Cooperative Cataloging Realistic? Thoughts of a Southeast Asian Bibliographer

Fe Susan Go

SUMMARY. Budget constraints, the geometric rise in available volumes, and the clientele's demand for instant access to all sources constitute the main issues confronting technical services in the final decade of the twentieth century. Cooperative cataloging not only nationally but also internationally offers the means to address these realities successfully. Such ventures can be achieved if directors of libraries mandate working together and provide the means to bring these massive efforts to fruition. True cooperation requires difficult team work and the ability to accommodate genuine personal and institutional differences–tasks not always congenial to the personality of most librarians. A small-scale precedent has been established by CORMOSEA, the Southeast Asian studies librarians of ten major universities. The challenge lies in pursuing the precedent to the directors' level and beyond.

To survive we must adapt; to remain as we are we must change.

–David Penniman
President
Council on Library Resources

Fe Susan Go is Southeast Asian Bibliographer and Head of the Southeast Asian Division, University of Michigan Libraries.

[Haworth co-indexing entry note]: "Is Cooperative Cataloging Realistic? Thoughts of a Southeast Asian Bibliographer." Go, Susan Fe. Co-published simultaneously in *Cataloging & Classification Quarterly* (The Haworth Press, Inc.) Vol. 17, No. 1/2, 1993, pp. 169-179; and: *Languages of the World: Cataloging Issues and Problems* (ed: Martin D. Joachim) The Haworth Press, Inc., 1993, pp. 169-179. Multiple copies of this article/chapter may be purchased from The Haworth Document Delivery Center [1-800-3-HAWORTH; 9:00 a.m. - 5:00 p.m. (EST)].

169

One of the most frequently discussed activities of libraries during the past thirty years has been that of cooperation in the acquisition and processing of library materials. A healthy, democratic spirit combined with a complicated structure of librarianship has resulted in a mixed bag of success and failure.

–Mark Grover
Latin American Bibliographer
Brigham Young University

THE DIRECTORS' HOLDING COMPANY FOR COOPERATION

Too frequently the entry and exit point for discussions of cataloging cooperation insures that they will be restricted to just that–discussions, shop talk which fails to lead to decisive action. Those in technical services often proceed as if the matter of cataloging resides solely in the domain of technical professionals without pressure from above. Such territorialism will not survive the ever more evident financial and informational pressures in the last decade of the twentieth century.

Financial strictures appear omnipresent. Mr. Grover correctly notes that "interest in cooperation has been higher during periods of financial difficulties, and commitment to national programs has waned during periods of budgetary growth and stability."[1] There was no need for administrators to be involved in cooperative agreements since there was no risk involved in this agreement nor pressure for it to succeed. All of us recognize the present as a time of financial troubles, but financial troubles come coupled with rapid and expensive computational transformation. Both signal human turbulence. Part of the perturbation originates with library directors, themselves under pressure from above, stressing consolidation, economizing, and efficiency. With current economic growth, nationally and globally, registering no meaningful improvement, the financial pressures along the chain of command within universities will only increase in the foreseeable future.

North American academic libraries play an integral role in the much larger but highly decentralized world of the contemporary university. The oft-repeated anecdote of Clark Kerr, former president of the University of California, asserts that universities are united only by their power plants. Today, Mr. Kerr's 1960s appear to us as a time more given to cooperation and less given to hyper-specialization than our own era. A spirit of cooperation at the level of overall leadership of the university community fails to register as a reality. Directors of libraries function in such an environment, and they see no decisive models of cooperation to emulate. The further down one goes in the organizational arrangements, the same lack of cooperation prevails. Until such time as the various components feel the absolute necessity to cooperate (in our world necessity equals a severe dwindling of funds), serious cooperation will not be forthcoming. In short, for cooperation among universities to be strengthened in a manner that helps though it hurts, sustained leadership and the investment of time and thought will have to come from the level of the director. Such an undertaking will necessitate a de facto holding company with library directors serving as members of the board. Such an embryonic organization already exists in RLG and the Committee on Institutional Cooperation (CIC), organizations composed primarily of research libraries with boards of directors. Only with such an arrangement will authority and funds be matched to confront the dilemma and augment the requirement of working together.

The above overarching frame of reference will increasingly serve as the environment in which all library decision-making, including that within technical services, will occur. This essay offers the example of a small organization of Southeast Asian librarians as protagonist in trying to grapple with these complicated dilemmas of library decision-making at the close of the twentieth century.

CORMOSEA AND COLLECTION DEVELOPMENT AS PRECEDENT

The Committee on Research Materials on Southeast Asia (CORMOSEA) constitutes the appropriate organization to serve as the cooperative link for our field of specialization to the so-called holding company. The ten research libraries (Arizona State, Cornell, Northern Illinois, Ohio, Yale, California-Berkeley, Hawaii, Michigan, Washington, and Wisconsin) which are represented in CORMOSEA presently act as the avenue for the exchange of ideas among Southeast Asian bibliographers. CORMOSEA's members also cooperate in seeking grants and in representation before the Association of Asian Studies.

The success of Southeast Asian cooperation to date has largely been in collection development, and success here has established a tacit precedent for working together on the more difficult task of technical services agreements. In all the library literature three factors are presented as reasons for the success of collection development: financial support, administrative support for cooperative agreement, and the will to cooperate that comes from all sides acting for mutual benefit. An unspoken generator of support for collection development is that university administrators, faculty, staff, and the public's centrally agreed purpose of a library is fulfilled with the development of a worthy collection. Put those books–more and more of them–on the shelf for the world to use. The success can also be attributed to the fact that collection development is quantifiable and thus can be proclaimed a numerical success–a fact much prized in our century.

Like other bibliographers responsible for different foreign areas, each Southeast Asian librarian since World War II has constructed his or her own basic collection with little real consultation with other members of the association. One's colleagues assume about themselves and each other that a strong basic collection has been constructed gradually in each of the member libraries. In this domain, the prize of mutual support has come so easily because no serious competition has been necessary.

Driven by the influx of serial publications from Indonesia, CORMO-SEA has decided to use electronic mail to inform its members of new subscriptions to serial titles. This arrangement, though informal, assures the bibliographers that at least one library within our group has subscribed to a publication that otherwise would not be available in North America.

The Southeast Asian Microfilming (SEAM) project is another cooperative collection development venture of the members of CORMOSEA. The day-to-day administration of SEAM resides with the Center for Research Libraries (CRL), but CORMOSEA makes the decisions regarding purchases and the recommendation of titles for microfilming. SEAM's independence in the selection and implementation makes its microfilming collection unique.

Yet actual cooperative collection development by CORMOSEA has been initiated in recent years. An agreement among CORMOSEA members was negotiated whereby pertinent Indonesian materials at the local and sub-provincial level would be collected by the group. We knew that these materials existed but no one, including the appropriate authorities in Indonesia, had been collecting them. None of the CORMOSEA members wished to assume collection responsibility by itself; therefore, we developed a plan among our members to assign an Indonesian province to each of the CORMOSEA member libraries. Each member library collects all local and sub-provincial level publications; a proviso for cataloging these materials was discussed but was not heartily approved by the members. Those libraries which have collected these materials do catalog them and enter records into the national databases. This policy of burden-sharing by CORMOSEA members successfully underscores the group's original mandate. Though not without difficulty, an activist plan of genuine cooperation came to be.

TECHNICAL COOPERATION AND STAFFING

CORMOSEA's commitment to informal cooperation and newly bargained formal cooperation has promoted vital professional relationships essential as prerequisites for working together in the difficult domain of cataloging. Cooperative cataloging traditionally has never been entertained as a worthy topic for discussion by CORMOSEA due to three factors. First, most of the old generation of post World War II bibliographers exhibited no interest in technical issues due to such matters being labeled outside their responsibility. These bibliographers conceptualized cataloging as part and parcel of technical services and thus an arena in which they had no voice. Their role consisted of recommending prioritization of titles to be cataloged. Second, during the early years of Southeast Asian studies, research libraries concerned themselves with recruiting specialized bibliographers and developing collections rather than technical concerns. Third, technical services departments make rules, and CORMO-SEA has demonstrated no taste for rule-making. This tradition of non-involvement, coupled with the contentiousness of technical decision-making in general, makes mutual agreement exceedingly difficult. To establish cooperation, nonetheless, becomes necessary given the manner in which internationalization of information technologies shapes the world and thus the library.

When we are forced to change focus from collection development to technical services issues, the fundamental energies and points of contention of librarianship manifest themselves. These nodal points meet where genuine finite agreement becomes more necessary and yet more problematic. The technical services tradition of rule-making affirms a belief that a sufficient number of rules can be created to fit each and every case. The addition of computers to technical library processes permits the reinforcement of these rule making beliefs. Yet, more rule making begets more exceptions. Furthermore, such propensities allow for very little of the variety of actual human decision-making in a library context. Such reasoning does not promote cooperation beyond a limited sphere. The fundamental deterrent for cooperation in cataloging thus becomes the incompatibility between ever increasing rules and the fact that all the rules simply will not accommodate all the exceptions. Approaching gridlock can be envisioned, and actualization of cooperation does not materialize. Nonetheless, the current environment dictates the political correctness of cooperation.

The word flies about, but to bring it to fruition requires perseverance, hard work, and, most significant, flexibility. In truth, these attributes necessitate the will and the incentive. At present, but only at present, no professional nor institutional risks exist for the failure to cooperate nor notable rewards for success.

Different libraries show a tendency not to accept, or at least to be suspicious of, the cataloging of other libraries. The working assumption would appear to be that people in my institution or under my control can do it better. Furthermore, within and between libraries contentions have arisen among the professionals regarding minimal level cataloging (MLC). The decision to streamline catalog records or even to adopt MLC in an environment which has by tradition fostered full USMARC standards faces strong opposition. Considerable numbers of professional librarians do not like minimal level cataloging records since they believe such formulations denigrate the profession as well as impair patron access. Such matters are presented as technical differences when in truth they are as much differences in personality reflected in the work place. In light of unprecedented acquisitions increases, picky debates regarding minimal versus full records will be resolved by the realities of the massive amount of materials at hand. Indeed, some libraries, including that of the University of Michigan, are comfortable with MLC, and its use has helped to eliminate backlogs–and the future holds no place for backlogs.

When cataloging became a necessity for Southeast Asian bibliographers due to accumulating backlogs, research libraries found few librarians available to become professional area studies catalogers. When libraries did recruit professional catalogers, they were taught the concept of correct and proper cataloging without concern for the need to reduce backlogs. When the present generation of bibliographers was recruited, they were told that their duties would include cataloging along with several other non-bibliographic tasks. These new bibliographers grappled with the new phenomena of recruiting and the training of paraprofessionals to do cataloging because few professionals had the required language expertise. Most libraries have resorted to using either paraprofessionals or students to undertake preliminary cataloging. The implicit question becomes: How well can you train paraprofessionals to do original cataloging? Some libraries are suspicious of records from other libraries that employ paraprofessionals to do their cataloging. Despite backlogs mounting to the point of being unable to be stored, the attitude seems to be: As long as what we can process is properly cataloged, who cares about backlogs? This mind-set appears set in concrete and hinders the promotion of cooperative cataloging. The use of paraprofessional staff has become the norm at some institutions that are trying to eliminate their backlogs. While other institutions still hesitate to use paraprofessionals to do original cataloging, the experience of the University of Michigan Library has made it evident that paraprofessionals are as competent to do original cataloging as professionals.

Perhaps not surprising given the above, actual technical cooperation has been stimulated from outside rather than from inside our institutions. A Luce Foundation grant was awarded to the University of Michigan's Southeast Asian Division to coordinate a project to catalog Vietnamese language materials. The project, known as the Vietnam Union Catalog (VUC), *forced* us to cooperate. Via this endeavor, uncataloged Vietnamese materials have been removed from backlogs and cataloged, and catalog records have been entered into the RLIN database.

The cooperating libraries have tolerated the VUC as long as no impingement on their local workflow occurred. There was little infringement on local operations, and thus the project has enjoyed success. Furthermore, given the absence of cooperative endeavors by other foreign area library organizations in the United States, this CORMOSEA venture could easily serve as a model. Yet, now in its final year, the maintenance and enhancement of the VUC is in jeopardy because CORMOSEA itself, as well as the leadership of the participating libraries, has not highlighted the VUC as a worthy example of cooperation. Once again, we see a demonstration of the absence of a sustaining commitment to a potential example of tangible cooperation. The potential benefits from established working relationships in cooperative cataloging become dissipated. Serious technical joint ventures await their historical moment.

CORMOSEA, TRANSLITERATION, WORD DIVISION, AND THE POWERS THAT BE

Librarians who never face the dilemmas of turning Burmese, Thai/Lao, or Khmer into the twenty-odd symbols of the Latin alphabet sometimes fail to appreciate the depth of the debates which the practice entails. None of the cultures or countries concerned has established a norm of romanization despite the supposed importance of western languages. Somehow, someway foreigners are held responsible for romanization. For example, Thais know real written Thai, and those Thais who need to know English study that language. As far as these Thais are concerned, the environment necessitates translation, not transliteration. The actual site of the problem is the Western world and its machines which can give back only stereotypical presentations, at least prior to our own age of advanced language software. Librarians accustomed only to the omnipresent English language or the familiar formations of French, German, or Spanish would do well to watch an educated Burmese or Thai struggle to read his or her own language in transliterated form. If we recall western resistance to the change of Chinese romanization in the 1950s from Wade-Giles to pinyin, we gain some understanding of the bafflement that ensues.

CORMOSEA's organizational face to the language issue in technical matters is pointed towards Washington D.C. and the Library of Congress (LC) rather than towards its member institutions. LC plays an important role in assembling or disassembling cooperation. The nexus point where CORMOSEA and LC convene for agreement and disagreement concerns transliteration where no definitive answers will ever be forthcoming. Thus, the topic to date offers no comfort to catalogers. Salvation may possibly come via the wonders of computer technology which will render any script into any format for any mode of print, and the need for transliteration will recede into history.

CORMOSEA's recommendations to the Library of Congress for a standardized transliteration scheme for romanizing Thai and Burmese met with agreement. The transliteration dilemma became more difficult with the advent of print technology. Words have to fit what the machine can accomplish. With the acceptance of CORMOSEA's transliteration plan, one would anticipate that the matter would be settled, but the reality is that the disagreement simply appears at the next lower level, namely, word division.

Agreement in this domain becomes significant for linguistic reasons and for machine readability. Inevitably, perspectives differ. Thai paraprofessionals at the University of Michigan Library, supported by American Thai linguists, suggested to the LC Thai cataloging staff during the annual meeting of the Association of Asian Studies in 1992 that to follow religiously the word divisions of the Royal Thai dictionary makes no sense to native catalogers. Furthermore, it is dysfunctional to establish arbitrary word divisions when words cannot be found in the Royal Thai dictionary. All searchers, including native speakers, encounter difficulties in accessing RLIN due to differences in word division, for the RLIN computers allow for no such idiosyncracies. Vested with no authority to alter the transliteration scheme, the LC cataloging staff adamantly proclaims the correctness of its word divisions. Moreover, the cataloging staff at LC would not even listen to CORMOSEA's reservations.

Furthermore, since libraries pay for each search they initiate with the RLIN system, it behooves the searcher to know the proper access procedures in order to make each and every search successful. Adherence to book knowledge rather than a comprehensive language competency will hinder not only access to RLIN and OCLC databases but also present to the clientele a simplified scheme of language transliteration and word division which does not conform to the realities.

While temporarily stymied, for by tradition LC's blessing must be forthcoming for change to be sanctioned, CORMOSEA will seek to continue to inform LC staff about the complexities of written language as actually practiced. We hope that our actions will serve as a proactive example for academic librarians affiliated with area studies programs in their dealings with LC.

The American Library Association (ALA) represents another influential organization whose bureaucratic propensities have delayed warranted changes. Small area studies organizations have no traditional venue to broach their issues with ALA. Part of our problem is that CORMOSEA as a body never deals directly with ALA. For CORMOSEA to recommend and adopt changes within the profession, it must ally itself with the Committee on Cataloging Asian and African materials of ALCTS, an already established committee of ALA. CORMOSEA's concern has to be precisely in step with that committee's agenda and, if not, wait in the queue for the appropriate time–a time which may never come.

The salient point seems obvious: both organizations, which supposedly work to promote ever more rapid and efficient access to research materials, defeat their own stated purposes by failing to agree to a workable standardization for transliteration and other technical matters. Individual research libraries do not help the cause by consistently waiting for the Library of Congress's seal of approval. The lack of influence of Southeast Asian area studies within the American Library Association hampers our ability to have an impact with recommendations to the Library of Congress.

COOPERATION BEYOND NATIONAL BOUNDARIES NOT WITHOUT COSTS

With each passing decade, scholars and publishers from Southeast Asia itself have come to play an ever more significant role in Southeast Asian studies. Indeed, academics and publishers from Asia, North America, and Western Europe have come to form a co-equal troika regarding their contribution to the field. Nonetheless, despite this contribution from Southeast Asia, CORMOSEA has yet to explore the possibilities of cooperating with librarians from the region. Neither has CORMOSEA made contacts with European libraries with Southeast Asian interests.

Cooperation with Southeast Asian countries can be achieved through the Congress of Southeast Asian Librarians (CONSAL). This organization of the Association of Southeast Asian Nations (ASEAN) can serve as the institutional focus for this cooperation. CORMOSEA should make every effort to ensure that these librarians feel themselves to be complete and equal members. This proposed cooperation can be achieved by mutually working together on projects that are beneficial to both sides. For example, the creation of pan-ASEAN bibliographies would be a logical first phase of cooperation.

Informal cooperative agreements have been established between COR-MOSEA and the Australian National Library (ANL). ANL seeks to stay abreast of the development of Southeast Asian studies in North America. This interest naturally includes technical library developments. ANL has been an integral part of the VUC consortium. Due to the trade embargo between Vietnam and the U.S., the Australians offered to take responsibility for making sure that Vietnamese records in Vietnam would be loaded into the Australian database. The dream of merging all Vietnamese language materials in one database was the unstated goal of VUC's agenda. With ANL responsible for loading Hanoi records and the collections of North American libraries already in RLIN, the merging of North American, Vietnamese, and Australian collections in one database is ready to take place. The VUC is the first project to be achieved through cooperation with a country halfway around the globe. Similar projects can be initiated and realized with CONSAL and European libraries.

Europeans have been slow to establish formal organizations which are involved with Southeast Asia.[2] Only as recently as 1992 have European scholars concerned with Southeast Asia organized themselves into a body called European Association for Southeast Asian Studies (EASEAS). European libraries have yet to undertake even this initial step. CORMOSEA hopes that European academics will lead the way for their library staffs. If such comes to pass, then the Europeans can come to effect a role concomitant with their traditional importance in the region and join with their colleagues in North America and Asia to form a genuine international network of research centers and scholarship.

In order to give actual international cooperation some tangibility, North American or European bibliographers with the support of their administrators could use part of their budgets to support the hiring of catalogers from each of the Southeast Asian national libraries. They would be responsible for cataloging titles procured by foreign institutions. If the availability of properly trained North American catalogers fails to meet demand, perhaps positions in the U.S. can be filled by professional indigenous librarians.

Other opportunities may exist for summer exchange programs. I myself have already participated in the short term training of a Vietnamese librarian in the methods of modern librarianship. Though future realities will vary, numerous opportunities for international cooperation should be forthcoming and encouraged. Given the importance of truly global telecommunications, libraries must actively seek serious international cooperative consortia, or libraries will lose out to more efficient and up-to-date methods of accessing information.

Yet international cooperation may place domestic staffs at risk. Internationalization can come to mean what it has meant in industry, namely, personnel redundancies under the watchwords of restructuring and rationalization. So-called divisional empires within the library world will decline once cooperation is achieved. Some CORMOSEA members have already experienced a loss of personnel due to more provincial financial constraints. If cooperation on a global scale truly comes, it is feared that more personnel will be cut, which will result in each bibliographer becoming more burdened by problems of global coordination as well as the practical matter of being his or her own staff. Thus, as in the world beyond the library, our age of global change offers little opportunity for free riders.

NOTES

1. Mark L. Grover, "Cooperative Cataloging of Latin-American Books: The Unfulfilled Promise," *Library Resources and Technical Services* 35:4 (October 1991): 406.

2. For a discussion of this topic, see: Paula Goossens, "Cooperation among Libraries in Europe: Current Realities, Future Prospects," in *In the Spirit of 1992: Access to Western European Libraries and Literature*, The Reference Librarian no. 35 (New York: The Haworth Press, Inc., 1992): 49-56.

The Cataloging
of Chinese Legal Materials

William Brokaw McCloy

SUMMARY. The cataloging of Chinese legal materials is described as a challenging field of specialization based on a complex variety of factors. The author proposes the three areas of **simplification, stabilization,** and **internationalization** as goals in effecting improvements in cataloging rules and practice.

The cataloging of Chinese legal materials is an interesting and challenging endeavor. Though to most of us the language of these publications is of course the most obvious hurdle to overcome, even an experienced Chinese cataloging specialist who is not a legal expert may easily be baffled by the subject matter and terminology of these materials. And to a legal expert, changes through the years in cataloging rules and practices, both for legal materials and for Chinese jurisdictional headings, can make interpreting historical catalog entries and creating correct, current cataloging at times appear to rival unraveling the Gordian knot in complexity.

The emphasis of this discussion will for the most part not be on practical solutions to the specific problems. Rather, a number of the challenges and complexities of cataloging Chinese legal materials will be laid out with the general purpose of promoting a better understanding of this area. Additionally, suggestions will be presented regarding some general direc-

Bill McCloy is Assistant Librarian for Comparative Law at the University of Washington Marian Gould Gallagher Law Library and is responsible for all aspects of a major collection of Chinese, Japanese, and Korean legal materials.

[Haworth co-indexing entry note]: "The Cataloging of Chinese Legal Materials." McCloy, William Brokaw. Co-published simultaneously in *Cataloging & Classification Quarterly* (The Haworth Press, Inc.) Vol. 17, No. 1/2, 1993, pp. 181-195; and: *Languages of the World: Cataloging Issues and Problems* (ed: Martin D. Joachim) The Haworth Press, Inc., 1993, pp. 181-195. Multiple copies of this article/ chapter may be purchased from The Haworth Document Delivery Center [1-800-3-HAWORTH; 9:00 a.m. - 5:00 p.m. (EST)].

181

tions in which the cataloging world might move in order to improve upon this situation. I shall not address the area of classification in this paper as the problems are equally complex. Further, the only classification schedules available as of this writing are a pre-publication draft issued by the Library of Congress in September 1991 (initially on floppy disk) and a looseleaf draft issued by the American Association of Law Libraries in 1992.[1] Both contain numerous errors and omissions (not always the same ones).

Few of the challenges of cataloging Chinese legal materials[2] are unique. Combine all the perverse and pesky problems found in cataloging other types of materials such as books, serials, and looseleaf publications with those found in cataloging **legal** publications and those found in cataloging **Chinese** publications, and you have quite a potent brew! However, as it is chiefly the special mix of problems that is unique, catalogers of other types of materials will undoubtedly find much that is familiar in this discussion. The cataloging challenges these materials present are magnified by the fact that many who catalog them are not legal specialists and that our Anglo-American legal systems are fundamentally different from the legal systems of the various Chinese jurisdictions.[3]

My particular perspective in this article is the cataloging of these materials within the RLIN database, thus from a North American perspective. Most of the problems I highlight and the suggestions I raise are undoubtedly applicable in other databases as well, but some are unique to RLIN. Additionally, it of course goes without saying that the approach to cataloging Chinese law books in France, Australia, or in China, for that matter, is likely to be very different from our own. Though my perspective on the issues is a very focused one, it is hoped that this viewpoint will provide some insights for those coming at this subject from a different angle and perhaps stimulate dialogue regarding the pros and cons of other systems as well.

CHINESE LEGAL SYSTEMS

The number and type of legal publications and the terminology used in them are closely tied to the nature of a country's legal system. Aside from the fact that the majority of the materials from these jurisdictions are written in Chinese, there is very little commonality to them otherwise. In imperial times–at least for those periods when China was unified–there was basically a single system of law and government, and in some areas of law one can still point to the influence of traditional Chinese law. Today, however, not only are the governmental and economic systems of Taiwan,

Hong Kong, and the People's Republic of China strikingly different, but also their legal systems stem from equally diverse models.

Though change is afoot and distinctions are blurring, in economic and political terms Taiwan and Hong Kong still stand on one side as democratic, free enterprise economies and the People's Republic of China on the other side as a socialist state. Yet their legal systems owe their origins to three separate and distinct paradigms. These differ not only in the content and organization of the laws themselves but also in the philosophies behind them and in the nature and function of legal institutions. The legal system of the People's Republic of China is based on a Russian model, typifying **socialist law**. In fact, many of the Soviet legal codes were translated into Chinese (some as early as the 1920s) and after the founding of the People's Republic of China in 1949 were adopted with very little change. On the other hand, the legal system of the Republic of China on Taiwan is a direct continuation of that in place on the Chinese mainland between 1912 and 1949. It is based on **civil law**, the European system which owes its origin to old Roman codes of law, and was heavily influenced in the early twentieth century by French, Swiss, and German models.[4]

Hong Kong alone follows the Anglo-American **common law** system, albeit with distinctly Chinese overtones. In this tradition, in contrast to civil and socialist law, legal precedent (previous judicial rulings on similar cases) carries as much weight as statutory law. The present Hong Kong legal system is an integral part of the legal order of the British Commonwealth.

Another important and parallel influence in Chinese law has been that of Japan. Beginning in the late Qing[5] Dynasty and continuing into the early years of the Republic of China, many legal scholars studied in Japan and many Japanese laws were translated into Chinese. Additionally, as Taiwan was ruled as a colony of Japan from 1895-1945, Japanese law (and the laws of other foreign countries filtered through the Japanese legal system) had a particularly profound effect in Taiwan.[6]

LEGAL TERMINOLOGY

As delineated above, the influence of foreign legal systems has been powerful in all three of these modern Chinese jurisdictions. Thus, with the influence of so many different foreign countries and strikingly different legal systems, it is not surprising that legal terminology is quite different among these modern jurisdictions as well as being different from that used in Imperial China. Though Chinese-Chinese and Chinese-English legal dictionaries have proliferated in recent years, it is important, especially for subject analysis, to have at least a basic understanding of the differences between the three major legal systems of the world (as the same term may mean something different in common law and civil law) as well as of the structure of the government in question. Most of us raised in North America, to the extent we are familiar with the law at all, are most familiar with common law terminology and institutions. Furthermore, though our descriptive and subject cataloging norms recognize and attempt to provide for most civil/common law discrepancies, there are areas where concepts do not translate well or where subject headings appropriate to the legal system in question have not been provided. An important example is the area called, in civil and socialist legal systems, economic law. Lacking such a subject heading (this is *not* **LAW AND ECONOMICS** nor is it **LAW–ECONOMIC ASPECTS**), the Library of Congress consistently assigns the subject heading **INDUSTRIAL LAWS AND LEGISLATION** to such works. However, the fact that this category includes banking laws, agricultural laws, foreign investment laws–in short, anything related to the economy–makes the lack of a more appropriate heading keenly felt. At any rate, an awareness of these problems is essential when cataloging Chinese legal materials.[7]

WHO'S DOING THE CATALOGING?

Who in the U.S. and Canada is cataloging Chinese legal materials? Although I am not familiar with any statistical studies, based on my experience with the RLIN database and personal contacts within the American Association of Law Libraries (AALL)[8] and the Committee on East Asian Libraries (CEAL),[9] I would say that most of the cataloging is being done by a small number of libraries, most of these being users of the RLIN system. Of course, the Library of Congress with its Far Eastern Law Division is by far the major producer, followed by a few academic law libraries with specialized collections such as Harvard, Columbia, and the University of Washington as well as a few large East Asian libraries such as the Hoover Institution, the University of Michigan, and the University of Toronto.

With the probable exception of the Library of Congress, this cataloging is of such comparably low volume that those who do it are generally not legal cataloging specialists. For the most part, either they catalog legal materials as only a very small part of a varied cataloging assignment, or they may fall into the Jack-of-all-trades model of a small specialized collection, doing collection development, acquisitions and perhaps reference in addition to cataloging, often in more than one language. In some cases, in fact, both patterns may be true. A cataloger may catalog the occasional law book interspersed with books on many other topics and perform general reference or collection development in the field of East Asian studies as well. Cataloging is frequently done by generalist catalogers (in both law and non-law libraries) who may be unfamiliar with either the Chinese language or with legal materials or both. Librarians may in some instances rely on clericals, students, or visiting legal scholars to catalog (particularly vernacular materials), with training and supervision provided by a cataloger or other librarian. Cataloging quality thus depends on a wide variety of factors.

Depending on the size and focus of the library and its cataloging staff, a cataloger may work with a single East Asian language or with several. It must be pointed out that in spite of superficial similarities, Chinese, Japanese, and Korean, the languages most commonly treated together in East Asian libraries and in East Asian legal collections, are very different languages. Cataloging East Asian materials correctly, at least according to North American standards, requires a high level of language and, in the case of Chinese, dialect sophistication, and it is the rare individual who can work effectively in more than one East Asian language.

LEGAL PUBLICATIONS: THE IMPORTANCE OF FORM AND PURPOSE OF ITEM

In cataloging legal publications more than perhaps with any other type of publication, it is important for a cataloger to understand first of all what the item-in-hand *is* (laws, regulations, cases, a code, a gazette, a treatise, a general collection, a topical collection, etc.) and what it *does*. Does it publish or update the laws? For what period? On what topic? Does it digest the case law? On what subject? For which court(s)? For which jurisdiction? Does it list the regulations? For what agency? For which law or laws? Further, quite frequently it is important to determine what the item supplements, cumulates, or supersedes. All the above is as much true for Chinese legal publications as for those of other governments. How each of these questions is answered has strong implications for choice of entry, serial vs. monographic treatment, and for subject analysis.[10]

THE COMPLEXITY OF ESSENTIAL CATALOGING TOOLS

As mentioned above, the problems of cataloging Chinese legal materials are a compendium of the problems of cataloging in general, those of cataloging legal materials and those of cataloging Chinese language materials. This in itself should connote a higher level of complexity. As for the issues of cataloging in general, the knowledge one needs to catalog well in this country is itself incredibly complex. A cataloger in a smaller collection, dealing with all types of publications, will need to refer to and, to a certain extent, master such lengthy and detailed reference tools and guidelines as *AACR2, Library of Congress Rule Interpretations, Library of Congress Subject Headings*, the Library of Congress's *Subject Cataloging Manual: Subject Headings, Cataloging of Looseleaf Publications, Cataloging Service Bulletin*, Library of Congress classification schedules (and their various supplements and cumulations, both official and commercially published), and the *CONSER Editing Guide*.[11]

Added to these are several necessary tools for legal and Chinese language cataloging, such as *Cataloging Legal Literature* mentioned above, romanization tables and guidelines, and the *AACR2 Workbook for East Asian Publications*.[12] Further, many catalogers will need to master manuals such as those on MARC tagging, terminal operation, *RLG Chinese Character Aggregation Guidelines*, and how to input Chinese characters into the database (my department uses at least eleven different RLIN manuals). Quite a lot of ground to cover to become a competent cataloger of anything! Now consider having to do all this part-time while doing collection development, reference, and other assorted duties for a specialized collection as well as find some time to train a part-time assistant to master all the above tools so that you will have time to do other things!

THE COMPLEXITY OF LEGAL CATALOGING RULES

Adding to the challenge a cataloger of Chinese legal materials faces is the difficulty of properly cataloging legal publications under *AACR2*. For example, in making the decision as to whether or not a publication should be entered under a corporate body (such as the name of a court or an administrative agency), under the name of a jurisdiction, under a personal name, or under title, a cataloger must weigh all the "normal" rules as to the number of names on the chief source of information, their function with respect to the publication, and the special rules for entry under a corporate body. However, it may also be necessary to answer several questions as to the nature of the contents and of the issuing jurisdiction, such as the following: Are these laws, regulations, or a collection of both? A single law and its implementing regulations? If regulations, are all issued by a single agency, or does the work contain the regulations of various agencies? Or is it a mixture of national legislation and both national and provincial regulations? Is the issuing jurisdiction one where regulations are considered laws?[13] Further, to determine the proper classification and whether or not a uniform title is called for, one must ask certain other questions, such as: Is this a topical compilation or a general compilation of laws? Would it be considered a code? And, if so, is it an annotated code (text and commentary)?

Note that in the Chinese context these questions may not be so quickly answered as in English. Linguistically, the Chinese language does not always distinguish clearly between editor and compiler. Further, a chief editor or compiler may be named on the chief source with, say, three other names not designated as chief. Is only one to be recorded? Traced? All four? Does this affect choice of entry? Additionally, the word for "regulation(s)"–*fagui (fa kuei)*–may also mean "laws *and* regulations," so it is necessary to examine contents carefully in order to determine which rules of entry apply as well as to weigh subject heading and classification information. Further, casebooks are often published with cases arranged in the order of the code they illustrate. Full or partial text of the laws may or may not be included. Are these codes? Digests? Casebooks? Law reports? Though sometimes clear-cut, often there are ambiguities.

THE COMPLEXITY OF CATALOG HEADINGS FOR CHINA

Determining and assigning the proper name and subject headings for the various Chinese jurisdictions can be complex and confusing, particularly for those not familiar with both modern Chinese political history and the history and philosophy of catalog entries used for these jurisdictions. The vast majority of Chinese legal materials are either entered under a jurisdictional heading, have a jurisdictional subject heading or subdivision, or both. Unfortunately, the choice of jurisdictional name is not always self-evident, and the two may not be the same because of the oddities of LC practice in cases where a distinction is made between the territory governed by a jurisdiction and the name of the jurisdiction itself. This is a subtlety seldom noted because in most cases, for the rest of the world, the headings used are exactly the same. Though the situation is highly complex, a few examples should suffice to illustrate the confusing nature of this area.

First of all, as changes were made through the years by the Library of Congress to the headings used for the People's Republic of China, the changes were not coordinated between the Subject Cataloging Division and the Descriptive Cataloging Division. For example, the Subject Cataloging Division dropped the use of the heading **CHINA (PEOPLE'S**

REPUBLIC OF CHINA, 1949-) in favor of **CHINA** in November 1973.[14] The Descriptive Cataloging Division continued using the former heading until the adoption of *AACR2* in 1981. For more than seven years the two divisions had different policies; the Descriptive Cataloging Division continued to use **China** to refer to the *Republic* **of China** (for both its mainland and its Taiwan periods) while in subject headings it referred to the *People's* **Republic of China.**[15]

The Descriptive Cataloging Division, in setting forth the headings to be used for China under *AACR2*, states: "For all governments that have controlled the mainland of China, use 'China' for all periods except 1931-1945."[16] The examples that follow illustrate the policy which is apparently still in force, giving seven different headings as valid for various governments active on the Chinese mainland and for the provincial government of Taiwan.[17] Then, though the Subject Cataloging Division restated and updated its 1973 policy in 1982, it gives subject equivalents for only three of these seven headings, those for the People's Republic of China, the Republic of China on Taiwan, and the Taiwan provincial government. Since in 1973 two of these three used subject entries *different* from the descriptive or jurisdictional entries (in 1982 only one is different), the cataloger is left to speculate as to what form of name to use for a collection of laws, for example, of the Chinese Soviet Republic (Jiangxi Soviet) or for the Japanese puppet government in Nanjing.

The Subject Cataloging Division's statement in 1982 further reiterates its 1972 policy as follows:

> The corporate heading **China (Republic : 1949-**) will be used by descriptive catalogers to designate the post-1948 Republic of China; the jurisdictional heading **Taiwan** will designate the province of Taiwan that is part of the Republic of China. *However, in subject cataloging practice, the jurisdictional heading* **TAIWAN** *will be used for both the post-1948 Republic of China and the island of Taiwan.*[18]

Consider the implications this policy has on headings for legal materials. A general collection of the laws of the Republic of China issued between 1912 and 1949 (the "mainland period" of the Republic of China or Guomindang government) will be entered under the heading **China** and will have the subject heading **LAW–CHINA**. After the move of the Republic of China government to Taiwan in 1949, however, the headings change. Though the government still calls itself the Republic of China, its laws have not changed, and it still claims jurisdiction over all of China; the extent of its jurisdiction is deemed to be limited to the Island of Taiwan

(Formosa). As **China (Republic : 1949-)** is defined as the jurisdictional heading used for governmental bodies and as main entry for collections of laws, etc., and **Taiwan** is defined as the name of the place or territory governed by the jurisdiction, the *same* code of laws mentioned above, reissued in 1951 after the move of the Republic of China government to the island of Taiwan, will be entered under **China (Republic : 1949-)** with the subject heading **LAW–TAIWAN**.

To complicate matters further, however, note that the use of **Taiwan** as a jurisdictional heading is also possible–with a different meaning! **Taiwan** is used in headings for the *provincial* government of Taiwan (as opposed to the *national* government of the Republic of China, both of which function as separate governmental units. It is also used as a main entry for laws of Taiwan during the Japanese colonial period.

These jurisdictional anomalies are particularly perplexing when applied to the Constitution of the Republic of China on Taiwan. Under LC's current practice, various editions of the Constitution entitled, for example, the *Constitution of China, Taiwan's New Constitution,* or the *Constitution of the Republic of China,* if issued in Taiwan after 1949, would all be entered under the main entry **China (Republic : 1949-)**, with the subject heading **TAIWAN–CONSTITUTION**. Although the scope note in *LCSH* provides for using the subdivision –CONSTITUTION under names of jurisdictions, with Taiwan, in fact, this practice is applied in a confusing manner. Because both **Taiwan** and **China (Republic : 1949-)** are used as jurisdictional headings, this subject treatment, in my way of thinking, makes it appear as though the constitution is for the *provincial* government of Taiwan (cf. the difference between the U.S. federal constitution and state constitutions). The subject heading **CHINA (REPUBLIC : 1949-)–CONSTITUTION** (not to mention the heading **LAW–CHINA (REPUBLIC : 1949-)** for collections of laws) would seem more consistent with logic, with realpolitik in Taiwan, and with other cataloging practices.

THE COMPLICATIONS OF CHANGES
IN HISTORICAL CATALOGING PRACTICE

All the above can be confusing, particularly to a new cataloger. Obviously, a current cataloger may in addition to newer cataloging consult older card catalogs, records cataloged online under earlier rules and practices as well as records input unchanged from old catalog cards. Even the same or equivalent materials may have been cataloged *very* differently, necessitating careful thought and the possibility of extensive recataloging to bring like materials together.

In addition to these confusions in applying jurisdictional headings to Chinese legal publications, there have been other major changes in the cataloging of legal publications which have also affected these materials. Though many of these are probably improvements, I shall cite one example here as evidence of the confusion factor that complex change brings about: the form subheading **Laws, statutes, etc.** and its approximate *AACR2* equivalent, the uniform title **Laws, etc.** Not only was the form heading changed to a uniform title and the wording of the (sub-) heading changed, the rules for when to use this heading were also significantly changed. To make matters worse (in terms of historical inconsistency, the change was actually for the better), in 1987, six years after *AACR2* was adopted, a long rule interpretation was adopted providing for qualifiers for **Laws, etc.** (From 1982-1986 the uniform title was qualified only in specific cases). Unfortunately, the title of one of the most useful compilations is still coded as a see reference on the old name authority record for **China (Republic : 1949-). Laws, etc.**[19] This, amazingly, seems to have kept LC from assigning the proper heading (under its own rule interpretation) to these works:

> **China (Republic : 1949-)**
> **Laws, etc. (Liu fa chᶜüan shu)**

This heading would bring together the various editions of these important codes.

PUBLICATION PATTERNS AND ROMANIZATION

Other complexities of cataloging Chinese legal materials shared by non-legal Chinese publications as well include differences of publication patterns among the three jurisdictions. Most notable is the different use of the word *ban* in Taiwan and the People's Republic of China. In China, this word is always used to denote edition; printing dates are separately noted in conjunction with the word *yinshua*. In Taiwan, on the other hand, where many publications are frequently issued in numerous printings, *ban* may mean either "edition" or "printing." It is necessary to rely on other clues, such as "revised," and on a careful examination of the work in order to make an educated guess as to whether a work is a new edition or simply a later printing. As a result of this ambiguity, many duplicate records have been entered into our cataloging databases.

Further, though changes in Chinese romanization practice through the years have been minimal, it is necessary to explain them to new catalogers who see (and try to copy) earlier cataloging. Moreover, in some online systems, such seemingly insignificant changes as the presence or absence of a diacritic can affect retrieval. For example, in the authority file of the WLN database, which is linked to bibliographic records, the presence or absence of the no-longer-used Chinese diacritics ^ or ⌣ can cause the same headings to end up in separate authority records, thus compromising the value of the linked authority file as a tool for search collocation and global heading change. RLIN displays a similar literality in its *also* command, used to narrow down a search result.

A far more serious challenge related to cataloging any Chinese materials also relates to romanization. First of all, the romanization system used for Chinese in this country is the old-fashioned Wade-Giles system, dating from the nineteenth century. Although this is the official system in Taiwan, it is not widely taught there. The system used in the People's Republic of China, which *is* widely taught, is a totally different one, called the Hanyu Pinyin system. An example of the difference is the word meaning "China": *Chung-kuo* (in Wade-Giles), *Zhongguo* or *Zhong guo* (in pinyin). Thus, even if a new untrained cataloger knows Chinese romanization, it is not likely to be the system needed for cataloging under present practice.[20] The United States and Canada are virtually alone in the world in their adherence to the Wade-Giles system for cataloging. Most other countries have adopted the pinyin system.

In addition, since Chinese is not written in an alphabetic script, romanization is based on pronunciation, and people tend to romanize the way they speak. With hundreds of significantly different dialects and regional accents in China, it often takes a long period of time for a native speaker to learn to romanize accurately enough to properly search a database or code a cataloging record unless that person happens to be an excellent speaker of Beijing dialect, the pronunciation upon which the standard is based. Learning to romanize properly assumes, of course, that he/she has someone to check and correct false attempts. Mis-romanizations in a database search retrieve the same result as misspellings: false hits or nothing. Without correction, guidance, and training, it is easy for a novice searcher or cataloger to assume that a title is not present in the database and to input a duplicate record. Furthermore, catalog users have the same problems retrieving our catalog records using romanized access points.

CATALOGING AS AN INTERNATIONAL ACTIVITY

The cataloging of Chinese legal materials in North America is essentially an international or cross-cultural activity. Not only are these publications of another language and culture cataloged according to an "Anglo-American" system, but also the vast majority of the personnel involved in cataloging them are native speakers of Chinese raised in a Chinese cultural environment, cataloging under "foreign" or "adopted country" rules. Even assuming native training in cataloging, there is very little carryover of norms. Romanization systems are different, as are cataloging rules, classification schemes, and subject headings. MARC formats differ in tags, in order of data fields, in subfield coding, and in the presence or absence and the location of romanized fields. One system used in Taiwan, for example, uses subfields for romanization rather than parallel or paired fields as we do. Even the character sets used for coding of Chinese characters are significantly different, and data input methods vary widely. The joint adoption of the *Anglo-American Cataloging Rules*, 2nd edition, and widespread international use of the Library of Congress subject headings have made the international exchange of cataloging tapes among English-speaking countries a useful activity. The same shared standards have made the carryover of cataloging experience from one country to another fairly easy and useful as well. Despite the international nature of Chinese legal cataloging, however, the same is not true in this area. This lack of international standardization contributes to the complexity of training new catalogers.

RECOMMENDATIONS FOR THE FUTURE

I have three overarching recommendations for improvement in the cataloging of Chinese legal materials: **simplification, internationalization,** and **stabilization. Stabilization of cataloging rules and practices,** the lack of which has caused so much of the confusion documented above, will, alas, be at least temporarily compromised if the other two recommendations are implemented. For even when change is for the better, it will in the short run imply discontinuity. Nevertheless, avoiding frequent and extensive changes would greatly simplify the training of catalogers.

Simplification, a concept already *de rigueur* in cataloging circles, should, quite simply, be a highly valued factor in all considerations of cataloging change. For legal materials, the complexities of choice of entry and the assignment of uniform titles come immediately to mind as prime candidates for simplification. The power and flexibility of computers to collocate access points in ways undreamt of in the days of the card catalog is, of course, the main reason simplified norms could work. Another is the exponential factor of increased expense in time and money and the reduced productivity that comes with each factor of added complexity of any task.

As for **internationalization** of cataloging, I speak broadly of the cataloging of Chinese language materials, not just legal materials. International harmonization of practice in Chinese language cataloging could bear the same fruits that the international collaboration on *AACR2* has done for English-speaking countries. It could provide for an easier exchange of cataloging records, use of those records with minimal change, and the more direct carryover of cataloging expertise from one country to another. This would likely require compromises on both sides of the Pacific. The first to fall on our side might well be our adherence to the outmoded Wade-Giles system of romanization, controversial as that issue has been.

More fundamentally, however, I would like to see a basic overhaul of how Chinese cataloging records are coded in computer records, something more akin to the Canadian handling of English and French records but taken to a further extreme.[21] Under current North American standards and practices, a Chinese cataloging record contains parallel (RLIN calls them paired) fields in romanization and in Chinese characters. On the RLIN database, a user of the multi-script workstation can select various types of displays, displaying all fields in the record or some combination of romanized, vernacular, and English-language fields. Obviously, this system is designed to reflect U.S.-based cataloging practices: English language subject headings and notes, a "standard" collation, etc. However, when the LCC (LC catalog card-like) or LONg display is selected and vernacular fields are displayed, the descriptive portion of the catalog record is *almost* completely intelligible to even an unsophisticated user of Chinese language materials. Why not go all the way to totally bilingual records?

Under present guidelines for multi-script cataloging, parallel fields must be word-for-word the same except for romanization replacing Chinese characters. If a cataloger quotes or constructs a note in English, no Chinese equivalent is allowed. If a cataloger quotes a Chinese note, only a virtually meaningless romanized version is allowed as a parallel. In fact, the Library of Congress does not use Chinese characters in notes at all. A quoted note is given in romanization only. Translation is not allowed.

Further, under current LC practice, a cataloger is not even supposed to code a parallel 100, 600 or 700 field for an author whose Chinese characters are known if for some reason that author has been established in a non-systematically-romanized form (e.g., **Chiang, Kai-shek** or **Confucius**). Moreover, under present LC rule interpretations, Chinese words like "Hong Kong" and "Taiwan" used as qualifiers for corporate headings or "[Peking]" used as a place of publication supplied by the cataloger must be in roman script even in vernacular fields. To say the least, in an LCC or LONg display–"public" displays intended for those who know Chinese–such

English renderings of Chinese words not only look strange but may also be confusing.

We have sacrificed the usability and intelligibility of the catalog record by insisting on exact one-to-one correspondence of every item in every field. Why not allow bilingual note fields rather than just "bi-script" ones? For example, common equivalencies could be established for notes like "Cover title: . . . ," "Frequency varies," etc. Words like et al. in the author statement (LC's choice over *AACR2's* allowable "equivalent in non-roman scripts") could be paralleled in vernacular fields by the Chinese equivalent *deng* (*teng*). Chinese terms could be used in the Chinese collation, as we occasionally see now in RLIN Chinese rare book cataloging; and form uniform titles like **Laws, etc.**, or **Treaties, etc.**, could be paralleled by equivalent fields in Chinese. One-to-one subject heading equivalencies could be set up similar to Canada's French edition of LC subject headings.[22] Together, such steps as these could lead to the creation of catalog records acceptable and intelligible on both sides of the Pacific, paving the way for increased sharing of records and a decrease in the need for costly original cataloging.

NOTES

1. *Library of Congress Classification: Class KL-KWX, Law of Asia and Eurasia, Africa, Pacific Area, and Antarctica: Cumulative Schedule*, AALL Publications Series no. 43 (Littleton, Colo.: F.B. Rothman, 1992-).

2. For the purposes of this paper, I define "Chinese legal materials" to refer to materials from Imperial China, the People's Republic of China, the Republic of China (in its Mainland period and on Taiwan), and Hong Kong. Though much, perhaps most, of what I say is valid for materials written in any language, I refer most particularly to those in Chinese.

3. I refer to the People's Republic of China, Hong Kong, and the Republic of China on Taiwan as jurisdictions rather than as countries or nations to focus on their differing legal systems and to sidestep the political issues of whether or not they should be considered separate countries.

4. Hungdah Chiu and Jyh-Pin Fa, "The Legal System of the Republic of China in Taiwan," in *Modern Legal Systems Cyclopedia* (Buffalo, N.Y.: Hein, 1984-): 2A.40.12.

5. Except when citing bibliographical sources, for the spelling of Chinese words I use the Hanyu Pinyin system of romanization (often abbreviated P-Y or pinyin). When necessary, the North American cataloging standard Wade-Giles spelling is given in parentheses.

6. Tay-sheng Wang, "Legal Reform in Taiwan Under Japanese Colonial Rule (1895-1945): The Reception of Western Law" (Ph.D. diss., University of Washington, 1992).

7. On problems of the translation of legal concepts and on the history of East Asian legal terminology, see, especially, articles by Chiu, Henderson, and Finkle-

stein in: Jerome Alan Cohen, ed., *Contemporary Chinese Law: Research Problems and Perspectives* (Cambridge, Mass.: Harvard University Press, 1970); and Dan F. Henderson, "Japanese Law in English: Reflections on Translation," *Journal of Japanese Studies* 6 (Winter 1980): 117-154.

8. Principal groups of the American Association of Law Libraries interested in Chinese legal materials include the Asian-American Law Librarians Caucus, the Asian Law Working Group, and the Foreign, Comparative, and International Law Special Interest Section.

9. CEAL is part of the Association for Asian Studies.

10. An excellent reference work in this field is: Peter Enyingi, Melody Busse Lembke, and Rhonda Lawrence Mittan, *Cataloging Legal Literature*, 2nd ed., AALL Publications Series no. 22 (Littleton, Colo.: F.B. Rothman, 1988). This publication not only provides clear guidelines for both descriptive and subject cataloging issues, but it also provides definitions of common types of legal publications and examples of their cataloging records (including older LC cataloging contrasted with *AACR2*-updated versions).

11. I very vividly remember a remark made some fifteen years ago by Elaine Woods, at that time coordinator of a serials conversion project at the Indiana University Libraries, in reference to *CONSER Editing Guide*, to the effect that "Anything that takes 300 pages to tell you how to do it is too hard!"

12. Subcommittee on Technical Processing, Association for Asian Studies, Thomas H. Lee, Beatrice Chang Ohta, ed., *AACR 2 Workbook for East Asian Publications* (Madison, WI: University of Wisconsin-Madison Libraries, 1983).

13. *Cataloging Legal Literature* gives some guidance in these areas.

14. *Cataloging Service*, bull. 110 (Summer 1974): 4.

15. Due to the policy of superimposition, the heading **China** (which under the pre-1967 ALA rules meant the **Republic of China**) continued to be used alongside the newly valid *AACR1* heading **China (Republic)**. The latter was used only for newly established headings.

16. *Cataloging Service Bulletin*, no. 18 (Fall 1982): 65.

17. Earlier under *AACR2*, LC had first announced a total of three headings (*Cataloging Service Bulletin*, no. 11 (Winter 1981): 86), then six headings (*Cataloging Service Bulletin*, no. 14 (Fall 1981): 42.

18. *Cataloging Service Bulletin*, no. 17 (Summer 1982): 38. Emphasis added.

19. The **Liufa quanshu**, coded on the authority record as follows:

> 110 10 **China (Republic : 1949-).$tLaws**, etc.
>
> 410 10 **China (Republic : 1949-).$tLiu fa ch^cüan shu**

20. An interesting article on this issue from the patron's viewpoint is: Joann S. Young, "Chinese Romanization Change: A Study on User Preference," *Cataloging & Classification Quarterly* 15:2 (1992): 15-35.

21. For a discussion of the several types of cataloging records created by the National Library of Canada, see the article by Virginia Ballance in this volume.

22. *Répertoire de vedettes-matière* [microform], Québec: Bibliothèque de l'Université Laval, 1988- .

The Languages of the Pacific

Nancy J. Morris

SUMMARY. The quantity of materials in languages of the Pacific is expected to increase in American and European libraries in the coming decades. This essay presents descriptions of the major language groups of Melanesia, Micronesia, and Polynesia and a discussion of issues which the cataloger will encounter in dealing with these materials. Also discussed are creole and pidgin languages of the Pacific, the body of literature in Pacific vernaculars, threatened languages, shared cataloging, meeting the special needs of library users, and dealing with Library of Congress classification and subject headings and with Dewey classification.

The islands of the Pacific are flung like pebbles over one third of the world's surface. Islanders and their cultures, however, remain relatively unfamiliar to many. If the predictions of futurists are correct, the coming decades will be characterized by a shift in orientation away from the Atlantic and toward the Pacific. As this happens, the flow into American and European libraries of Pacific island vernacular materials created by ethnologists, linguists, administrators, and islanders themselves will undoubtedly increase. This essay is addressed to cataloging librarians who must deal with these materials. It is intended as an overview of the major Pacific island language groups with notes on cataloging aids and a discussion of cataloging issues.

Nancy J. Morris is Head, Manuscripts and Archives, Special Collections, and Curator of the Jean Sharlot Collection, Hamilton Library, University of Hawaii, Honolulu, HI 96822.

[Haworth co-indexing entry note]: "The Languages of the Pacific." Morris, Nancy J. Co-published simultaneously in *Cataloging & Classification Quarterly* (The Haworth Press, Inc.) Vol. 17, No. 1/2, 1993, pp. 197-205; and: *Languages of the World: Cataloging Issues and Problems* (ed: Martin D. Joachim) The Haworth Press, Inc., 1993, pp. 197-205. Multiple copies of this article/chapter may be purchased from The Haworth Document Delivery Center [1-800-3-HAWORTH; 9:00 a.m. - 5:00 p.m. (EST)].

Ethnologists classify the islands into three broad cultural groups: Melanesia, Micronesia, and Polynesia. The languages of the islands (with certain exceptions) belong to a large category which linguists call Austronesian. Scientists now believe that the Austronesian languages were originally carried by expanding agricultural populations from south China and Taiwan into Southeast Asia and on to the Pacific into regions that were either empty or sparsely inhabited by foraging peoples.[1]

MELANESIAN LANGUAGES

Geographically, Melanesia includes independent Papua New Guinea, the Indonesian province of Irian Jaya located in the west of the island of New Guinea, Vanuatu (formerly New Hebrides), the Solomons, New Caledonia, the Loyalty Islands, Fiji, and Rotuma. Aside from the Polynesian outlier languages within Melanesia, the languages of Melanesia are classified into two groups: Austronesian and non-Austronesian (earlier linguists called non-Austronesian languages Papuan).

The New Guinea Austronesian languages are nearly all coastal, undoubtedly the languages of immigrants who did not penetrate inland. Elsewhere on the island of New Guinea some 600 non-Austronesian languages are in use, and the linguistic situation can best be described as a modern Babel although linguists now have categorized many of the non-Austronesian languages into perhaps five major families.

The Austronesian family of languages on Fiji, most of the Solomons, and on Vanuatu have been classified by linguists as "Melanesian languages par excellence." The languages of New Caledonia and the Loyalty Islands also belong to the Austronesian-Melanesian family. A scholarly guide to the complexities of the Melanesian linguistic situation is included in *Linguistics in Oceania.*[2] Fraiser McConnell's article on the languages of Melanesia treats the subject from a cataloger's point of view.[3]

MICRONESIAN LANGUAGES

Micronesia encompasses an area larger than the continental United States and includes over 2,100 islands, islets, and atolls. The political units within Micronesia include the Republic of Kiribati (formerly the Gilbert Islands), Tuwalu (formerly the Ellice Islands), the Republic of Nauru, the Territory of Guam, the Commonwealth of the Northern Mariana Islands, the Federated States of Micronesia, the Republic of the Marshall Islands, and the Republic of Palau. The four last named entities were formerly the Trust Territory of the Pacific Islands.

There are about eighteen Micronesian languages, the actual number depending on how one counts language as opposed to dialect. Byron Bender's essay on the languages of Micronesia provides a clear guide to a complex linguistic situation.[4] In Bender's scheme Micronesian languages are classified into "nonnuclear," "questionable," and "nuclear" groups. Nonnuclear Micronesian languages are of two types: Indonesian (Chamorro and Palauan) and Polynesian (Nakuoro and Kapingamarangi). The questionable nuclear Micronesian languages are Yapese and Naruan. Bender identifies seven nuclear Micronesian languages: Ulithian (there are three Ulithian dialects: Sonsorol, Ulithi, and Woleai), Carolinian (this group of languages was carried from the islands of Satawal, Pulusuk, Puluwat, Pulap, and Namonuito to Saipan by migrants who thereafter mingled with Chamorro speakers), Trukese, Ponapean, Kusaiean, Marshallese, and Gilbertese.

The passing of the colonial era in Micronesia has been accompanied by orthographic reforms and changes of place names. These changes in turn affect the nomenclature of language names since language names often correspond to island names. Catalogers will be required to perform mental gymnastics in relating names rendered on pieces in hand to be cataloged to older spellings and/or to older political designations and then in turn to the appropriate official authority lists used by various library institutions. Consider, for example, the problems posed by a vernacular text in Chuuk. Catalogers must relate this language to the nuclear Micronesian language Trukese (and still so called Trukese by the Library of Congress). Similarly, *Belau* is the modern spelling of *Palau*, and *Ponape* might be transcribed in modern vernacular texts as *Pohnpei* or *Bonape*. The Kiribati language was once called Gilbertese; the language of the Ellice Islands was once Tuwalu.

For those libraries which wish to assemble a basic collection of Micronesian grammars and dictionaries for the use of scholars as well as catalogers, Goetzfridt and Goniwiecha have contributed a useful compilation.[5] Their list also includes information on where to buy these tools and on prices.

POLYNESIAN LANGUAGES

Sailing about the Pacific, early Western explorers were intrigued by the similarity of languages in such isolated areas as Hawaii, Easter Island, and New Zealand; and, indeed, the notion of one Polynesian language with a number of dialects persisted into the twentieth century. Today, however, linguists prefer to speak of some twenty-six distinct Polynesian language groups; if all identified Polynesian dialects were listed, this number would more than double. Bruce Biggs's essay, "The Languages of Polynesia," is recommended as an introduction to these languages.[6] Biggs lists the following Polynesian languages located within the Polynesian triangle: Cook Islands, East Futuna, Easter Island, Ellicean (now called Tuwaluan, Hawaiian, Mangarevan, Marquesan, Neo-Tahitian, New Zealand Maori, Niuean, Penrhyn, Pukupukan, Rapa, Samoan, Tongan, and Tuamotuan. The Polynesian languages spoken in isolated islands in Melanesia and Micronesia include Futuna-Aniwa, Kapingamarangi, Northern outliers (Nukumanu, Nukurai, Luangiua Takuu, Sikaiana), Mukuoro, Pileni, Mae, Mele-Fila, Tikopia, West Uvea, and Rennellese.

CREOLE AND PIDGIN

Linguists define pidgin as speech that is not the mother tongue of any who use it. Pidgin develops in situations where speakers of two or several languages have contact with one another and need to communicate. In contrast, creole is a mother tongue of speakers. Both pidgin and creole languages are common in the Pacific, and especially in Melanesia pidgin English has become the lingua franca of the islands. Critics have denounced pidgin as a debased corruption, and during New Guinea's colonial era Australia went so far as to try to outlaw it. Pidgin survived such onslaughts because of its usefulness.

In Melanesia there are three main dialects of pidgin, each associated with three neighboring independent Melanesian countries: Tok Pigin in Papua New Guinea, Pigin in the Solomons, and Bislama in Vanuatu. Pidgin is accepted as an official language of these countries and is widely used in administration, schools, newspapers, and everyday commerce.

Elsewhere in the Pacific pidgins also thrive. In Hawaii a school of writers has dedicated its talents to recording and preserving the colorful pidgin that developed among immigrant groups working together in the sugar and plantation fields. Those who wish to experience Hawaiian pidgin will enjoy sampling such works as Darrell Lum's *Pass On No Pass Back*.[7] A scholarly analysis of Hawaiian pidgin is Elizabeth Carr's *Da Kine Talk*.[8]

A note about cataloging policy and the evolution of social attitudes about pidgins: With the fifteenth edition of *Subject Headings*, the Library of Congress granted to Bislama, the national language of Vanuatu, a note of dignity lacking in earlier editions. Bislama was earlier called Beche-de mer, literally the term for the Pacific Islands sea slug but one that came to refer to the contact language between islanders and foreigners. For many years the Library of Congress used the demeaning term **BECHE-DE-MER JARGON** before at last taking note of the correct designation of this language. *Tangkyu tumas*, LC!

THE BODY OF LITERATURE
IN PACIFIC VERNACULARS

To Western missionaries belongs the credit for transcribing the oral languages of the Pacific Islands into written form. The first written materials produced were religious tracts, Bibles, and literacy tools for indigenous students. Especially in Polynesia, Pacific islanders set about with enthusiasm in learning to read and write. In the nineteenth century islanders produced a large volume of vernacular texts; such resources as Maori and Hawaiian language newspapers provide scholars with an invaluable alternative perspective on Pacific history from the indigenous rather than the western colonial point of view. Serious Pacific island library collections will also include a body of legal and administrative materials in Pacific vernaculars.

By the turn of the twentieth century, islanders had become somewhat disenchanted with the ability to write in their own languages. Such ability was, after all, not the key to the white man's magic; and in many areas, by choice and by western edicts, the emphasis shifted to literacy in western languages or, in the case of Micronesia, in Japanese. After World War II a corps of American administrators and Peace Corps volunteers tried valiantly to promote literacy in the native vernaculars. Somewhat the same process went on in Melanesia, encouraged by British and Australian administrators. A large body of vernacular materials is being produced by such institutions as the Summer Institute of Linguistics, an international organization with a Pacific branch headquartered in Ukarumpa, Papua New Guinea. The Institute has contributed greatly to the recording and study of little known languages. In other areas of the Pacific such as Samoa, Tonga, and Fiji, the indigenous languages remained strong and vital. The passing of the Pacific colonial era has brought other changes with respect to the vernacular literature now being produced, and there is a developing indigenous tradition of poetry and prose in the language of the native Pacific peoples.

THREATENED LANGUAGES

Linguists have made the gloomy prediction that within a century 90 percent of the languages of the world will be eliminated. Pacific languages in particular are in danger of being swallowed up by what Pacific language specialist George Grace called the "growing world monoculture." In view of the seriousness of the situation, catalogers have an important social role to play in documenting, preserving, and providing proper access to the Pacific island language materials that pass through their charge. The complexities of this task call for all the best skills that catalogers can muster.

SHARED CATALOGING

Tapping into the cataloging records created by libraries specializing in the Pacific requires a bit of shopping through the various electronic networks available to the thoroughly modern cataloging librarian of today. Many librarians will turn first to OCLC, but there are other choices. The University of Hawaii Pacific Collection, which holds the most comprehensive collection of Pacific Island language materials of any American library, contributes records to OCLC but, because of protocols applicable to tape loading of records into OCLC, has experienced difficulty in transferring some types of materials. Records for serials, for example, cannot be loaded by tape into OCLC although OCLC reports that progress is being made to eliminate this problem. A complete display of University of Hawaii records is available through the CARL network, which can be accessed by off-site users through Internet.

Included in the University of Hawaii holdings is the unique Tsuzaki/Reinecke Collection of pidgin and creole linguistics, much of which is related to Pacific island creoles and pidgins. This collection of 2,200 items was fully cataloged using Title IIC grant funds from the U.S. Department of Education's Strengthening Research Library Resources Program; full cataloging records are displayed on the CARL network. A printed catalog of these records is available from the University of Hawaii Library.

MEETING THE SPECIAL NEEDS OF USERS

In working with Pacific language materials, catalogers must face the question of user needs. If library collections are assembled for the use of scholars and academics, catalogers will no doubt rely on the standardized classification schemes and subject headings offered by the Library of Congress and Dewey. If, however, library users are native speakers, other considerations arise.

In Hawaii a cultural renaissance among native Hawaiians is underway as a young generation struggles to perpetuate a culture threatened by western influences. Islanders are filling Hawaiian language classes and are unwilling to pronounce the Hawaiian language as moribund as had once been feared. This renewal of interest has occasioned a pride in preserving the accurate rendering of the language in its written form. In Hawaiian this means attention to diacritics indicating the glottal stop (a ' or upside down comma) and elongated vowels (indicated by macrons over vowels). Unfortunately, in this age of computerized cataloging, there are technical problems associated with the inputting and display of diacritics. In an interesting confrontation between user rights and library practice, the University of Hawaii Library received an angry letter from Hawaiian language students demanding that cataloging records show proper diacritical markings. The Library at length obliged, and now there is a special terminal with the capacity of displaying proper diacritics.

Libraries in New Zealand have given unprecedented attention to the needs and sensitivities of indigenous users of language collections. New Zealand libraries have accepted the concept that Maori language materials entrusted to their keeping are in fact part of the cultural heritage of the Maori people. This realization has led to changes in the organization of materials and patterns of bibliographic access. Maoris, for example, find western-style histories of their people meaningless and often offensive. The Maori approach to history is through tribal identification. All Maoris belong to one of about fifty tribes, or *iwi*, broad descent groups tracing ancestry back to the real or first mythical canoe landings of the Maori people in New Zealand. Typical modern Maori library users want to know the history of *their* tribes and will often toss aside materials relating to other tribes.

New Zealand libraries have responded to this pattern by attaching tribal designations to subject headings. Maoris, moreover, find little meaning in such standard library terms as **BEADWORK, MAORI**. To bridge such communication gaps, a comprehensive Maori thesaurus of subject headings has been published by the Alexander Turnbull Library of New Zealand. Scope notes are in English and Maori. The thesaurus also attempts to link scientific terms with Maori words as, for example, terms for birds. In creating the thesaurus, Maori elders have joined with librarians. The innovative measures ongoing in New Zealand represent honest attempts by librarians to deal with the rightful indignation of Maoris who feel that they were alienated from their intellectual property as they were from their lands.[9]

LIVING WITH THE SYSTEM

Most American libraries will take only an academic interest in these issues raised by native speakers of Pacific island languages. Library administrators, increasingly alarmed by the rising costs of the processing of library materials, will argue for conformity to standard library cataloging practices. For many librarians this will mean reliance on Library of Congress practice and Dewey schedules. There are references in library literature to objections which librarians have taken to Library of Congress and Dewey inadequacies with respect to the cataloging and classification of Pacific island language materials,[10] but in fact these national authorities often prove responsive to suggestions and revisions from the field. An example is the willingness on the part of the Library of Congress to establish new MARC language codes when librarians in the field can offer evidence of the existence of twenty titles in a given language.

CONCLUSION

Most libraries, of course, do not have the types of specialized Pacific language collections that are available at the University of Hawaii and other Pacific area libraries. One goal of this essay has been to provide background information for catalogers who must handle materials in Pacific island languages when there is little or no expertise in the specific languages available in their own libraries. It is also important that librarians be aware of the wealth of material in and about these languages and that they be dedicated to collecting, cataloging, and preserving these linguistic and cultural resources for future generations.

NOTES

1. Peter Bellwood, "The Austronesian Dispersal and the Origin of Languages," *Scientific American* 265:1 (July 1991): 88-93.

2. *Linguistics in Oceania*, vol. 8 of *Current Trends in Linguistics* (The Hague: Mouton, 1971), 240-425.

3. Fraiser McConnell, "Languages of Melanesia: Problems and Proposals for Classification," *Cataloging & Classification Quarterly* 5:3 (Spring 1985): 57-66.

4. Byron W. Bender, "Micronesian Languages" in *Current Trends in Linguistics* (The Hague: Mouton, 1971), 8: 426-465.

5. Nicholas J. Goetzfridt and Mark C. Goniwiecha, "Language Dictionaries and Grammars of Guam and Micronesia," *Reference Services Review* 18:1 (Spring 1990):17-38.

6. Bruce Biggs, "The Languages of Polynesia" in *Current Trends in Linguistics* (The Hague: Mouton, 1971), 8: 466-505.

7. Darrell Lum, *Pass On No Pass Back* (Honolulu: Bamboo Ridge Press, 1990).

8. Elizabeth Carr, *Da Kine Talk* (Honolulu: University Press of Hawaii, 1972).

9. Wharehuia Hemara, "Whakakautoro: Reaching Out," *Turnbull Library Record* 23:1 (May 1990): 34-38. Comments in this paragraph are also based on an oral interview, March 20, 1992, with Sharon Dell of the Alexander Turnbull Library.

10. See, for example, articles by Fraiser McConnell: "Classification of Melanesia: Proposal for Revision of DDC, Table 2," *Cataloging & Classification Quarterly* 5:1 (Fall 1984): 53-60; "Peoples of Melanesia: Proposals for Revision of DDC 19, Table 5," *Cataloging & Classification Quarterly* 5:4 (Summer 1985): 47-51.

NON-SPECIFIC LANGUAGES

Cataloging
Non-English Government Publications
in a Medium Research Library

Kerry A. Keck
Barbara Stewart

SUMMARY. The authors provide a brief review of recent literature addressing cataloging of non-U.S. government publications (with an emphasis on publications in languages other than English) and discuss issues specific to bibliographic processing of official government publications, including poor internal bibliographic control, restrictive or unusual government policies, unusual government structures and practices, and highly irregular publishing schedules. They summarize a survey of cataloging copy availability conducted for non-English, non-U.S. government publications in the OCLC database, and conclude with a discussion of practice in dealing with these materials in place in one medium-sized library.

Kerry A. Keck is Coordinator for Collection Development & Electronic Information Resources, and Barbara Stewart is Documents Librarian, Fondren Library, Rice University, Houston, TX.

[Haworth co-indexing entry note]: "Cataloging Non-English Government Publications in a Medium Research Library." Keck, Kerry A., and Barbara Stewart. Co-published simultaneously in *Cataloging & Classification Quarterly* (The Haworth Press, Inc.) Vol. 17, No. 1/2, 1993, pp. 207-217; and: *Languages of the World: Cataloging Issues and Problems* (ed: Martin D. Joachim) The Haworth Press, Inc., 1993, pp. 207-217. Multiple copies of this article/chapter may be purchased from The Haworth Document Delivery Center [1-800-3-HAWORTH; 9:00 a.m. - 5:00 p.m. (EST)].

INTRODUCTION

The bibliographic control of official government publications presents unique challenges and opportunities not only for librarians responsible for cataloging those publications but also for public service librarians committed to providing high quality reference assistance to the users of those publications. The problems associated with the dissemination and control of publications of the United States government are well documented in the literature and continue to be the focus of discussion and research by various professional organizations. For purposes of this article, attention is turned to the cataloging of official publications of foreign governments–that is, publications produced by countries other than the United States.

A survey of the current literature produced surprisingly little in terms of attempts to address the problem of cataloging foreign government publications. In 1980 Mohammed M. Aman compiled and edited a series of articles addressing the intricacies involved in cataloging non-Western material.[1] The contribution of this work to the problem at hand is significant for two reasons. First, many of the specific obstacles confronted by catalogers of foreign government publications (i.e., changes in names of countries and government agencies) are addressed in this book. A second and perhaps more valuable contribution of this work is its very thorough discussion of the problems associated with language and cultural differences in non-Western material, both of which profoundly impact the organization of official publications.

The establishment of Canada's cataloging-in-publication data for Canadian government publications is outlined in a 1979 article by Maedythe Martin.[2] The advantages for the cataloger of making CIP data available are discussed, but, more important, the author provides insight into the conditions which must exist within the government and the library community in order to implement a project of this nature successfully.

By providing updated information on the resources currently available to catalogers and by sharing our library's approach to the problem, the authors hope to add to the body of knowledge in this area. Before that can be accomplished, however, it is necessary to review the broad issues which affect *all* non-English language publications.

The first hurdle faced by catalogers of non-English language publications is, of course, the language barrier. In theory, acquiring the necessary language expertise in the cataloging department would at least somewhat alleviate this problem. In fact, as discussed below, Fondren Library has found this a viable solution in some instances. There are, however, particular areas of the world which are more troublesome than others in compensating for the language barrier. An otherwise routine task such as determining who authored a work becomes a significant problem when dealing with material published in regions like Africa and India where multiple languages are in use and customs within the regions allow many individuals to use the same name or to change names at will.

Other aspects of non-Western publications can also result in some confusion for catalogers. Title page construction can vary from country to country, and different bibliographic information is emphasized depending on the publishing practices, library attitudes and procedures, and the culture or traditions within a given country or region. For instance, Chinese monographs may or may not include title pages. In those cases when a title page is included, the elements standard to title pages in English language publications are typically dispersed throughout the Chinese monograph. Hebrew publications also tend to be problematic with regard to identification and interpretation of title page information.

The difficulties faced by professional groups in establishing bibliographic standards and in achieving worldwide or even regional compliance with those standards are at least partially the result of a wide range of practices and procedures in libraries throughout the world. Examples of the variations which occur are evident in almost every aspect of library work. Historically, libraries in China and many of the Arab nations have preferred a title main entry catalog. The practice in the Southeast Asian countries has been to maintain separate catalogs for collections in different scripts. The standardization problem is therefore exacerbated by the fact that many nations are not utilizing *AACR2* conventions and accordingly are not contributing to the development of standard or uniform catalog entries. Conversely, the superficial treatment by Western-based cataloging conventions of non-Western cultures has been a source of concern in the library community for some time.

The preceding discussion is intended to serve as a foundation for those unfamiliar with the issues. Although many of the problems encountered by the cataloger of non-Western publications stem from the differences in language, culture, and library procedures discussed above, there are other issues specific to the task of cataloging foreign government publications which are addressed in the following paragraphs.

ISSUES SPECIFIC TO DOCUMENTS

Government publications, regardless of language or country of origin, pose a distinctive set of challenges from acquisition to processing. The issues that can trouble the acquisitions librarian also affect the cataloger. Factors such as minimal internal bibliographic control, restrictive or un-

usual government policies, and irregular publishing schedules can bedevil
the processing of these materials as well as their acquisition by U.S.
libraries. As Rozkuszka says:

> The United States is a complex society where information is valued
> at a premium, and where one-half of the economy is related to the
> information industry. There are strong assumptions that if a need is
> defined, there are resources available to answer that need. *This is not
> the case for resources from a large part of the Third World.* An
> expectation for much of what may be wanted by a researcher will
> probably be unrealistic.[3]

Bibliographic control. Many of the developing nations have poor internal bibliographic control. Where a national bibliography exists, it frequently does not include the publications of the central or state governments.[4] The librarian frequently is dependent, therefore, upon the
necessarily selective bibliographies available from commercial sources
and/or the Library of Congress. The lack of internal bibliographic resources hinders the acquisition of materials, of course, but also restricts the
secondary-source information available to the cataloger trying to deal with
language difficulties and cultural variances as to what information can be
found on title and/or verso pages.

Of course, many nations have significant bibliographic access for their
official publications. As mentioned before, Canada has provided CIP data
for publications generated at both the national and provincial level. Brazil
and Columbia are two other western hemisphere countries providing CIP
in their official publications.

Subject analysis. Exceptions do exist, of course, but there tends to be a
core of subject matter which comprises the majority of a government's
publication base. There will be a standard array of statistical publications,
planning documents, censuses, and legal materials. Application of standard subject headings will usually be straightforward for the bulk of this
literature. Consequently, the largest body of subject analysis will be a
non-issue for government publications.

Corporate headings. The cataloger dealing with government publications will become intimately familiar with the *AACR2* rules and LC interpretations dealing with forms of entry and access points for these materials. Although *AACR2* rules and LC interpretations both place increased
emphasis on recognition of personal authorship, catalogers of government
publications will continue to find themselves attributing many publications to the authorizing agencies.

Especially crucial to main entry construction for government publications is chapter 24, ruling the choice of corporate names and the structure used. Proper application of the rules may be equally dependent upon an in-depth understanding of the political and cultural conditions in the country. A country may have a history of frequent reorganization of the government. Although this may be due in some cases to political turbulence, in other situations it is a standard means of operating. Some of the Caribbean countries, for example, practice a form of floating ministerial portfolio: the group of agencies for which a minister is responsible changes from year to year.

In certain countries, the government may be the sole publisher. Conversely, the publications recording the government's activities may be generated through a quasi-official body such as a university or research institute. A thorough grounding in the political culture of the nation is therefore necessary for original cataloging of non-U.S. government publications.

A major challenge for original cataloging of government publications is construction of the entry in a proper fashion vis-à-vis independent versus subordinate entries. *AACR2* rules 24.13 and 24.18 outline the criteria by which the cataloger may determine when the entry for a government body should be constructed as a subordinate or related body. Rule 24.13 describes the criteria for bodies not entered under the parent government and 24.18 for bodies entered under the parent government. The distinction between the two categories can be somewhat fine and can impact on entries for quasi-governmental organizations in those countries that publish through these bodies.

Non-unique titles and frequent title changes. Banes for the serials cataloger, non-unique titles and frequent changes of title are seemingly fundamental to the nature of government serials. Titles such as *Rapport annuel* and *Memoria annual* are all too frequent. Title marking of the publication may vary from issue to issue, so that *Boletin mensual* becomes *Boletin mensual de estadistico* and the *Boletin mensual* once again. These changes, official or otherwise, complicate the task of tracing the origin and/or termination of a serial title.

In the face of the challenges of acquisition and processing these materials, many U.S. libraries still seek to add the publications of other governments to their collections. Frequently invaluable information sources, non-U.S. government publications are in increased demand. The growing globalization of our economies (if not all aspects of our cultures) is driving the American demand for access to detailed data on the economies, cultures, and governmental policies of other states and nations.

As experience has shown us, however, physical possession alone of these valuable printed documents is insufficient to provide our libraries' users access to the needed information. Bibliographic control of these publications through centralized library record systems provides that access. Recent experience in a number of U.S. libraries has demonstrated the effect of introducing cataloging records for major microform sets (such as Evans' *American Bibliography* microform set) and U.S. government publications into central library catalog systems. Various sources have reported increased usage of the materials of several orders of magnitude.[5]

AVAILABILITY OF CATALOGING COPY FOR NON-U.S. GOVERNMENT PUBLICATIONS

Few librarians would disagree with the desirability of a single central record of all library holdings, including any non-U.S. government publications. Practical considerations such as the ranking of priorities which we all face (e.g., processing of current materials with good cataloging copy available versus retrospective conversion of materials requiring original work) do intrude. Government publications, both U.S. and non-U.S., are frequently perceived as belonging among the latter category. Cataloging of foreign government publications remains a low priority for libraries (including the Library of Congress)[6], and progress will continue slowly. Much has been done, however, to improve the availability of high-quality cataloging for these materials.

The authors took a sample of available cataloging copy for 248 non-English, non-U.S. government publications in June 1992. Our goal was to determine (1) the availability in the most widely used cataloging utility (OCLC) of copy for the basic publications generated by a nation's government and (2) the availability of an authority record for the core agencies. We operated on the premise that the average academic or public library wishing to build a collection from a given nation will likely begin with the basic publications (legislative materials, economic statistics, etc.). Further, although such a library will go on to acquire materials for which cataloging copy is unavailable, established personal and/or corporate author headings can significantly minimize difficulties in the cataloging process.

The authors took the sample of publications from the *Guide to Official Publications of Foreign Countries.*[7] The *Guide* provides a body of government publications which form the core of any country's published literature. We sampled 248 of the publications listed which met the following criteria:

- the government issues basic publications in a language other than English (bilingual publications were accepted leading to inclusion of Canada but exclusion of Kenya)
- publications are by a governmental or quasi-governmental body in the country in question (e.g., U.S. publications *about* the country were excluded).

Although the *Guide* frequently includes OCLC numbers, the authors researched each sample title to confirm the presence of a record and to further determine the source of the copy (DLC or member copy). In addition, all personal and corporate authors that could be identified were searched for an established authority record. The results of the sample are summarized in Table 1. The results of the sample demonstrate a positive record of copy availability for government publications in languages other than English. A solid core of these records originated from the Library of Congress or have been reviewed by that body. Ranging from almost 89 percent of the publications generated in North America, the Library of Congress has provided authoritative copy for the publications of nations

TABLE 1

Cataloging Copy on OCLC
For Non-U.S., Non-English Government Publications

	N=	% with records		% with authority	
		Yes	DLC	w/o copy	All
Africa	54	84.6	57.7	60.0	84.6
Central America	17	94.1	70.6	66.7	82.4
East Asia	31	90.3	67.7	75.1	77.4
Europe	76	84.2	63.2	83.2	82.9
Middle East	15	73.3	60.0	100.0	86.7
North America	9	100.0	88.9	90.0	88.9
Oceania	10	66.7	33.3	80.0	88.9
South America	24	92.9	46.4	100.0	92.9
South Asia	13	100.0	66.7	58.0	88.9

from all regions. The Library's contributions for the materials originating in Oceania and South America have been less, yet high-caliber copy is being provided by research libraries building collections in these areas.[8]

More encouraging yet than the percentages of copy for these publications was the finding regarding the availability of authority records for the central corporate authors represented in the *Guide*. The publications described in the *Guide* will likely represent the first materials to be acquired by public and academic libraries. Having begun to collect, however, we will likely go on to acquire additional, "secondary" literature from these same governmental bodies. The consistently high rates of established authority records for these bodies provide a stable framework for the cataloging staffs working to provide access.

The authors' survey demonstrates the improving environment for cataloging of government publications. Cataloging copy on OCLC for certain titles was identified by the authors in June 1992; these titles had not yet been cited in the *Guide* (published in 1990). Some of this copy was new and reflects ongoing work around the country. The authors speculate that at least some of the copy existing before publication of the *Guide* went uncited due to the difficulty of identifying non-unique titles using the search key system previously required by OCLC. The recently introduced search capabilities of OCLC, such as title scanning, provide greater access to these non-unique titles.

The authors must acknowledge the potential for error in their own findings. We suspect that these findings may themselves be a conservative estimate of copy available as, unfamiliar with certain languages and conventional names of governmental entities, we may have missed available authority records.

LOCAL PRACTICE AT RICE UNIVERSITY

Fondren Library at Rice University acquires a moderate collection of non-English, non-U.S. government publications. A medium-sized research library, Fondren Library's collection is composed largely of the type of basic documents described in the *Guide* and included in the authors' sample. The cataloging department is composed of three and one half FTE professional and ten paraprofessional staff. Languages read include Russian, Hebrew, Chinese, and Latin, as well the major modern European tongues.

All non-English publications currently being acquired by the Fondren Library are cataloged through the OCLC cataloging utility and added to the library's online catalog (NOTIS's integrated system, known locally as LI-

BRIS). A retrospective conversion of the library's card catalog is largely complete with the exception of a relatively few dead serials and some monographic titles in non-roman character sets (Greek, Chinese, Russian, etc.). Transliteration and conversion of these non-English materials into LIBRIS continue at a slow pace as other duties allow staff to deal with the materials.

As might be predicted from the authors' sample, many of the non-English publications, governmental and otherwise, being acquired at Fondren Library have DLC or high-caliber member copy available. Using LIBRIS's acquisition module in conjunction with OCLC, our catalogers locate a bibliographic record for the title, transfer the record to LIBRIS, and use the record to create a printed order to the originating agency or (more likely) an appropriate vendor. The LIBRIS record is updated upon receipt to initiate payment and to reflect the availability of the publication in the library. The system is used to record receipt of serial publications and to initiate claims upon non-receipt. In short, processing procedures for non-English government publications are the same at Fondren Library as those for commercial publications in English.

In the absence of quality cataloging copy in OCLC for a foreign government imprint, catalogers enter provisional records into LIBRIS from which to initiate the orders. Upon receipt of the material, full original cataloging is initiated. In this procedure there is obviously no difference in treatment of the materials. It is at this point, however, that the difficulties previously discussed can arise.

One of our greatest weapons in dealing with the difficulties is the language and cultural expertise of our cataloging staff. As with many other libraries, however, the expertise of our staff is not as broad as the range of languages and cultures represented in the collection. Fondren Library has been able to draw upon the expertise of the large population of foreign students and faculty at Rice University. Most recently, a university research associate was hired on a contract basis to work with one of our catalogers to process a collection of Arabic materials acquired by Fondren Library. The research associate has the language skills and cultural background to support the cataloging skills of the library staff member. Previously, junior faculty have volunteered their service in similar capacities; library staff have worked to ensure recognition of the scope of this university service during tenure review of these scholars.

Fondren Library has also explored collaborative cataloging and "outsourcing" cataloging projects when necessary language skills have been unavailable to us. Collections of special material may be processed by contracting with a library services firm for these specialized skills.

CONCLUSION

The task of providing full bibliographic access to non-U.S. government publications may appear daunting for the average public or academic library, which may nonetheless possess such jewels in its collections. The difficulties are genuine and reflect the challenges facing academic and public libraries in the U.S. The information expectations of our libraries' users are increasing at a greater rate than the resources available to meet those expectations. At the same time that demand for increasingly sophisticated information grows, budgetary constraints limit the ability of the Library of Congress to aggressively pursue and process such materials and limit the ability of academic and public libraries to attract employees with the skills to take up the burden.

Counter-balancing these pessimistic factors, however, is the positive fact of a solid base of work contributed over the last several decades by the Library of Congress and major research libraries across the continent. The Library of Congress and other major U.S. research libraries have been contributing cataloging records for the official publications of other nations, as well as authority records for the corporate components of those nations, into the OCLC and RLIN databases where they are available for use by small and medium libraries.

Small and medium U.S. libraries which are interested in building collections of the basic publications of the non-English government publications of other nations will find a solid body of specialized literature relating to acquisition of these materials. The growing interest in this type of resource by the average library may explain the recent increase in discussion of these specialized acquisitions issues in the general professional literature. The authors hope to see these more widespread discussions of acquisition of non-English language, non-U.S. documents followed by a corresponding increase in expert discussion of bibliographic access for these invaluable information resources.

NOTES

1. Mohammed M. Aman, ed., *Cataloging and Classification of Non-Western Material: Concerns, Issues, and Practices* (Phoenix: Oryx Press, 1980).

2. Maedythe Martin, "Canadian Cataloguing-in-Publication (CIP) Data for Government Publications," *Ontario Library Review* 63 (March 1979): 34-38.

3. W. David Rozkuszka, "Status of Government Documentation and Publishing in the Third World," *Government Publications Review* 19 (1992): 4.

4. For a recent listing of bibliographic sources for publications of other governments, see: Lawrence Hallewell, "Government Publishing in the Third World:

A Bibliography of Works about Official Publishing in Developing Countries," *Government Publications Review* 19 (1992): 23-58.

5. For information on increases in usage of U.S. document collections experienced after loading records for these collections into central online catalog databases, see footnote 25 of Myrtle Smith Bolner and Barbara Kile, "Documents to the People: Access through the Automated Catalog," *Government Publications Review* 18 (1991): 51-64.

6. "Cataloging Priorities and Levels of Cataloging," *Cataloging Service Bulletin* 51 (Winter 1991): 3-4.

7. American Library Association. Government Documents Roundtable, *Guide to Official Publications of Foreign Countries* (Bethesda, Md.: CIS, c1990).

8. For a brief overview of major research libraries which are acting as libraries of record for certain regions of the globe, see: John Bruce Howell, "Implications of Government Publishing in the Third World for Library Collections and Services," *Government Publications Review* 19 (1992): 11-22.

Cataloguing in the Official
and Heritage Languages
at the National Library of Canada

Virginia Ballance

SUMMARY. The National Library of Canada's main mandate is to acquire, catalogue, and promote Canadiana regardless of language or place of publication. Since Canada has two official languages, English and French, the National Library aspires to bilingual bibliographic control. Technological advances that link bilingual authority files and allow a language-specific user interface make bilingual cataloguing of individual items unnecessary. The National Library's cataloguing policy for materials in both official languages is outlined, as well as policies governing cataloguing in languages other than English and French. As a resource-sharing agency, the National Library also operates a separate Multilingual Biblioservice (MBS) collection to assist public libraries across the country in providing heritage-language material to their users. The MBS currently has collections in thirty-two languages and several scripts, all of which are catalogued in the vernacular. The automated MBS-MINISIS system is a pioneer multilingual, multiscript integrated library application.

SOMMAIRE EN FRANCAIS. La Bibliothèque nationale du Canada (BNC) a pour mandat l'acquisition, le catalogage et la promotion

Virginia Ballance, BA (Hons.), Carleton University, MA, University of London, and MLS, University of Western Ontario, is former Head of Cataloguing and Automation in the Multilingual Biblioservice of the National Library of Canada.

[Haworth co-indexing entry note]: "Cataloguing in the Official and Heritage Languages at the National Library of Canada." Ballance, Virginia. Co-published simultaneously in *Cataloging & Classification Quarterly* (The Haworth Press, Inc.) Vol. 17, No. 1/2, 1993, pp. 219-232; and: *Languages of the World: Cataloging Issues and Problems* (ed: Martin D. Joachim) The Haworth Press, Inc., 1993, pp. 219-232. Multiple copies of this article/chapter may be purchased from The Haworth Document Delivery Center [1-800-3-HAWORTH; 9:00 a.m. - 5:00 p.m. (EST)].

de Canadiana, peu importe la langue ou lieu de publication. Puisqu'au Canada, il existe deux langues officielles, soit le français et l'anglais, la BNC aspire au contrôle bibliographique bilingue. Grâce aux progrès technologiques qui lient les fichiers d'autorité bilingues, et qui permettent une interface dans la langue choisie par l'usager, le catalogage individuel n'est plus nécessaire. Un aperçu de la politique de la Bibliothèque nationale du Canada sur le catalogage des langues officielles est présenté, ainsi que celle sur le catalogage des langues d'origine. Dans le cadre de la mise en commun des ressources, la Bibliothèque nationale du Canada fournit aussi une aide aux bibliothèques publiques d'un coin à l'autre du pays en leur offrant des matériaux dans la langue d'origine de leurs usagers, et ce, par l'intermédiaire des collection du Biblioservice multilingue (BSM). Le BSM possède présentement des matériaux en trente-deux langues et plusieurs systèmes graphiques, ou alphabets, le tout catalogué dans la langue d'origine. Le système automatisé MINISIS-BSM est un chef de file mis en place au Biblioservice multilingue. Ce système permet l'exploitation de plusieurs systèmes graphiques automatisés.

THE NATIONAL LIBRARY OF CANADA
AND BILINGUAL CATALOGUING

The National Library of Canada, established in 1953, is the Canadian federal cultural institution responsible for ensuring that the nation's published heritage is gathered, preserved, and made accessible to all Canadians, whether it is published at home or abroad. The National Library's mandate also includes the promotion of Canadian studies and of the Canadian heritage and resource-sharing and library development across Canada.

Born of the union of French and English cultures, Canada is by political circumstance a bilingual country. Since the adoption of the Official Languages Act in 1969, English and French have been declared to be the official languages of Canada. The Act does not mean that every Canadian must know both languages (although many do); rather, it officially mandates "institutional bilingualism," requiring all federally-regulated institutions, as well as certain provincial and municipal bodies, to provide services to the public in both official languages.

In complying with the Act, the National Library must provide bilingual reference services. It must also ensure that all its communications are available in both languages, such as *Canadiana* (the national bibliography) and other bibliographic services, and indeed all published products, whether printed or electronic: reports, exhibition catalogues, union lists, directories, online catalogues, and so on.

Bilingual Cataloguing of French and English Works

Canadian libraries use the same descriptive catalogue code, classification systems, and subject headings as their counterparts in the United States; however, the bilingual requirements of Canadian society present special problems. The National Library of Canada has had to interpret the cataloguing code to allow flexibility in the handling of bilingual bibliographic data as well as to adapt the classification systems and subject headings lists which were not adequate for the subject analysis of Canadian materials, particularly in law, history, and literature.[1]

The 1972 report of the Task Group on Cataloguing Standards suggested that the National Library of Canada keep its bilingual community in mind "particularly when data is prepared for inclusion in the database from which various bibliographic services for the whole country will be generated."[2] The specific recommendation was that the National Library use both the English and French versions of *Anglo-American Cataloging Rules* for descriptive cataloguing.

A truly bilingual catalogue would be one in which every title, regardless of its language of publication, would be catalogued twice, once in English and once in French. This ideal has probably never been attained by any library, for practical considerations such as the cost and time required to catalogue every title twice, and the doubled overhead of computer storage costs (or card filing). However, the technological advances of an automated catalogue with linked bilingual authority files and a language-specific user interface make full double cataloguing unnecessary.

Thus, in keeping with the spirit of the official languages legislation and the recommendations of the Task Group on Cataloguing Standards, the National Library has adopted a simple cataloguing policy: the language of the publication determines the language of the descriptive cataloguing of a title.[3]

The first rule is that titles in French are catalogued in French according to the French-language *Règles de catalogage anglo-américains,* deuxième édition, révision 1988 (*RCAA*-1988), the French version of the revised second edition of the *Anglo-American Cataloguing Rules* (*AACR*2-1988). In addition to the French main-entry and added-entry headings, subject headings are added in French and English.

The second rule is that all other publications are catalogued in English according to *AACR*2-1988. As with French-language publications, subject headings in both languages are added to the record. Titles published in two separate editions, one in each of the two official languages, are catalogued separately, once in English and once in French, including subject headings in both languages. The relationship between the two records is indicated through linking "Also published in French," "Aussi disponible en anglais" notes, and added entries are provided for the title in the other language.

The uniquely bilingual aspect of the National Library's cataloguing policy is more evident in its treatment of bilingual books, meaning works in any format that combine text in both official languages within one publication. The National Library's descriptive cataloguing policy treats bilingual English-French titles, or multilingual titles containing substantial portions of text in both English and French, by cataloguing twice, once in English and once in French.

The *tête bêche,* or tumble, format, in which French and English halves of one bound volume are printed upside-down and in reverse order relative to each other, provides two front covers and title pages; therefore each title is catalogued according to the language of its own title page. Subject headings are supplied only in the language of cataloguing.

On the other hand, treatment of a bilingual title published in parallel-page or other mixed format is less obvious. The cataloguing code states that when transcribing parallel titles, the first stated language on the title page should be listed first in a single catalogue record. At the National Library of Canada, a parallel-format title in French and English or vice versa, would be catalogued twice, once in each of the two languages, including interpolations in the appropriate language. Again, subject headings are provided only in the language of cataloguing. Although the resulting records may at first glance appear more or less the same, there would be differences of language in the publication statement, collation, notes areas, and subject headings.

Beyond Bilingualism: Third-Language Works in the Main Collection

The National Library cataloguing policy treats the following two cases in a special fashion: language-instruction materials and titles published entirely in Latin. The language of cataloguing is determined by the language of the intended audience of the materials. For example, a book teaching English and which is entirely in English would nevertheless be catalogued only in French if it is intended for a French audience. Similarly, Latin titles intended for a French audience would be catalogued in French, and for an English audience, in English.

The cataloguing of materials in languages other than English or French is more difficult to decide upon in a bilingual environment. The title, of course, must be presented in the language of the publication, but in what language should the notes and other information be given–in English or

French? The language of the intended audience cannot be used as a guide, as with works in Latin, a classical language. The National Library's policy is to catalogue works in living third languages for the main collection in English, with roman script transliterations of titles and main entries where required. The policy gives rise to the situation where a title in Italian and French would be catalogued in French, whereas a title only in Italian would be catalogued in English! The name authorities for main and added entries would use both English and French forms of transliteration for titles published in non-roman scripts.

The treatment of materials in aboriginal languages deserves special notice. There are fifty-three native Indian and Inuit languages identified as being spoken in Canada. According to analyses of Canadian census data, daily use of these languages has fallen over the past twenty years. Although many aboriginal languages have only an oral tradition, whatever publishing does occur in these languages is collected by the National Library and is included in *Canadiana*. All entries are transliterated from syllabics to the roman script. The notes and interpolations in the catalogue record are provided in English.

Serials in a Bilingual Cataloguing Environment

Serial publications present an interesting challenge to bilingual bibliographical control at the National Library of Canada, owing to their ever changing formats and publication patterns. Cataloguing policy for serial titles, as for monographs, is that they are catalogued in the language of publication. In the case of serials with both French and English content under a single or parallel title, two cataloguing records are produced.

If a serial is issued in two editions, one French and one English, there would be four bibliographic records created for the serial title: (i) in English for the English edition, (ii) in English for the French edition, (iii) in French for the French edition, and (iv) in French for the English edition. The notes on the four records would be constructed according to the relationship of the record to the title being described; for example, the two records describing the English edition are considered equivalent records, whereas the two records catalogued in French are for variant editions of the same work.[4]

Bilingual Name Authorities and Subject Headings

Authority control in a bilingual library can be handled quite easily when using an automated system as long as all language-specific access points have been established in both languages. At the National Library of Canada, parallel authority headings in French and in English have been established for all names of corporate bodies (if they exist in standard reference sources), names with additions (such as honorifics), place names, and transliterations. As well, uniform titles are established for titles in transliteration, the classics (pre-1501), any title with qualifying information, such as [**Selections**], all acts and laws, treaties, sacred works, and so on.

The National Library of Canada has published a list of subject headings, *Canadian Subject Headings*, that takes into consideration the particular Canadian needs of subject access to materials on Canadian history, geography, law, literature, and works on specifically Canadian institutions, such as the National Research Council.[5] As well, the Université Laval has formulated a list of subject headings in French to parallel *Library of Congress Subject Headings* and *Canadian Subject Headings*. The list is called the *Répertoire de vedettes-matière* and has been produced with the assistance of the National Library of Canada. These two uniquely Canadian cataloguing tools are in wide use in Canadian libraries.

Occasionally problems are encountered when applying bilingual subject headings, as non-equivalent relationships may exist between the English and French headings. For example, the topical heading **ADMINISTRATIVE AGENCIES–CANADA** is rendered in French as a geographic heading, **CANADA–ADMINISTRATION PUBLIQUE**. Or a heading in one language may give rise to two headings in the other language according to a differing logical analysis or because of the lack of a single, exact terminological equivalent in the target language.[6] For example, the French heading **ORFEVRES** translates into two headings in English: **GOLDSMITHS** and **SILVERSMITHS**.

Bilingual Library Automation

The National Library's automated system, DOBIS, serves as both the Library's in-house database and Canada's national union catalogue. Although it is scheduled to be replaced within the next two years with a fourth-generation relational database (recently baptized AMICUS), the DOBIS database, with over 8 million bibliographic records and nearly 500,000 authority records, has served the needs of the Canadian library community admirably for the past twenty years. Users may choose to search the database in either English or French, and the online display and user dialogue are in the language of choice.

By means of a special built-in language equivalence relationship, equivalent French and English bibliographic or authority records may be linked online, thus enhancing retrieval. A subject heading search will retrieve records in both languages, and the linkage will lead the user to related records. For example, a search on the subject heading **JESUITS–CANADA–HISTORY** will retrieve records in both English and French.[7]

THE ACQUISITION AND CATALOGUING
OF CANADIANA PUBLISHED OUTSIDE CANADA

Canadians are often pleasantly surprised to discover that their country, its cultures, history, and institutions are the subject both of study by academics and of popular publications in other countries. Canadiana published outside Canada, particularly in languages other than English and French, are collected and catalogued by the National Library. Through a cooperative project with the International Council for Canadian Studies (ICCS), increased comprehensiveness has been achieved in recent years.

The NLC-ICCS project, which was initiated in 1988, has become a viable means of promoting the Canadian studies focus of the National Library's mandate. It entails gathering information, acquiring and cataloguing copies of Canadiana produced abroad, and transferring the books and bibliographic information to the National Library.

The ICCS librarian follows National Library of Canada cataloguing policies, rendering cataloguing in either English or French, according to the language of the publication. Titles in non-roman scripts are romanized or transliterated according to the accepted ISO or LC standard for the language. The content summaries and subject analysis are provided by language consultants. Eventually, all fully-catalogued titles are input into the DOBIS database.[8]

HERITAGE-LANGUAGE CATALOGUING
AT THE MULTILINGUAL BIBLIOSERVICE

The Multilingual Biblioservice (MBS) operates as a self-contained division within the Public Services Branch of the National Library of Canada. The MBS mandate is to provide the twelve provincial and territorial public library systems with books in the non-official, or heritage, languages spoken in Canada, not including aboriginal tongues. MBS was established in 1973 in response to the ever-growing needs of Canadian public libraries for materials in the languages of the one-third of the Canadian population of immigrant origins other than English and French.

It has been estimated that there are between eighty and one hundred non-aboriginal heritage languages spoken by Canadians. MBS currently provides materials in thirty-two of these: Arabic and Urdu, Chinese and Japanese, Vietnamese and Filipino (also known as Tagalog), Russian, Ukrainian, Polish, Slovak and Czech, Hungarian and Finnish, Estonian, Latvian and Lithuanian, German, Dutch, Danish, Swedish, Norwegian, and Icelandic, Welsh and Gaelic, Maltese, Greek, Italian, Spanish and Portuguese, Hindi, Gujarati and Panjabi. Ten languages of the thirty-two are written in non-roman scripts.

The mandate of MBS is to provide Canadian public libraries with browsing collections of leisure reading, predominantly fiction. Given the popular nature of the materials collected, MBS cataloguing policy reflects a mixture of internationally-accepted principles and pragmatism. In particular, the emphasis on full cataloguing and the provision of complete English and French records found in the NLC main collection on DOBIS are noticeably different in the more than 130,000 records on the MBS-MINISIS database.

Cataloguing in the Vernacular

The first principle of cataloguing at MBS is that materials in the MBS collection are catalogued in the vernacular, which means in the language and script of the publication. When MBS was established, this guideline was seen to be quite unusual as it went against the established practices of all academic, public, and special libraries, where a single integrated roman-script catalogue was deemed to be the only means to bibliographic control. Given that the purpose of MBS was to provide books in the language of the reader, accessible through the library catalogue, it follows, then, that the catalogue should also be in the language and script of the reader. Transliteration or other transcriptions into the roman script of bibliographic data often render the cataloguing unintelligible to the ordinary reader of the language and only somewhat useful to the librarian.

Thus, MBS was certainly among the first to apply ISBD(M) and the Anglo-American cataloguing rules regarding the language and script of description! Rule 1.0E1 of *AACR2*-1988 states that information be transcribed from the item itself in its own language and script (wherever practicable) in areas 1 (title and statement of responsibility), 2 (edition area), 4 (publication and distribution area), and 6 (series area) of the bibliographic record.

Transliteration and Romanization

There are many limitations inherent to transliteration and romanization schemes.[9] They are often "target-language-dependent," as they are based on the sounds of a particular language, most often English, into whose script the source information is being converted. In addition, there are many differing national transliteration tables, and attempts at encouraging the use of international tables have not been successful. Furthermore, it is often impossible to successfully convert from the transliteration back to the original script.

Despite all of these drawbacks, MBS transliterates (or romanizes) the main entry and title information for each book because this information may be useful to the librarian (who may not know the language) or may be used to create an entry in a roman-script catalogue (whether automated or manual). MBS provides this information in an "Author romanized" and/ or "Title romanized" note. In most Canadian libraries, transliteration or romanization is done according to the ALA/LC romanization tables, where they exist.[10] And, as is the prevalent practice in North America, MBS follows Wade-Giles romanization for Chinese and Hepburn for Japanese.

Level of Description

Minimal-level cataloguing is applied to the MBS collection for a variety of reasons. First of all, the nature of the material precludes the necessity of full cataloguing. Approximately 75 percent of the collection consists of fiction and children's books, which require only minimal-level description. Second, MBS hires language consultants on contract to catalogue the collections. They are hired primarily for their knowledge of the language and literature, not necessarily for their skills in librarianship. Third, collections include much material of current interest, so it is important to have the materials speedily catalogued, processed, and distributed to the provincial and territorial library systems rather than to have complete cataloguing and the resulting slower delivery. All in all, minimal-level cataloguing allows considerable bibliographic control to be exercised over a collection that does not warrant the high costs of full cataloguing.

In keeping with minimal-level descriptive cataloguing, authority work at MBS is also minimal. The rule-of-thumb is to transcribe an author main entry exactly as it appears in the chief source of information (or title page). In the unautomated past this practice worked fine, as the language consultant could compensate for inconsistencies in the fullness of the author's name by interfiling main entry cards. With the advent of automation at MBS, computer-generated indexes eliminated that kind of judgement. It has thus become necessary to standardize main entries for particular authors, depending on the number of variants in spelling and fullness of the names on the chief sources of information. Prior to automation, authority files had been established for some languages where it was deemed necessary, particularly Urdu and Arabic, where variants and additions to names always presented problems. In the same vein, at MBS non-western names are not force-fit to the rules and practices of western librarianship. For example, commas are not inserted in names that are naturally inverted (Vietnamese, Hungarian, Japanese, and Chinese) nor are non-inverted names inverted (Arabic, Urdu, and Panjabi).

Subject Access

Providing subject access to a multilingual collection presents several problems. Traditional Library of Congress subject headings may not offer specific enough headings to distinguish between parts of the collection, nor may they be accurate or current enough to describe book contents. As well, any cultural bias inherent in the headings may render them inappropriate for a multilingual, multicultural collection. A further issue is whether readers would use the subject catalogue if it were not in their language or, indeed, whether the libraries even use the same list of subject headings. MBS has opted to annotate all of its materials.

A brief content summary note or annotation gives the reader or the librarian the gist of the book, both as to its genre and its intellectual content. MBS provides these annotations in both English and French. A further refinement has been to develop a list of some 500 standard short annotations, such as "Short stories," "Novel of adventure," "Novel about the immigrant experience," and "Spy novel" that can be applied to the majority of fiction in the MBS collection. Children's books are not annotated unless they have significant subject content, such as "An illustrated Lithuanian-English dictionary."

As an improvement made possible by automation, the annotations are available directly in the book, on a 3 × 3 label that is glued to the book pocket. This gives both the reader and the librarian direct access to a summary of the content of the book, on the shelf as well as in the catalogue.

The usefulness of providing content summary notes for multilingual materials–or any library material for that matter–has grown since online systems now allow word-by-word access to the notes. The MBS automated system allows each and every word to be accessed, thereby allowing cross-language subject access to collections. It is also interesting to note that there has recently been a general movement in the library world to providing subject access to collections of fiction, as anticipated by the MBS short annotations for fiction.

Classification

In Canada, as in the United States, the Dewey Decimal Classification (DDC) is used most frequently by public libraries, whereas Library of Congress Classification is used in academic and special libraries. MBS classifies its subject-oriented materials using the 20th edition of DDC; but to accommodate the varying practices of public library systems, the classification number is truncated to a maximum of three places after the decimal point. Every call number is preceded by a three-character language code based on the *Canadian MARC Communication Format: Bibliographic Data* list of languages and language codes. Thus, the call number DAN 641.563 would be assigned to a Danish-language book on vegetarian cooking.

To Integrate or To Separate?

Prior to automation, MBS maintained separate shelflist, main entry, and title catalogues for each language. Alphabetical card catalogues followed the filing rules of the language in question: e.g., *ch* following *c* in Spanish, *ö* as *oe* in German. And a word of caution that only a native Welsh speaker was allowed to file Welsh!

Since automating its catalogue, MBS continues to maintain a separate shelflist for each language. Collections are shelved by language at MBS as they are in the deposit libraries. However, the burden of filing according to the rules of specific languages has been taken over by the computer.

Automation

Planning for the automation of the MBS catalogue was a challenge because the system of choice had to have the ability to maintain data in the extended roman script as well as in non-roman scripts.

After a survey of the alternative systems available on the market, MBS settled on MINISIS. In addition to being capable of managing data in the extended roman script as well as many non-roman scripts, MINISIS is an internationally available and supported Canadian system, is not expensive to acquire, is flexible, and supports MARC records. The MBS-MINISIS system is a pioneering effort in that it is a multilingual, multiscript application that supports all functions of the library from acquisitions through cataloguing to circulation. Records in the MBS-MINISIS database conform to the *Canadian MARC Communication Format: Minimal Level*.

Since mid-1990 MBS has implemented a graphical interface to MINI-

SIS using Microsoft Windows 3.0 that allows bibliographic records in the extended roman script, Arabic script, and Greek and Cyrillic alphabets to be entered and displayed online as well as printed via a laser printer. More recently, the character sets needed for Hindi and Panjabi have been developed and implemented.

CONCLUSION

The National Library of Canada has developed expertise in the provision of library services in both of Canada's official languages. Its bilingual cataloguing policy produces bibliographic records in English or French based on the language of publication and makes them available to libraries, whether in Canada or abroad, through its national database on DOBIS and through the MARC Records Distribution Service. Bilingual French and English authority records afford bilingual access to a major portion of titles in the DOBIS database without reference to the language of cataloguing. The National Library's main collections contain catalogued Canadiana in many languages from around the world, with English and French-language access points.

In addition, through the use of flexible cataloguing procedures in the vernacular at its Multilingual Biblioservice, the National Library serves the special needs of many readers throughout Canada with library materials in their heritage languages. Innovative subject access and a multilingual, multiscript automated database place this service in the vanguard of international cataloguing.

NOTES

1. These were among the issues raised by the Canadian Task Group on Cataloguing Standards in its report in 1972.

2. Canadian Task Group on Cataloguing Standards, *Cataloguing Standards* (Ottawa: National Library of Canada, 1972), 19.

3. The complete text of the National Library of Canada Bilingual Cataloguing Policy has been reproduced in: Lynne C. Howarth, *AACR2 Decisions and Rule Interpretations*, 5th ed. (Ottawa: Canadian Library Association, 1991).

4. For a thorough treatment of the subject, see: Wayne Jones and John Clark, "Bilingual Serials Cataloguing at the National Library of Canada," *The Serials Librarian* 12:1-2 (1987): 53-62.

5. *Canadian Subject Headings*, 3rd ed. (Ottawa: National Library of Canada, 1992).

6. Paule Rolland-Thomas and Gerard Mercure, "Subject Access in a Bilingual Online Catalogue," *Cataloging & Classification Quarterly* 10:1-2 (1989): 141-163.

7. Donna J. Dinberg, "DOBIS and the Canadian Union Catalogue," *Cataloging & Classification Quarterly* 8:3-4 (1988): 165-186.

8. *National Library News* 20:7-8 (1988): 11; 21:7-8 (1989): 6.

9. Hans Wellisch, "Bibliographic Access to Multilingual Collections," *Library Trends* 29:2 (1980): 223-244.

10. Cataloguers of multilingual collections welcomed two recent publications: *ALA-LC Romanization Tables* (Washington, D.C.: Library of Congress, 1991) and Sally Tseng, comp., *LC Romanization Tables and Cataloging Policies* (Metuchen, N.J.: Scarecrow Press, 1990).

SELECTED REFERENCES

Aliprand, Joan M. "Nonroman Scripts in the Bibliographic Environment." *Information Technology and Libraries* 11:2 (1992): 105-119.

Allen, Bryce. "Bilingual Catalogues: Challenges and Options." *Technicalities* 9:10 (1989): 12-15.

Aman, Mohammed M., ed. *Cataloguing and Classification of Non-Western Material: Concerns, Issues, and Practices.* Phoenix: Oryx, 1980.

Canadian Subject Headings. 3rd ed. Ottawa: National Library of Canada, 1992.

Canadian Task Group on Cataloguing Standards. *Cataloguing Standards.* Ottawa: National Library of Canada, 1972.

Delsey, Tom. "Retrospective Conversion in a Bilingual Context." *IFLA Journal* 16:1 (1990): 44-48.

Dinberg, Donna J. "DOBIS and the Canadian Union Catalogue." *Cataloging & Classification Quarterly* 8:3-4 (1988): 165-186.

Howarth, Lynne C. *AACR2 Decisions & Rule Interpretations.* 5th ed. Ottawa: Canadian Library Association, 1991.

International Federation of Library Associations and Institutions. *ISBD (M).* Rev. ed. London: IFLA Universal Bibliographic Control and International MARC Programme, 1987.

Jones, Wayne, and John Clark. "Bilingual Serials Cataloguing at the National Library of Canada." *The Serials Librarian* 12:1-2 (1987): 53-62.

Jover, Barbara. "The Review of the International Standard Bibliographic Descriptions (ISBDs) and Non-Roman Script Publications." In *Automated Systems for Access to Multilingual and Multiscript Materials: Problems and Solutions,* 205-212. München: K.G. Saur, 1987.

Piggott, Mary. *A Topography of Cataloguing: Showing the Most Important Landmarks, Communications and Perilous Places.* London: The Library Association, 1988.

Rolland-Thomas, Paule, and Gerard Mercure. "Subject Access in a Bilingual On-line Catalogue." *Cataloging & Classification Quarterly* 10:1-2 (1989): 141-163.

Slater, Ronald. "Authority Control in a Bilingual OPAC: MultiLIS at Laurentian University." *Library Resources and Technical Services* 35:4 (1991): 422-458.

Wellisch, Hans. "Bibliographic Access to Multilingual Collections." *Library Trends* 29:2 (1980): 223-244.

Zielinska, Marie F., ed. *Multicultural Librarianship: an International Handbook.* München: K.G. Saur, 1992.

Cataloging at the Bibliothèque Nationale

Nicole Simon
Monique Choudey

SUMMARY. The Bibliothèque Nationale acquires about 45,000 non-French documents in roman script annually; these are cataloged online in the BN-OPALE database. A MARC format, INTER-MARC, is used. Standards and format are consistent with international standards (ISBD, *AACR2*, UNIMARC) so that conversion and loading of records from a CD-ROM network and from RLIN can be done without difficulty. In 1995 the Bibliothèque Nationale will become the Bibliothèque de France, housing in a new building books, periodicals, and audiovisual and electronic materials; the old building will maintain all other items (manuscripts, maps, engravings, coins, printed music, and materials on the performing arts). Then another computerized system with new abilities will replace the present one; concerning cataloging, for example, there will be a project for linking bibliographic records to scanned summaries of books and to scanned documents.

RESUME. Il entre environ 45.000 documents étrangers à la Bibliothèque Nationale par an. Seuls ceux qui sont publiés en caractères latins sont catalogués dans la base BN-OPALE. Un format MARC, INTERMARC, est utilisé. Les normes et le format utilisés sont compatibles avec les normes internationales (ISBD, *AACR2*, UNIMARC), si bien que l'on peut sans difficulté faire la conversion et le

---

Nicole Simon is Head, Département des Entrées étrangères (Foreign Accessions Department), and Monique Choudey is Head, Département des Entrées étrangères, Service étranger (Foreign Division), Bibliothèque Nationale, 2 rue Vivienne, 75084, Paris, Cedex 02, France.

[Haworth co-indexing entry note]: "Cataloging at the Bibliothèque Nationale." Simon, Nicole, and Monique Choudey. Co-published simultaneously in *Cataloging & Classification Quarterly* (The Haworth Press, Inc.) Vol. 17. No. 1/2, 1993, pp. 233-256; and: *Languages of the World: Cataloging Issues and Problems* (ed: Martin D. Joachim) The Haworth Press, Inc., 1993, pp. 233-256. Multiple copies of this article/chapter may be purchased from The Haworth Document Delivery Center [1-800-3-HAWORTH; 9:00 a.m. - 5:00 p.m. (EST)].

233

déchargement de notices d'un réseau de CD-ROM et de RLIN. En 1995, la Bibliothèque Nationale deviendra la Bibliothèque de France, qui abritera dans un nouveau bâtiment les livres, les périodiques, les documents audiovisuels et électroniques; l'ancien bâtiment conservera les autres documents (manuscrits, cartes, estampes, monnaies, musique imprimée, arts du spectacle). Un autre système informatique, disposant de plus de possibilités, remplacera le système actuel; en ce qui concerne le catalogage, par exemple, il y a le project de lier des notices bibliographiques aux sommaires numérisés de livres ou à des documents numérisés.

As we began to write this article, we were astonished to find so few French references on the topic of cataloging of non-French language materials. It has been several years since an article on this topic has appeared in a French librarianship periodical. Cataloging, in fact, is often treated as a "poor relation" in these periodicals; none is especially dedicated to cataloging. The most important article on this subject was published in the *Bulletin des bibliothèques de France* in 1989, with the notable contribution of Isabelle Dussert-Carbone about the comparison between French cataloging standards and *AACR2*.[1] We also searched in the PASCAL database with French videotex Minitel and found 442 references with the term *cataloging*; only twenty-three were from French periodicals, primarily from two: the *Bulletin des bibliothèques de France* and the *Bulletin d'information de l'Association des bibliothécaires français*. It is a paradox for the country that was host to the Paris Conference (or, to be more precise, the International Conference on Cataloguing Principles, in 1961),[2] whose principles have led to *AACR*, ISBD, and many national cataloging codes, to have produced so little on the topic of cataloging.

In this article we shall explain the practices of the Bibliothèque Nationale (BN) in the cataloging of non-French materials. We shall see that we are not so far from the dream of the principles of the Paris Conference. The idea of a unique international cataloging code may be utopian, but the national and international sharing of cataloguing data on a large scale is, in fact, already taking place.

For a better understanding of our paper, however, we must first review what is now the Bibliothèque Nationale, its objectives, its acquisitions (and, above all, its non-French acquistions), and its computerized systems. One must also bear in mind that the Bibliothèque Nationale will be fundamentally modified in 1995. Then it will be split into two locations: the Bibliothèque de France, in the Southeast of Paris, will maintain the printed books, periodicals, and audio-visual collections and will be more encyclopedic than the actual BN; and the old building of the Bibliothèque Nationale, in the same place, will house the specialized departments of the BN and some Parisian art libraries.

THE BIBLIOTHEQUE NATIONALE

Following are some important dates and figures about the Bibliothèque Nationale:

Dates

- 1368: King Charles V assembles about 1000 manuscripts of his library in a tower of the Louvre Palais.
- 1537: Legal deposit of printed documents founded by King François I.
- 1692: First attempt to open the library to the public (scholars only).
- 1789-1799: Confiscations made during the Revolution bring the number of documents held by the Bibliothèque de la Nation (the Nation's Library) to over 300,000.
- 1868: Main Reading Room built by Henri Labrouste for printed books is opened.
- 1981: Publication of volume 231, the last volume of the *Catalogue général des livres imprimés de la Bibliothèque Nationale*, which was begun in 1897.
- 1988: Cataloging online in BN-OPALE done for the first time.
- 1988: French President François Mitterand announces that the Bibliothèque de France will be built.

Figures

In addition to administrative and technical services, the Bibliothèque Nationale is divided into ten departments for conservation and providing access to the collections:

- Printed books: 12,000,000 items
- Periodicals: 350,000 titles dead and alive
- Maps and plans: 650,000 items
- Engravings and photographs: 15,000,000 items
- Manuscripts: 350,000 items
- Coins, medals: 300,000 items
- Printed music: 1,500,000 items
- Sound archives and audio-visual documents: 1,100,000 items
- Performing arts: 3,000,000 items
- The Arsenal Library: more than 1,000,000 documents (manuscripts, printed materials, etc.)

Annual Accessions

The following data are extracted from the 1990 annual report of the library; updates are indicated in parentheses:

Legal deposit (for all items published in France)

- Books: 44,636 (1991)
- Official publications: 34,647 (1991)
- Periodicals: 32,000 titles (1991)
- Maps: 2241
- Engravings and photographs: 44,771
- Coins and medals: 2502
- Recordings: 24,500

Purchase, gift, exchange

- Books: 45,000 (1991)
- Periodicals: 8000 titles (1991)
- Manuscripts: 2486
- Engravings: 7342
- Maps: 1683
- Coins and medals: 1182
- Printed music: 2309
- Sound archives: 4511
- Performing arts: 18,044
- The Arsenal Library: 578

Reader services

- 400,000 readers
- 1,250,000 documents consulted in 16 reading rooms

Staff

- 1245, of whom 42.5% are library professionals; others are clerical and support staff, skilled workmen (photographers, restorers, etc.)

NON-FRENCH ACCESSIONS
OF THE PRINTED BOOKS AND PERIODICALS DIVISIONS

The Bibliothèque du Roi (Royal Library) was eager to acquire and purchase non-French books and documents as early as the seventeenth century. Nicolas Clément, Keeper of the Library from 1691 to 1712, wanted "to establish correspondents in all places where printing is the most widespread" and asked d'Avaux and d'Alancé to buy books in the Netherlands, d'Obeil and Hans Sloane in England, and de la Piquetière in Sweden. In the eighteenth century, under Father Louvois, duplicate copies of engravings in the library were exchanged for books from the famous bookseller, Leers, in Rotterdam.

At this time and until the beginning of the twentieth century, assembling a universal collection of human knowledge was the library's goal. Because of the enormous increase in the quantity of printed materials and ongoing budget problems, however, the collection policy has been limited to acquiring academic and learned materials in the human sciences (philosophy, theology, sociology, ethnology, linguistics, philology, art, literature, history, human geography, history of law, history of sciences, psychology, and economic and social sciences). Also acquired are all materials dealing with France and its place in the world as well as materials about French-speaking communities. This is the present collections policy of the Bibliothèque Nationale.[3] With the establishment of the Bibliothèque de France in 1995, the library will once again be encyclopedic in its acquisitions.

Documents, books, periodicals, microforms, and CD-ROMs come from almost all nations in the world (111 countries in 1991, in about sixty languages, among them many in non-roman scripts). They are acquired and processed in the Département des Entrées étrangères (Foreign Accessions Department) for the Printed Books and Periodicals Divisions. (It is not our purpose in this paper to discuss acquisitions in the other specialized departments of the Bibliothèque Nationale). The Foreign Accessions Department is divided into four sections, together employing ninety-five staff, most of whom are library personnel (forty-four senior and thirty-four assistant librarians). Two sections, the Purchasing Division and the Gift Division, are responsible for acquisitions; one section, the Foreign Division, catalogs documents in western languages; and another, the Slavic and Oriental Division, has the integrated responsibility for acquiring and cataloging documents.

COMPUTERIZATION IN THE BIBLIOTHEQUE NATIONALE

The computerization of library functions in the Bibliothèque Nationale began in 1981. An Automation and Organization Division was created in July 1982 and now employs about thirty staff. Automated functions (cataloging and OPAC at the present time and acquisitions and the loading of records soon) are carried out with in-house hardware. There are two databases with online public access: BN-OPALE and BN-OPALINE; a third, BN-SYCOMORE, is used for circulation control.

The Hardware

Two GEAC 9000s: BN1 is dedicated to legal deposit management and to the processing of books, periodicals, and microfilms in the BN-OPALE database:

- 7 processors, 32 megabytes central memory
- 14 gigabytes for data storage (16 disks)
- 400 terminals

BN2 is dedicated to online public access of the BN-OPALE database:

- 3 processors, 12 megabytes central memory
- 10 gigabytes for data storage
- 30 terminals

The Ethernet network links all the workstations to both GEAC systems. One BULL 7000-705 is dedicated to the processing of specialized documents (maps, music, engravings, sound archives, etc.) in the BN-OPALINE database and to management functions and will soon be used for automated acquisitions:

- 2 processors, 64 megabytes central memory
- 22 gigabytes for data storage on disks
- 150 terminals
- monitor GC OS 7
- DSA network
- database IDS2

Each computerized system, GEAC and BULL, can be reached via TRANSPAC.

One HP 9000/832S is dedicated to circulation control and also to inventory control in the Printed Books and Periodicals Divisions; this database is called BN-SYCOMORE:

- single processor under UNIX
- 24 megabytes central memory
- 2.6 gigabytes for data storage on disks
- 98 terminals, 36 printers, 57 notebooks Portfolio/Atari

- 8 front-hand machines for driving terminals, each one with 16 Mb for central memory and one with 300 megabytes for data storage on disks
- relational and Client/Server architecture Sybase

One NOVELL network, version 3.11, at the present time has two Meridian Data CD314, storage capacity 14 disks each. The access server software is supplied by the German company Holthaus+Heinisch. About 40 workstations are connected, using the BN Ethernet network. The network stores CD-ROMS of national and specialized bibliographies and library catalogs, which are used primarily by the acquisitions system and reader services.

BN-OPALINE AND BN-SYCOMORE DATABASES

Since they do not fit the topic of this paper, we shall add only a few words about the BN-OPALINE and BN-SYCOMORE databases.

BN-OPALINE[4] is the multimedia bibliographic database of the Bibliothèque Nationale, operational since 1987. It includes four subsets: maps and plans, engravings and photographs, sound archives, and printed music. It has the following functions: authority files, legal deposit management, automated shelf numbering, shared cataloging, multilevel description, series management, piece-analytic records, window ability for creating authorities during a cataloging session, subject headings RAMEAU management, keyword searching, and OPAC. BN-OPALINE was developed in house by the Automation Division of the Bibliothèque Nationale and now includes 220,000 bibliographic records and 170,000 authority records with about 1,000,000 access points indexed.[5]

BN-SYCOMORE[6] was born in 1991. The software was developed by ALCATEL-TITN Answare. The aims are, on the one hand, the management of inventory control of all the books and periodicals (about 12,000,000 items) before moving to the new building in 1995, and, on the other hand, the automation of circulation control. Only shelf numbers are automated in BN-SYCOMORE. Links will be made with the holdings statements of all the records of the computerized BN catalogs and with the ongoing retrospective conversion of the catalogs prior to 1969.[7]

BN-OPALE

BN-OPALE is the most important BN bibliographic database, implemented with the library GEAC systems. The automated cataloging system was developed specifically for the Bibliothèque Nationale and is a little different from the software package (GEAC BPS, developed after BN-OP-ALE). A notable difference with the GEAC software package is the automated legal deposit system linked to the cataloging system and specific to BN-OPALE. It is the common database for all printed materials, both French and non-French.

BN-OPALE is organized in three files:

- bibliographic file for monograph and series records
- location file with document holdings
- authority file, unique as far as computerization is concerned, including four separate subsets: personal authors, corporate names, uniform titles, and a subject file with proper names and common names.

Cataloging online in BN-OPALE began in 1985 for authority records and in January 1988 for bibliographic records. As of January 20, 1993, the database included 1,420,234 bibliographic records and 829,539 authority records (552,424 personal authors, 129,192 corporate authors, 144,714 subject headings, and 3209 uniform titles). The database increases by 110,000 bibliographic records and 55,000 authority records annually. About 400 staff work online in the database.

Recently fourteen academic libraries began to share this database to create records for loading into their local systems. For non-French documents they create or locate records according to whether or not they find records in BN-OPALE; for French documents they need only to locate records in BN-OPALE since the French database is complete for French records.

BIBLIOGRAPHIC PRODUCTS OF BN DATABASES

The *Bibliographie nationale française (French National Bibliography)* is one of the most important products of the Bibliothèque Nationale. It collects and describes French production resulting from legal deposit. It was first published in 1811 and is now published in two forms:

- *Printed:* the book part, published twice a month, about 33,000 records in 1991. Includes four specialized publications: series (about 7000 records), government publications (about 3000 records), music (about 1200 records), maps and plans (about 200 records)
- *CD-ROM:* for books and serials since 1970, quarterly, 650,000 records.[8]

The *Liste des acquisitions de la Bibliothèque Nationale: ouvrages entrés par achat, don, échange (Accessions List of the Bibliothèque Nationale)* has been monthly since 1984 and succeeds a similar publication, published from 1874 to 1951.

Authority files are issued in two forms: the microfiche includes corporate names (60,000 records) and personal names and uniform titles (150,000 and 1500 records, respectively). The subject heading file is published in *RAMEAU*, the national authority for subject headings. All BN authority files will be available on CD-ROM in 1994.

THE NATIONAL BIBLIOGRAPHIC UTILITY (SBN)

The National Bibliographic Utility (Serveur bibliographique national, SBN) has been operational since January 1992. Via a QUESTEL host, BN-OPALE and BN-OPALINE bibliographic records can be loaded into local systems. SBN is jointly owned by the Bibliothèque Nationale and the Ministry of Culture. The goals of the utility are to reduce original cataloging in French libraries and to offer authority records. Component parts of the database are BN-OPALE (for French and non-French books and serials) and BN-OPALINE (for audiovisual archives). About thirty access points are available. Libraries can order records online, which are loaded overnight onto a magnetic support, online by electronic transfer, or on hard copy. Costs are three francs for a monograph record and five francs for an audiovisual record. Telecommunications charges are 170 francs per hour and 35 francs for TRANSPAC, by which libraries are connected to BN-OPALE. Before the end of 1993 a new important step will take place with access via the French videotex MINITEL. Thus anyone will be able to consult BN databases from remote locations.[9]

CATALOGING NON-FRENCH DOCUMENTS IN BN-OPALE

Loading of records from external databases into BN-OPALE began in 1993 and is linked to the implementation of an automated acquisitions system. Until now the library has done only original cataloging. There are two levels of original cataloging: full level and less than full level records depending on the type of document. The INTERMARC format is used. Non-French publications receive middle level cataloging.

For publications in non-roman characters, two different practices coexist. For books and periodicals acquired by legal deposit, records are transliterated according to ISO and input into the *Bibliographie nationale française* and BN-OPALE. If ISO standards do not yet exist for particular languages (for example, Korean), then the library applies transliteration systems used in France. On the other hand, books acquired by purchase, gift, or exchange are still cataloged manually on cards in the original script. Although this may seem illogical, we explain it in terms of the recent date of BN automation. Specialists hope for a cataloging system that will allow for the input of original characters. Aware of the benefits of the Chinese-Japanese-Korean (CJK) system, they have opposed inputting of records in transliteration. We agree entirely, knowing well the Tower of Babel that can result from works in transliteration only. We await the solution from the future Bibliothèque de France automation system.

In the Foreign Accessions Department, there are specialists in the majority of the most important languages. When a permanent specialist is lacking, we temporarily hire an expert with needed language expertise to assist in cataloging.

Standards and Rules and the CCBT

Different from *AACR2*, the French cataloging rules are published in different fascicules, each with a topic: either a part of the record (e.g., bibliographic description, access points) or a type of document (e.g., monographs, serials, maps). At regular intervals AFNOR (Association française de normalisation) publishes a compilation of these fascicules.[10] These standards are elaborated by committees of experts from various types of libraries working as part of AFNOR. They follow ISBD and take into account such widely used codes as *AACR2*.[11]

In 1987 an important change in cataloging procedures occurred in the Bibliothèque Nationale. Multilevel description of multipart monographs was ceased.[12] As is now possible in the revised French standard for bibliographic description of monographs (AFNOR Z 44050), a publication is either described independently with the common title in the series area, or multiple parts are itemized in the contents area. The implementation of this policy brings the Bibliothèque Nationale a step closer to conformity with *AACR2*.

Another useful implementation for BN catalogers is the *Guide to Cataloging* issued by the CCBT (Centre de coordination bibliographique et technique) with the collaboration of the best experts of the BN. The CCBT has multiple roles: coherence of the authority files, elaboration of guidelines for catalogers, participation in standards committees (AFNOR, ISO), and administration of the data files. The purpose of the *Guide to Cataloging* is to help catalogers in applying standards, to solve problems not previously encountered, and, above all, to link standards and format; it uses the fields and subfields of the INTERMARC format.[13]

There are as many INTERMARC formats as there are types of documents and/or records. INTERMARC (A) is used for authorities, (M) for monographs, (S) for serials, (MUS) for printed music, (C) for maps, (IM) for fixed images, and (AV) for audiovisual materials. A document for coins and medals is being prepared. CCBT has begun to merge all these INTERMARC formats into one unique INTERMARC as is the case with USMARC.[14] All external electronic products of BN-OPALE and BN-OPALINE, however, are in UNIMARC format for ease of loading records in France as well as abroad.

Cataloging in Middle or Minimal Level

As in *AACR2*, there exists in French standards provisions for doing abridged cataloging. Generally, there are complete bibliographic descriptions for all French documents received in the library from legal deposit. It is clear that the Bibliothèque Nationale has a responsibility to provide full cataloging for French documents for the national and international needs of libraries wishing to load French records. Old documents (before 1800) are currently cataloged with extensive description, following the French standard, which has adapted the ISBD(A).[15]

For non-French books, however, the mission of BN is not the same. The middle level cataloging rule (AFNOR Z 44073), equivalent to *AACR2* second level, is used. This standard is now commonly used in academic and public libraries in France for creating records when they are not available for loading from various databases (e.g., BN-OPALE, BN-OPA-LINE, OCLC, SIBIL). Non-French serials are also input with an abridged format. Minimal level cataloging (third level in *AACR2*) is less frequently used in current cataloging–only for the mass cataloging of important gifts.

Headings and Authority Files

All cataloging services at BN add to the same authority files during online cataloging. The decision-making process for establishing French and non-French headings is the same. Because of the increasing number of records to be created, however, the library cannot afford to create complete authority records in all circumstances. In order to save time and cost of staff employed in cataloging, CCBT and cataloging services have mutually agreed which fields to include in records for non-French headings.[16]

Personal and Corporate Authors

For non-French books complete authority records are not created for new authors. The BN GEAC system automatically creates headings from the 100 or 110 fields. Full authority records, however, are created if the library receives books in French by the same authors. Exceptions are made, on the other hand, for complex names. For compound surnames (e.g., most Spanish names), full records are always created with related terms. For names from countries with non-roman scripts, books are sent to language specialists, who transliterate headings, if necessary, and create full authority records. Authority records are also created in the case of names that have the appearance of being based on non-roman languages– for example, an author with an apparently Chinese name who is in fact French or English. Full records are also always done for non-unique names; catalogers must link all records in the database to authority records for non-unique headings.

Subject Headings

The subject headings list used at BN since 1980 is *RAMEAU (Répertoire d'autorité de matières encyclopédique et alphabétique unifié)*. This list has been developed by the Bibliothèque Nationale. Its main source is the subject authority file of Laval University, which derived and translated the list from *Library of Congress Subject Headings (LCSH)*. It was adopted in 1987 as the national subject authority file and is now managed by a committee of the Ministry of Universities. Since 1990 an agreement between Laval University and the Bibliothèque Nationale and Ministry of Universities provides for establishing cooperation and exchange of all newly created authority records. Most of the records created in *RAMEAU* come from the BN subject authority file, but many academic libraries are also creating records in *RAMEAU* for works in fields in which the Bibliothèque Nationale does not acquire large numbers of titles (principally in law and scientific and technical fields). All external creations are submitted to national committee experts.[17]

The structure of *RAMEAU* is similar to *LCSH*. The similarity of these two subject lists makes it easier for catalogers to handle books from the United States. Librarians and patrons used to both *RAMEAU* and *LCSH* will find familiar search structures in both. The same kinds of criticisms that can be applied to *LCSH* can, of course, also be applied to *RAMEAU*: complex, not always up-to-date, and difficult and time-consuming to learn. It is, however, important to have a national subject authority file which is a variant of a list whose use is as widespread as *LCSH* and which provides similarly well controlled subject access for users in most French libraries. Subject access will be improved when we have keyword and Boolean searching. Patrons are today demanding more efficient subject access. We are hoping for solutions with the future Bibliothèque de France information systems.

Classification

The Bibliothèque Nationale does not provide Dewey classification numbers in its records. This is a significant deficiency since Dewey is generally used in all public libraries and many academic ones. This inadequacy will be resolved with the Bibliothèque de France project. An abridged UDC number (three positions) is input into the 008 field for the needs of printed bibliographic products.

There are two special classifications used in the Bibliothèque Nationale. One is applied to books on the history of France. It was developed from the old BN shelf number system, created in the seventeenth century by Nicolas Clément, librarian of the Royal Library (Bibliothèque du Roi). This shelf number system, based upon a subject classification and represented by the letters of the alphabet (from A, Holy Writ, to Z, mixed subjects), is still used in the Bibliothèque Nationale for assigning call numbers to documents. It cannot, however, be termed a classification such as the Library of Congress system. Except for the letter concerning the history of France (L for King Louis XIV!), the Histoire de France classification was developped in the mid-nineteenth century and includes 914 subdivisions. At present about 775,000 documents have been indexed with this system. With automation it was revised. It presently includes 480 subdivisions, and new ones are created according to need (Figures 1 and 2).

The second classification is more recent and was created by the Periodicals Department in 1989 for indexing serials. It is called *PIRANAS (Procédé d'indexation de recherche alphabétique et numérique appliqué aux séries)* and is based upon UDC classification. *PIRANAS* replaced *RAMEAU*, which was used from 1983 to 1987 for indexing serials. *RAMEAU*, however, was judged not to be adequate for the indexing of most serials, especially for the many legal deposit French serials dealing with politics and associations.

Summary

Even with abridged bibliographic description and some simplification in the creation of name authorities, as explained above, the cataloging of

FIGURE 1. Extract of the History of France classification

LG <u>HISTOIRE DES RELATIONS EXTERIEURES DE LA FRANCE</u>

$a	LG 100	Diplomatie française : généralités $x mémoires diplomatiques généraux recueils généraux de traités
	LG 200	Diplomatie française par époque
	LG 210	Des origines à 1870 $z *chronologie*
	LG 220	De 1871 à 1944 $z *chronologie*
	LG 230	Depuis 1945 $z *chronologie*
	LG 300	Relations extérieures par pays $y *nom du pays* $z *chronologie*
	LG 400	La France dans l'Europe $z *chronologie* $x construction de l'Europe institutions européennes en France élections européennes

non-French books is always expensive and time-consuming. We continue to search for ways in which to save time. First is a reorganization of the most important cataloging services, now complete (see discussion below). The other, the loading of records from different databases, was implemented this year.

WHOLE BOOK CATALOGING IN THE FOREIGN SERVICE

The Service étranger (Foreign Service) in the Foreign Books Division is in charge of cataloging books in western languages. Until 1990 it was divided into two sections: one for descriptive cataloging (25 staff) with language subdivisions and the other for subject cataloging (10 staff) with subdivision by subject and language. It was an organization with an assembly line approach.

In 1991 the library decided the time was right to reorganize and introduce whole book cataloging. We had principally two aims: to reduce the steps in the cataloging process in order to offer improved service to

FIGURE 2. INTERMARC record with subject headings (600) and History of France
classification (681)

```
FC : RCN 00614732 MON                    DEGRE 2 SECTION:BIBSE
GUIDE : ETAT : n VALEUR: STATUTS   :  0am AUTR. CODES:
001 [      ] frBN006147320
008 [      ] 881021s1988    us   5 6          enga   1 01 93

015 [     ]  $a58903398
020 [     ]  $a 0-87169-180-9
100 [00416765] < $w.0..b.....$a Hill $m Peter P. >
245 [     ] 1  $a French perceptions of the early American Republic 1783-1793 $f Peter P. Hill
260 [     ]  $a Philadelphia $c American philosophical society $d 1988
280 [     ]  $a XV-196 p. $d 26 cm
295 [00461092] 1 $a Memoirs of the American philosophical society $x 0065-9738 $v 180
300 [     ]  $a Bibliogr. p. 179-189. Index
410 [00461092] < $x 0065-9738 > $v 180
600 [     ] 7 [00152026] < $a Etats-Unis > [00212602] < $x Commerce extérieur
             > [0152147] < $y France > [00343580] < $x Histoire $z + * 1700......- 1799...... + :18e siècle: >
600 [     ] 7 [00152147] < $a France > [00212602] < $x Commerce extérieur > [00152026]
             < $y Etats-Unis > [00343580] < $x Histoire $z + * 1700......- 1799...... + :18e siècle: >
600 [     ] 7 [00177386] < $a Etats-Unis $x Histoire $z + * 1783......- 1815...... + :1783-1815: > [00413619]
             < $x Opinion publique française >

Données locales
001 [      ] frBN006147320

036 [     ]  $a Acq. 88-11238
090 [     ]  $cBN$dImpr.$a4-R-8149 (180)
681 [     ]  $aLG 300$y Etats-Unis $z 1783-1793
681 [     ]  $aLG 210$z 1783-1793
681 [     ]  $aLA 410
```

readers and to create more interesting work for staff and allow them to
attain a higher qualification level. The time was also right for other reasons. After three years of cataloging online, the staff was well trained;
descriptive cataloging alone was beginning to be tedious and repetitive for
a well educated staff with good language expertise. The plans for the new
Bibliothèque de France, which will be organized in thematic departments,
have provided the impetus for reorganization.

We were able to hire a pilot team of eight staff to do integrated cataloging for what has become the Bibliothèque de France project. During
the period from January 1991 to June 1992, twenty-eight persons acquired subject cataloging training. The basic training period given by
CCBT is twenty-five hours for subject cataloging and thirty-four hours
for descriptive. Each subject cataloger of the Foreign Service then reviews the work of two or three new staff; the review process lasts for a
year.

We believe that this experiment has been successful. Newly trained
staff are able to process most of the books; difficult problems are passed

on to the subject cataloging instructors, who continue to do subject cataloging for 60 percent of new receipts. Staff have appreciated being able to attain a higher qualification level and are more cohesive in the work they do. From the quantitative standpoint, productivity, as expected, fell at first–about 5 percent in 1991. Productivity rose again in 1992.

TOWARD NEW CHANGES: LOADING RECORDS FROM FOREIGN DATABASES

We anticipate considerable increase in productivity and efficiency with the loading of records from foreign databases, which we have begun in 1993. It is obvious that efficiency is improved by using available cataloging, but only this year has the Bibliothèque Nationale begun to take advantage of it. There are many reasons for the delay. Automation at BN is recent, and the library's first priority has been to catalog French materials and to manage the legal deposit and, by so doing, provide original cataloging of these materials for the national and international library communities. For a long time, also, the number of non-French acquisitions was not so high; and, likewise, funds for buying books and periodicals were low. In 1991, however, the library acquired two times more foreign materials than it had the year before without adequate staff for processing these documents.[18] These increased acquisitions were also a powerful impetus for the Bibliothèque de France project.

We decided in 1990 to implement an acquisitions system coupled with a system for loading records from other databases. During a planning phase, the Automation Division has done systems analysis for establishing the needs of the Acquisitions, Gift, and Foreign Services. As it was difficult to link the GEAC acquisitions system in our specific software (we already had an acquisitions system with the legal deposit management), it was decided that the design and implementation of the system would be done in house by the Automation Division with our other mainframe, BULL, and with in-house software, BN-OPALINE.

As records sources we have chosen CD-ROMs and RLIN as an online database. CD-ROMs allow a quasi-exhaustive records source for a country's production. They are not too expensive and, of course, there is no telecommunication cost. They are mounted in a CD network NOVELL with mainframe from Meridian Data (two CD314s) and specific software from the German company Holthaus+Heinisch. Mounted CD-ROMS are at readers' and staff's disposal with about forty workstations already linked. Some impediments, however, have limited the number of CD-

ROMs used as records sources. First we must do format conversions for each database. It is a long and expensive process and difficult for some databases that do not use the 2709 standard and, above all, for those that do not have a MARC structure.

Cataloging rules can also be a problem–for example, the multilevel description of the *German National Bibliography*. There are also terms and conditions for database use with, as the case may be, fees that must be paid for networks, tranfer, or use. Given all these parameters and also the results of match tests, we chose Library of Congress CD-MARC and the *Deutsche Nationalbibliographie* CD-ROM, both affording good coverage for the most important part of our foreign acquisitions (books coming from the USA, Canada, and Great Britain represent 26 percent of our acquisitions; from Germany, 18 percent). Our agreement with RLG will allow for online record transfer.

As can be seen in Figure 3, records are processed on workstations inside the NOVELL network. Files are constituted on a PC from the loaded record and converted from the original formats into two records: one in order format for the acquisitions process and the other in INTER-MARC format for addition to the BN-OPALE database for eventual processing by catalogers (Figure 4).

FIGURE 3. CD-ROM Network Structure

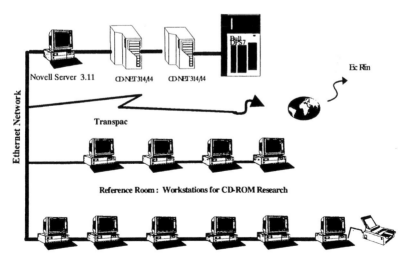

Foreign Accessions Department: Workstations for Unloading Records from CD-ROM and Online Databases

FIGURE 4. Workflow of records from acquisition system to cataloging system

```
┌─────────────────┐   ┌─────────────────┐   ┌─────────────────┐
│  CD-ROM server  │   │     On line     │   │     others      │
│                 │   │  Bibliographic  │   │  (booktrades...)│
│                 │   │    databases    │   │                 │
└─────────────────┘   └─────────────────┘   └─────────────────┘
```

```
              ┌─────────────────────────┐
              │       workstation       │
              │ ----------------------- │
              │    exporting records    │
              │     (retrieving and     │
              │        loading)         │
              │  (Marc or other formats)│
              └─────────────────────────┘
```

```
┌──────────────┐   ┌──────────────┐
│  workstation │   │    server    │
│ ------------ │   │ ------------ │
│    order     │   │    order     │
│    record    │   │    format    │
│   created    │   │  conversion  │
└──────────────┘   └──────────────┘
```

```
                   ┌──────────────┐          ┌──────────────┐
                   │     Bull     │          │     Bull     │
                   │ ------------ │          │ ------------ │
                   │    order     │          │  INTERMARC   │
                   │  management  │          │ full format  │
                   │              │          │  conversion  │
                   └──────────────┘          └──────────────┘
                 document delivery
```

```
                   ┌──────────────┐          ┌──────────────┐
                   │     Bull     │          │  workstation │
                   │ ------------ │  (OR)    │ ------------ │
                   │ Order record │          │  acquisition │
                   │   become     │          │    number    │
                   │  INTERMARC   │          │    added     │
                   │    record    │          │              │
                   └──────────────┘          └──────────────┘
```

```
                   ┌──────────────┐
                   │     Bull     │
                   │ ------------ │
                   │  BN-OPALINE  │
                   │     file     │
                   └──────────────┘
```

```
                   ┌──────────────┐
                   │     Geac     │
                   │ ------------ │
                   │   BN-OPALE   │
                   └──────────────┘
```

```
┌──────────────┐   ┌──────────────┐   ┌──────────────────┐
│     SBN      │   │     OPAC     │   │ printed products │
└──────────────┘   └──────────────┘   └──────────────────┘
```

Figures 5 to 7 show a US-MARC record and its INTERMARC conversions. It is clear that catalogers will save time in the descriptive analysis, which is nearly the same in both formats. Since headings structure is similar, work with access points will be easier even though catalogers will face the time-consuming task of creating authority records for personal and corporate names, series, and subjects (Figures 8 to 12). It is our hope that international authority files will soon be available, thus fulfilling our dream of diminishing cataloging tasks.[19]

THE BIBLIOTHEQUE DE FRANCE INFORMATION SYSTEM

As we write this paper, work continues on the future Bibliothèque de France information system. It will be an integrated system unlike the

FIGURE 5. Exported US-Marc record (on the workstation)

```
Leader00749cam 2200217 a 4500
001  $a  83000984 //r892
005  $a19890530000000.0
008  $a830118s1983   nyu    b   s00010 eng
020  $a0866980628
043  $ae-it---
050 0 $aB3279.H49$bG677 1983
082 0 $a190$219
100 10$aGrassi, Ernesto.
245 10$aHeidegger and the question of Renaissance humanism :$bfour studies /$cby Ernesto Grassi.
260 0 $aBinghamton, N.Y. :$bCenter for Medieval & Early Renaissance Studies,$c1983.
300  $a103 p. ;$c23 cm.
440 0$aMedieval & Renaissance texts & studies ;$vv. 24
504  $aIncludes bibliographical references.
600 10$aHeidegger, Martin,$d1889-1976.
650 0$aRenaissance$zItaly.
650 0$aHumanism$xHistory.
```

FIGURE 6. INTERMARC converted record (on the workstation)

```
Leader $a *****n6am    1
019    $a US  $b LC  $c  83000984
008    $a     s1983   us  5        enga
676 0  $a 190 $v 19e (éd. complète)
100    $a Grassi  $m Ernesto
245 1  $a Heidegger and the question of Renaissance humanism $r : four studies / by Ernesto Grassi
260    $a Binghamton, N.Y.  $c Center for Medieval & Early Renaissance Studies  $d 1983
280    $a 103 p.  $d 23 cm
295 1  $a Medieval & Renaissance texts & studies  $v v. 24
300    $a Includes bibliographical references
620 0  $a Heidegger, Martin, 1889-1976
620 6  $a Renaissance -- Italy
620 6  $a Humanism -- History
```

FIGURE 7. INTERMARC original cataloging record (BN-OPALE)

```
FC : RCN 01427360 MON [LOC]              DEGRE 2 SECTION:BIBSE
GUIDE : ETAT : n VALEUR: 1 STATUTS : 0am AUTR. CODES:
001 [    ] frBN014273607
008 [    ] 920616s1983  us 5 6        enga 1 01 1
015 [    ] $a59215099
100 [00326056]  <$w 0  b   $a Grassi $m Ernesto>
245 [    ] 1 $a Heidegger and the question of Renaissance humanism $e
           four studies $f by Ernesto Grassi
260 [    ] $a Binghamton (N.Y.) $c Center for Medieval and early
           Renaissance studies $d 1983
280 [    ] $a 103 p. $d 22 cm
295 [00342040] 1 $a Medieval and Renaissance texts and studies $v 24
410 [00342040] $v 24
600 [    ] 0 [00158410]<$a Heidegger $m Martin $d 1889-1976>[00449127]<$x
           Attitude envers l'humanisme>
600 [    ] 6 [00161358]<$a Philosophie de la Renaissance>[00212053]<$x
           Influence>
600 [    ] 6 [00169675]<$a Humanisme>[00152982]<$y Italie>[00212053]<$x
           Influence>
```

FIGURE 8. INTERMARC series record (BN-OPALE)

```
FC : RCN 00342040 COL [LOC]              DEGRE 2 SECTION:BIBSE
GUIDE : ETAT : c VALEUR: 1 STATUTS : 1as AUTR. CODES:
001 [    ] frBN003420408
008 [    ] 840630c1981  us  6          enga   820   ?xxm

015 [    ] $a58419617
019 [    ] $aFR$bMCP5$c58419617
110 [00029365]  <$w.0..b.....$aCenter for medieval and early Renaissance
           studies $c Binghamton, N.Y.>
245 [    ] 1 $a Medieval and Renaissance texts and studies $f Center for
           Medieval and early Renaissance studies
255 [    ] $a 1
260 [    ] $a Binghamton (N.Y.) $c Center for Medieval and early
           Renaissance studies $d 1981 -
280 [    ] $d 23 cm
326 [    ] $a Collection
745 [    ] 24$a MRTS
```

present system at the Bibliothèque Nationale. As can be seen in what we have written, the implementation of automation in the library has given priority to a traditional cataloging system with traditional printed materials (books and periodicals) and, above all, for French documents of legal deposit. Providing this cataloging access is the primary mission of the Bibliothèque Nationale. Because of this goal and the inadequacies of our specific GEAC system, other automated systems and databases have been built with the BULL mainframe and BN-OPALINE database for cataloging specialized documents, for acquisitions management, and for loading

FIGURE 9. Personal name INTERMARC authority record (BN-OPALE)

```
FC  : RCN 00326056 APP                    DEGRE 1 SECTION:AUTAPP
GUIDE : ETAT  : c VALEUR: 2 STATUTS  : 0 a AUTR. CODES : p
001 [      ] frBN003260569
008 [      ] 860101920107xxeng        19020502 19911222

017 [      ] BDF.001621056
100 [      ] $w 0  b   $a Grassi $m Ernesto
400 [      ] $w    b   $a Grassi $m Ernest
600 [      ] $a Ecrit aussi en allemand et en italien
600 [      ] $a Philosophe $a Fondateur à Munich du Centre italien
             d'études humanistes et philosophiques, professeur aux
             Etats-Unis à partir de 1970 $a Directeur aux éditions Rowohlt
             de la collection "Bibliothèque humaniste"
610 [      ] $a Folly and insanity in Renaissance literature / Ernesto
             Grassi and Maristella Lorch, 1986
610 [      ] $a Kurschner 1983 $a Livres hebdo, n°1, 1992-01-03, p.
             54-55
```

FIGURE 10. Corporate name INTERMARC authority record (BN-OPALE)

```
FC  : RCN 00029365 ACO                    DEGRE 4 SECTION:AUTACO
GUIDE : ETAT  : c VALEUR: 2 STATUTS  : 1 a AUTR. CODES: c
001 [      ] frBN00029365X
008 [      ] 841003930121useng  e3

017 [      ] BDF.000145259
019 [      ] $aBN$bCNA$c00029308
110 [      ] $w.0..b.....$aCenter for medieval and early Renaissance
             studies $c Binghamton, N.Y.
410 [      ] $w1...b.....$a State university of New York $b Center for
             medieval and early Renaissance studies
410 [      ] $w....b.....$a State university of New York at Binghamton $b
             Center for medieval and early Renaissance studies
610 [      ] $a WL, 1992.
```

records. Another database will soon exist and will include about 6,000,000 records after a retroconversion project.

Since February 1992, CAP SESA Tertiaire, BULL and GEAC have been working together with the Bibliothèque de France and Bibliothèque Nationale experts to design the future automated system, which will include administrative, transfer of documents, communication, and circulation control in addition to processing services and OPAC. With regard to the cataloging of non-French books, the most important improvement will be the integration of records with non-roman characters into the future unique catalogue with public access. Providing better subject access is also necessary. Much has been written about the need for additional subject access, and the Bibliothèque de France project is exploring some ways to succeed in this area. Among them the classic way is to use a searching

FIGURE 11. Subject heading INTERMARC authority record (BN-OPALE)

```
FC : RCN 00169675 AMA              DEGRE 3 SECTION:AUTMM
GUIDE : ETAT : c VALEUR: 2 STATUTS : 0 a1 AUTR.CODES: m
001 [        ] frBN00169675X
008 [        ] 820527920407        1

017 [        ] BDF.000686510
166 [        ] $w.12.b.....$a Humanisme
301 [00211340]   <$w.12.b.....$a Civilisation>
301 [00211389]   <$w.12.b.....$a Enseignement classique>
301 [00154136]   <$w.12.b   $a Philologie classique>
301 [00163541]   <$w.12.b.....$a Renaissance>
301 [00154307]   <$w 12 b   $a Savoir et érudition>
301 [00449127]   <$w.12.b.....$a Attitude envers l'humanisme>
301 [00186830]   <$w.12.b.....$a Humanisme $z + * 1900......- 1999...... +:20e
                 siècle
302 [00169676]   <$w.14.b.....$a Etudes classiques>
302 [00190022]   <$w 13 b   $a Hellénisme
302 [00155935]   <$w 14 b   $a Humanisme islamique>
302 [00171119]   <$w 12 b   $a Morale humaniste>
466 [        ] $w.14.b.....$a Humanisme $z + * 1400......-
                 1599...... +:Renaissance:
502 [00152587]   <$w.12.b.....$a Culture>
502 [00173000]   <$w.12.b.....$a Education humaniste>
502 [00161358]   <$w.12.b.....$a Philosophie de la Renaissance>
602 [        ] $a Sous cette vedette, on trouve les ouvrages qui concernent
                 le mouvement des idées à la Renaissance. On trouve les
                 ouvrages sur l'aspect moderne et philosophique de l'humanisme
                 sous Humanisme -- 20e siècle
620 [        ] $a Humanism (May Subd Geog) $v LCSH, 1991-09
```

FIGURE 12. Subject heading INTERMARC authority record (BN-OPALE)

```
FC : RCN 00161358 AMA              DEGRE 3 SECTION:AUTMM
GUIDE : ETAT : c VALEUR: 2 STATUTS : 1 a1 AUTR. CODES:m
001 [        ] frBN001613586
008 [        ] 810429921116   0
017 [        ] BDF. 000607947
166 [        ] $w.12.b.....$a Philosophie de la Renaissance
300 [        ] $r Voir aussi les vedettes du type Philosophie [ + adjectif de nationalité] --
                 16e siècle, par ex : Philosophie française -- 16e siècle.
620 [        ] $a Philosophy, Renaissance $v LCSH, 1992-03
302 [00169675]   <$w.12.b.....$a Humanisme>
466 [        ] $w.14.b.....$a Philosophie $z + * 1400......-
                 1599...... +:Renaissance:
466 [        ] $w.14.b..... $a Philosophie $z + * 1500......- 1599...... +:16e
                 siècle:
466 [        ] $w.14.b.....$a Philosophie moderne $z + * 1500......-
                 1599...... +:16e siècle:
```

system, such as OKAPI, where keyword access has different weight depending upon frequency in a record. Another way, newer but expensive, is to enrich records by links to scanned summaries or scanned documents themselves.

NOTES

1. Isabelle Dussert-Carbone, "Comparaison entre les normes françaises et les règles anglo-américaines de catalogage," *Bull. Bibl. France* 34:4 (1989): 352-361.

2. *Report [of the] International Conference on Cataloguing Principles, Paris, 9th-18th October 1961* (London: Organizing Committee of the International Conference on Cataloguing Principles, 1963).

3. Elisabeth Vilatte, "Le Service des Acquistons du Département des Entrées étrangères," *Bulletin d'informations de l'Association des bibliothécaires français* 153 (1991): 13-15.

4. Pierre-Yves Duchemin, "Opaline: étapes d'une évolution," *Bulletin d'informations de l'Association des bibliothécaires français* 148 (1990): 51-52.

5. These figures are current as of January 1993.

6. Ghyslaine Duong-Vinh, "BN-Sycomore ou l'automatisation de la communication et du récolement dans les départements des Livres Imprimés et des Périodiques," *Bulletin d'informations de l'Association des bibliothécaires français* 153 (1991): 27-31.

7. Jacqueline Solomiac, "La conversion rétrospective à la Bibliothèque Nationale," *Bulletin d'informations de l'Association des bibliothécaires français* 153 (1991): 20-22.

8. Françoise Bourdon, "Le contrôle bibliographique courant en France: état en 1989," *International Cataloguing and Bibliographic Control* (April-June 1989): 19-24.

9. Annick Bernard, Michel Schutz, "SBN: les bases de l'écrit et du son en direct," *Bulletin d'informations de l'Association des bibliothécaires français* 157 (1992): 11-15.

10. *Recueil de normes françaises. Documentation*, 4th ed., 2 vols. (Paris: AFNOR, 1990).

11. Françoise Leresche, "La normalisation du catalogage en France," *International Cataloguing and Bibliographic Control* (April-June 1989): 24-27; "L'évolution des normes de catalogage," *Bulletin d'informations de l'Association des bibliothécaires français* 146 (1990): 37-39.

12. Annick Bernard, "Sur l'abandon du catalogage à niveaux par la Bibliothèque Nationale," *Bulletin d'informations de l'Association des bibliothécaires français* 141 (1988): 26-27.

13. *Guide pratique du catalogueur à la Bibliothèque Nationale: services participant à la base Opale* (Paris: Bibliothèque Nationale, 1987-).

14. Following is a list of Bibliothèque Nationale publications about formats: *INTERMARC (A): notice d'autorité*, 1992; *INTERMARC (M): notice bibliogra-*

phique de monographies, édition revisée, 1991; *INTERMARC (S): notice bibliographique de publications en série*, édition revisée, 1988, janvier; *INTERMARC (MUS): notice bibliographique de la musique imprimée et manuscrite*, 1987, juin; *INTERMARC (C): notice bibliographique de documents cartographiques*, 1985, décembre (review in progress); *INTERMARC (IM): notice bibliographique des images fixes*, 1987, septembre; *INTERMARC (AV): notice bibliographique de documents audiovisuels*, 1991.

15. *Imprimeurs-libraires, XVIe-XVIIIe siècles: guide pour la rédaction des notices d'autorité en format INTERMARC*, Etudes, guides et inventaires, 8 (Paris: Bibliothèque Nationale, 1987); *Manuel de catalogage automatisé des livres anciens en format INTERMARC*, Etudes, guides et inventaires, 6 (Paris: Bibliothèque Nationale, 1987).

16. Marcelle Beaudiquez et al., "Les fichiers d'autorité de la base BN-OPALE," *Bulletin d'informations de l'Association des bibliothécaires français* 148 (1990): 30-44.

17. *Guide d'indexation RAMEAU* (Paris: Bibliothèque Nationale, Ministère de l'Education Nationale, 1992); Suzanne Jouguelet, "L'accès par sujets et le marché de l'information bibliographique en France," *International Cataloging and Bibliographic Control* (April-June 1990): 29-32.

18. Nicole Simon, "Le chantier acquisitions," *Bulletin d'informations de l'Association des bibliothécaires français* 153 (1991): 17-19.

19. Françoise Bourdon, "How Can IFLA Contribute to Solving Problems in Name Authority Control at the International Level?" *IFLA Journal* 18:2 (1992): 135-137.

Cataloging Non-English Materials at Cleveland Public Library: A One Hundred Twenty-Four Year History

Edward Seely

SUMMARY. Cleveland Public Library has cataloged non-English materials for its collection since its establishment in 1869. To this day, Cleveland continues to have areas of high ethnic concentration. The Library now catalogs materials in forty-five languages and has one of the largest non-English collections among public libraries in the United States, consisting of 214,000 volumes in its Foreign Literature Department. Materials for new immigrants from Eastern Europe and the Near and Far East have expanded the non-English collections as CPL has responded to the information and reading needs of the new arrivals. Cataloging procedures have been streamlined to move materials as quickly as possible to circulation shelves. Cleveland Public budgets over $130,000 for non-English materials, and support from library administration continues to be high.

CLEVELAND'S ETHNIC HERITAGE

From the very beginning of its existence in 1869, the Cleveland Public Library has handled the cataloging of non-English materials as part of its normal work. In its formative years Cleveland, Ohio, began to develop areas of high ethnic concentration. When it was incorporated as a village

---

Edward Seely is Head of Technical Services, Cleveland Public Library.

[Haworth co-indexing entry note]: "Cataloging Non-English Materials at Cleveland Public Library: A One Hundred Twenty-Four Year History." Seely, Edward. Co-published simultaneously in *Cataloging & Classification Quarterly* (The Haworth Press, Inc.) Vol. 17, No. 1/2, 1993, pp. 257-265; and: *Languages of the World: Cataloging Issues and Problems* (ed: Martin D. Joachim) The Haworth Press, Inc., 1993, pp. 257-265. Multiple copies of this article/chapter may be purchased from The Haworth Document Delivery Center [1-800-3-HAWORTH; 9:00 a.m. - 5:00 p.m. (EST)].

257

in 1814, Cleveland had been populated mostly by New Englanders and continued so until it entered into an era of great expansion and prosperity brought about by the construction of the Ohio Canal in the 1830s. Prior to the Ohio Canal, it was as eastern in its character as a city could be. The construction of the canal drew upon thousands of hard-nosed, hard-working immigrants for its laboring force who stayed on as permanent residents.[1] The first major foreign language speaking immigrants were German, and even today this is reflected by the fact that the largest non-English language collection in the Cleveland Public Library is German.

A new flood of non-English speaking immigrants came to the city in the middle of the nineteenth century, including Bohemians and Italians, followed by other waves of immigrants from eastern Europe, such as Poles, Hungarians, and Slovaks. It was common for these new residents of Cleveland to cluster together in their own nationality centers, continuing to speak their own languages and to school their American-born children in the languages of their forebears. Soon after the founding of the Cleveland Public Library in 1869, German language materials were being purchased for German-speaking residents. One of the leading book vendors in Germany, Otto Harrassowitz, has accounting ledgers dating back to the 1870s showing sales of German language books to the Cleveland Public Library. The library is Harrassowitz's second oldest United States library customer, a relationship that continues to this day. Some of the titles purchased from Harrassowitz in 1870 undoubtedly resulted from a gift from the German Citizens of Cleveland, a local organization which honored the hundredth anniversary of the birth of their countryman, Alexander von Humboldt, the famous scientist and explorer. The gift amounted to $1,000, a considerable sum when it is recalled that the entire receipts for the library in its first year were less than $6,500.[2]

So even from its earliest days, Cleveland Public Library had non-English materials as a part of its collection. As additional waves of immigrants came to the city, the library routinely provided materials in their native languages. Prior to 1924, non-English materials were shelved in the Sociology Department, where many immigrants came for citizenship materials. In April 1924 the Foreign Literature Department became a separate division. By 1939, twenty-nine non-English languages were represented in a circulating collection of about 66,000 volumes. During this period the Foreign Literature Department became a resource for libraries throughout the United States. Librarians consulted the Cleveland Public Library staff for help with book selection and acquisition.

A new wave of European immigrants after World War II brought increased necessity for non-English materials. In response to demands in the

1960s, the Foreign Literature Department established Korean, Swahili, and Turkish collections. Vietnamese was added in the late 1970s. The 1970s and 1980s brought more demand for oriental languages and an increase in Russian language materials as many Soviet émigrés moved into the area. In 1992 six more languages joined the collections: Bengali, Farsi, Hindi, Marathi, Thai, and Urdu.

PROFILE OF THE CPL NON-ENGLISH COLLECTION

Cleveland Public Library's Foreign Literature Department began in 1969, by mutual agreement with other public libraries, to be the resource center in Cuyahoga County for non-English materials. The department regularly provides three-month bulk loans to area public libraries which have high concentrations of non-English speaking patrons. Although many of these libraries buy non-English materials, they still rely on the Cleveland Public Library collection to help fill their needs. Due to the CLEVNET network of twenty public libraries which use the Cleveland Public Library's database as a shared catalog and through computer dial-up capabilities to the online catalog by area residents, access to and knowledge of the large non-English collection in the library have increased circulation of the materials. In 1991, the circulation of non-English materials was 94,370, approximately 8 percent of the circulation of the Main Library.

In 1991 the non-English collection in the Foreign Literature Department consisted of 214,811 volumes in forty-five languages. The largest collections are in German (31,476), French (25,969), Spanish (22,014), Russian (20,372), Polish (12,356), and Hungarian (10,540). Non-roman language collections are now outdistancing the lesser European languages. There are now 4,214 Arabic and 3,288 Chinese items. Another Asian language, Vietnamese, is represented by 3,654 volumes. The last survey of non-English collections in major public libraries published in *Library Trends*, Fall 1980, revealed that Cleveland Public Library had the second largest collection.[3] The largest collection was in the Los Angeles Public Library which held that distinction by only a few more thousand volumes.

While the Foreign Literature Department houses the majority of cataloged titles, the Special Collections Department in the library also purchases a number of titles in non-English languages for its chess materials collection, which is the largest in the world, and for its substantial holdings in folklore and Orientalia. Rare books, many in non-English languages, are purchased for the library's research collection and are available in the Special Collections Department.

From the 1992 Main Library budget of $1,566,000 for monographs and audio media, the Foreign Literature Department received $113,310, or approximately 7 percent. The department also got around $20,000 for the purchase of serials and periodicals from other parts of the materials budget.

The Collection Development Policy of the Cleveland Public Library for the Foreign Literature Department states:

> The collections for specific languages are designed to meet the prac-
> tical needs and interests of the heterogeneous, cosmopolitan popula-
> tions of Cleveland which includes: new immigrants who require
> language-learning materials and information in their native tongue to
> meet immediate day-to day, practical, educational, and recreational
> needs; bilingual or multilingual individuals who wish to improve
> and continue their language skills and to transmit their ethnic heri-
> tage to succeeding generations; students of foreign languages from
> primary through graduate levels and people who use the collections
> for their studies or business purposes.

Acquisition priorities include dictionaries and general encyclopedias; beginning grammars and readers; literary works of significant authors in the original languages; basic educational materials written in the vernacu-lar; books concerning American culture, literature, and history in transla-tion from English when suitable material is not available in non-English language originals; standard works, such as Bibles, introductory subject material, and popular treatments of current social, economic, and scientific issues, depending on demand and availability; and general reference tools, acquired selectively to meet the reference and materials selection needs of the department. Monographs are primary purchases, but the department also carries a number of periodicals, both popular and literary, based on public demand. Language learning sound recordings are also acquired for the forty-five language collections. Sound recordings of plays, poetry, and stories are also purchased to supplement print materials.

Shelving of the collection is done by language. In a study by David Kaser on the work of the library's Foreign Literature Department in 1981, he described it as an "aggregation of some thirty-nine small-town public libraries, each serving a community of 10,000-50,000 speakers of a partic-ular language. Each of these thirty-nine collections is arrayed by subject although shelved separate from the others, and each comprises perhaps two-thirds popular literature and perhaps one-third 'reference' literature."[4] Professor Kaser's comments on the nature of the collection are notable:

> Many libraries nationwide possess the works of Goethe, or Racine, or Tolstoi in the originals, but few American libraries have reason to acquire the next echelon of quality below those stellar authors. In many cases moreover European libraries may no longer possess the works of such authors because of the destruction their collections sustained during two World Wars. Thus among such works especially it is possible that CPL's books may be unique artifacts.[5]

THE CPL CATALOGING PROCESS

The Cataloging Department at Cleveland Public Library for 1992 had a staff of twenty-three. In 1991 the department created 61,456 new bibliographic records for the library's online catalog. It also added 17,563 records for the twenty libraries which share the Cleveland Public database as members of the CLEVNET network. In order to maintain and to control a quality catalog, CPL does not allow members of CLEVNET to add or edit bibliographic records. All requests or changes must be handled by the CPL's Catalog Department. Most CLEVNET members provide catalog workforms for input when original cataloging is needed. Of the titles added to Cleveland Public's collection in 1991, 7,365 were in non-English languages, 10 percent of the Catalog Department's work.

All but six of the forty-five non-English language collections were added to in 1991. Book acquisitions continue to dominate for European languages. After over 120 years of purchases in the German language, titles acquired continue to be high, ranking second in 1991 with 627 additions. The highest was in the Russian language with 1,300, corroborating the fact that Russians are voracious readers. This has been reflected by the demand for more Russian language materials by recent Soviet émigrés to Cleveland. Other significant European language purchases were Polish (419), Spanish (360), Hungarian (398), Ukrainian (308), and French (275). The influx of immigrants from the Near and Far-East is evidenced by the increases in acquisitions for Chinese (357), Vietnamese (278), and Arabic (292) languages.

How is the Catalog Department organized to handle the cataloging for a wide range of non-English language materials? Unlike some other public libraries with large non-English language collections, CPL has opted not to catalog in non-roman scripts. All of this material is transliterated using Library of Congress standards. There is no special unit devoted to cataloging these materials. The Catalog Department strives, as much as possible, to incorporate non-English materials into its regular cataloging work. For the past five years the Catalog Department has made a determined effort to decentralize cataloging responsibility. In the past, catalogers worked mainly in their areas of subject expertise. Support staff assisted in cataloging routines but made no judgment regarding copy cataloging.

As part of the streamlining process for cataloging, copy cataloging teams were organized in 1987. The teams accept cataloging copy within established guidelines from LC MARC bibliographic records available from our automation vendor, Data Research Associates, or from OCLC. Copy cataloging not meeting standards and materials needing original cataloging are forwarded to professional catalogers. Catalogers check RLIN before creating original cataloging records. Cataloger teams have been established by dividing up the Library of Congress classification so that two catalogers share a part of the classification schedule, thus assuring continuity of cataloging during vacations and sickness and providing for consultation with each other on classification problems.

How is non-English language cataloging handled, given this departmental arrangement? Every cataloging team, in addition to being responsible for part of the LC classification schedule, also catalogs non-English language materials based upon language knowledge for the entire LC classification schedule. For example, one cataloger is Canadian who is proficient in French; another is from the Middle East and knows Arabic. Only one of the eight professional catalogers deals mainly with non-English cataloging. Her area of expertise is in Slavic and Eastern European languages. Since much material is purchased in these languages, most of her time is spent cataloging non-English materials even though she is still part of a cataloging team for the LC classification schedule. Another professional cataloger who handles Special Collections cataloging, because of the nature of the materials, spends at least 30 percent of her time on non-English languages, and she, too, is part of a team.

Patrons who read in non-roman scripts would, of course, welcome access to catalog records in the original scripts. However, the decision not to enter the materials in the catalog in non-roman scripts is based on the following practical reasons: Cataloging in non-roman scripts can be labor intensive; reproducing bibliographic records and providing access to them in an online catalog can be expensive. From a staffing viewpoint, transliterated materials provide for easier retrieval by reference librarians and simplify shelving for pages. Since the Foreign Literature Department arranges its collections by language, providing for an aggregation of separate small libraries, most patrons browse the collections. For non-roman titles that must be rebound, CPL has an arrangement with its bindery to retain the non-roman scripts on the spines of the books so that the titles may be identified by browsers.

The library's policy is to accept Library of Congress classification without modification in order to move materials as quickly as possible and to take advantage of the cataloging done by LC and other libraries whose cataloging is acceptable to CPL. Therefore, no additional subject analysis is done, nor is any modification done for local need. The library relies on the staff of the Foreign Literature Department to know the collection and to provide reference service for those patrons who need help.

Any library that catalogs non-English materials in as many languages as Cleveland Public Library does needs all the assistance it can get. Catalogers with language expertise do help, and CPL is fortunate to have European and East European languages, including Russian, covered by existing staff. It is the policy to exhaust all available cataloging utilities before turning to original cataloging by CPL's language-proficient professional catalogers. Book vendors are always chosen for high fulfillment expectation and cost effectiveness, not for any cataloging support they may have. However, since languages in non-roman scripts pose the biggest cataloging problems, the library has turned to vendors who also can supply cataloging. Currently, oriental books are purchased with basic cataloging information from Pan Asian Publications, Inc. The cataloging has been generally satisfactory although their work is carefully reviewed to see that it meets Library of Congress cataloging standards. As for English language materials, all non-English language items are searched in OCLC and RLIN. Search hits are best for West-European languages with 60 percent success. For East-European languages, those in non-Roman scripts, and rare books, the hit rate is 25 percent.

As stated previously, non-English language books are included in the normal cataloging flow of the department. With training it has been possible to have copy catalogers do searches for non-English titles and to export LC or acceptable member copy records from OCLC into CPL's online catalog. Records that match but do not meet CPL cataloging standards are referred to professional catalogers who enhance them for OCLC input. No editing is done on LC MARC records. This policy has worked well for West-European languages, which pose few problems for copy catalogers. When a copy cataloger begins transferring non-English records to the online catalog, all additions are checked by a professional cataloger. When the staff person becomes error free, checking is no longer done. In order to move materials along quickly, copy catalogers with higher level positions do less than full original cataloging (K level) in OCLC for fiction and certain non-fiction items of minor research value. A subject heading may be added. The K level records are verified by professional catalogers. All other research materials and titles in non-roman scripts are referred to the professional catalogers.

In 1991, reflecting the shift in immigration patterns in the 1980s and in the non-English languages materials added for the Special Collections Department, cataloging in non-roman scripts has increased to 38 percent. One of the professional catalogers is proficient in Russian and can handle other Cyrillic scripts; thus over 1300 titles of the 2800 in non-roman scripts are handled routinely. Other significant numbers of titles in non-roman languages are in Arabic, Chinese, Japanese, Korean, and Hebrew. Always on the lookout for help in cataloging in these languages, CPL has tried to get assistance with transliteration from local universities and colleges which have foreign students with needed languages skills. Recruitment, however, has not been successful. At times, materials have been sent out for transliteration. Armenian and Sanskrit titles have been contracted out with mixed results. Since 1989 CPL has been fortunate to hire two part-time professional catalogers who work thirty hours per month each on Arabic, Chinese, and Korean books. A librarian from the People's Republic of China works for the Catalog Department three days a week. Her stay in the USA has been extended to the end of 1993. Recently, a patron volunteered to transliterate Hebrew books. Her assistance was a big help to the catalogers who were able to clear up the backlog quickly.

Admittedly some non-English titles languish for quite a few months, and a few even for years, while an attempt is made to procure the language proficiency necessary to get them transliterated and cataloged. In spite of problems, CPL has had measurable success in handling non-English additions to the catalog. With all of the options available, and the determination to get the materials cataloged, the Catalog Department has only a modest 1,100 non-English titles in its backlog.

CPL has had over 120 years of experience dealing with non-English titles as part of the catalog. Past directors and library administrators over the years have recognized the importance of these materials to the diverse ethnic populations of Cleveland and have acknowledged the collections of the Foreign Literature Department as an important part of library service to the community. The policy continues to this day: as long as there is a need to serve non-English speaking residents and students wishing to acquire foreign language skills or others wanting to become proficient in foreign languages, the library undoubtedly will be responsive to these patrons.

NOTES

1. George E. Condon, *Cleveland: The Best Kept Secret* (Garden City, N.Y.: Doubleday, 1967), 47.

2. C. H. Cramer, *Open Shelves and Open Minds: A History of the Cleveland Public Library* (Cleveland, Ohio: The Press of Case Western Reserve University, 1972), 24.

3. Natalia B. Bezugloff, "Library Services to Non-English-Language Ethnic Minorities in the United States," *Library Trends* 29:2 (Fall, 1980): 280.

4. David Kaser, "The Foreign Literature Department in the Cleveland Public Library" (Report, Cleveland Public Library, 1981), 5.

5. Ibid., 12.

The Role of Subject Headings in Access to Information: The Experience of One Spanish-Speaking Patron

Marielena Fina

SUMMARY. This article examines the role of subject headings in providing access to information for the Spanish-speaking population of the United States. Such tools for assigning subject headings as *Library of Congress Subject Headings (LCSH)* and *Bilindex* are examined and their effectiveness assessed. A plea is made to technical services librarians to go beyond standardized methods of cataloging in order to assure meaningful access for Spanish-speaking patrons.

Marielena Fina is an attorney and, at the time that this article was written, was a student at the Graduate School of Library and Information Science at Simmons College.

The author wishes to thank Professor Sheila Intner, who always encouraged her to do her best, and Elena Margolis for her support and help in proofreading the article.

[Haworth co-indexing entry note]: "The Role of Subject Headings in Access to Information: The Experience of One Spanish-Speaking Patron." Fina, Marielena. Co-published simultaneously in *Cataloging & Classification Quarterly* (The Haworth Press, Inc.) Vol. 17, No. 1/2, 1993, pp. 267-274; and: *Languages of the World: Cataloging Issues and Problems* (ed: Martin D. Joachim) The Haworth Press, Inc., 1993, pp. 267-274. Multiple copies of this article/chapter may be purchased from The Haworth Document Delivery Center [1-800-3-HAWORTH; 9:00 - 5:00 (EST)].

267

RESUMEN. Este artículo examina el uso de los encabezamientos de materia y como estos contribuyen o no ha hacer asequible la información en las bibliotecas a los Hispano parlante en los E.E. U.U. El artículo tambien examina los vehículos designados como guía para establecer los encabezamientos tales como son la lista de la Biblioteca del Congreso y *Bilindex*. Su effectividad se explora. A los bibliotecarios y bibliotecarias se les pide que usen cualquier método que sea necesario para establecer los encabezamientos para que la información en las bibliotecas este al alcance de los Hispano parlantes de una manera significativa y provechosa.

INTRODUCTION

Em Claire Knowles and Linda Jolivet have written:

By the year 2000, the majority of the population of the US will be members of underrepresented racial and ethnic groups. They will consist primarily of Americans from the following racial and ethnic groups: African-American, Asian-American, Latino(a) and American Indian. In order for the new emerging majority to become productive members of society, their information needs must be addressed, and their access to information must be insured.[1]

These words have been echoed by authors such as Mary Huston and Joe Williams,[2] Hans Wellisch,[3] and Robert Haro.[4] Yet, in spite of the statistics, information in libraries remains largely inaccessible for the Spanish-speaking patron.[5]

This article examines the role of subject headings used to catalog books for Spanish-speaking patrons and the role that the headings play in promoting access to information for the Spanish-speaking population in the United States. Catalogers accomplish the task of subject analysis, of course, with such tools as *Library of Congress Subject Headings (LCSH)*, *Sears List of Subject Headings*, and, in some instances, by creating their own authority files, such as the *Hennepin County Library Cataloging Bulletin* in Minnesota. For administrative convenience and for budgetary reasons, however, most libraries use *LCSH* or Sears. Rarely do libraries, especially small public libraries, use their own cataloging and authority file systems.[6]

Careful analysis and assignment of subject headings for appropriate access to information by all patrons are important. Some of the principles that apply to the assignment of subject headings are, according to David

Judson Haykin, "readers focus," "usage," and "specificity."[7] In other words, the ways in which a reader would most naturally search for information should be given priority over considerations of convenience to the librarian. In spite of Haykin's principles and the mission of the library as stated by the American Library Association, information remains largely inaccessible to the Spanish-speaking population in the United States.[8]

It has been argued that subject catalogers, and in particular those who use *LCSH*, in their haste to standardize and save money have, in the process, limited access to information in our libraries to many cultural and ethnic minorities.[9] Whether this limitation to access information is the product of a conscious effort, apathy, or simply carelessness is beyond the scope of this article. Suffice it to say that this author does not subscribe to the conspiracy theory but tends to agree that, for whatever reason, it is clear that information organized according to *LCSH* shows a bias that is, for the most part, white, male, Anglo-Saxon, and Protestant to the exclusion of other views and other sensitivities.[10]

THE PROBLEM

It is well documented that the Spanish-speaking population in the United States has minimal access to information in our libraries. From public libraries to academic libraries, members of the Latina(o) community are not being properly served.[11] Much of the analysis regarding the lack of access to information by members of cultural and ethnic minorities and the failure of current cataloging practices to fulfill Cutter's principle of cataloging comes from people like Sanford Berman. Berman feels that "users, including those whose primary language may not be English, should be able to find desired subjects on the first try, and should not be prejudiced, confused, misled or 'turned off' by terminology used to denote specific topics."[12] For the Spanish-speaking patron, the fulfillment of this principle is far from reality.

My own experience in doing research for this article illustrates the biases found in the subject headings system. Having obtained one book on the subject of this article, I had hoped to work backward from it to find subject headings that would lead me to more information. In the card catalog of a Boston-area academic library, I found a card with the heading **LIBRARIES AND THE SOCIALLY HANDICAPPED** (having been changed from **LIBRARY SERVICE TO THE CULTURALLY HAND-ICAPPED**) to cover the topic of access to information by a Latina(o) in 1972. Twenty-one years later the same card remains in the catalog. And even more incredible, **CULTURALLY HANDICAPPED** and **SOCIAL-**

LY HANDICAPPED are still listed in *LCSH* as acceptable headings! Except for the fact that I was looking for a particular work by author, I would not have found any information at all in this library. Not even in my wildest dreams would I have thought that I was "culturally" or "socially" handicapped for being Latina, nor would it have occurred to me to search under such a heading for subject information.

The subject headings in this catalog are antithetical to what Berman and Cutter suggest. Not only would I have failed to find information on the first or second try, but "turned off" is an understatement for how this heading made me feel when I discovered it. One can easily see how this characterization of the subject would discourage patrons from seeking further access to information.

This situation is not unusual. My visit to two local public libraries in Latina(o) areas of Boston confirms and parallels the findings of two studies conducted on access to information by the Spanish-speaking in 1972 and 1980.[13] In these two libraries that I visited, I searched first for books written in English about Latina(o) people. The microfiche catalog in one of this libraries listed books of this nature under such headings as **SOCIALLY HANDICAPPED**. I brought my concerns about this subject heading to a librarian. Although she assured me that the microfiche was very old and that such a heading would not appear now, the date of the microfiche was Winter 1990.

At both of these libraries, there are also collections of books written in Spanish. However, not only are these collections rather small given the number of Spanish-speaking people in these communities, but the books are not cataloged in any systematic way. There is no access to books except by browsing on disorganized shelves. The books are not even shelved alphabetically by author. On one shelf books about motorcycle repair are mixed with cookbooks. One of the libraries, at least, has two signs on the shelves that read (in English): **Fiction** and **Non-Fiction.**

To see the role that subject headings play in promoting access to information in this library, I pulled a 1984 book off the shelf in one of the libraries and asked the librarian if she could find it in the microfiche catalog since I could not. She could not find it either until she used the online terminal at her desk. This was the only online computer in this library, linked online to the Boston Public Library, and was not available for use to patrons. The librarian was able to find the book by author but not by subject heading in spite of the fact that the heading **HISPANIC AMERICAN WOMEN** is listed in *LCSH*. A search for subject headings used by the Boston Public Library also failed to retrieve this book. Since this library does not own *LCSH*, it is difficult for patrons and librarians alike to do any sort of meaningful subject heading search. Thus in that instance, even if *LCSH* provided appropriate subject headings, only my training as a librarian kept me from walking out of that library empty-handed.

These examples illustrate some of the ways in which subject cataloging with *LCSH* fails to provide adequate access for Spanish-speaking library patrons. First, at least in public libraries in Boston and surrounding areas, there is a general lack of cataloging of books in Spanish and books about Spanish-speaking peoples. When books are cataloged, the subject headings are often inadequate or biased to such an extent that a Spanish-speaker would never find the appropriate headings. Finally, offensive subject headings such as **SOCIALLY HANDICAPPED** often remain in the catalogs even if they have been changed in *LCSH*. This practice actually deters the Spanish-speaker from utilizing the subject heading system at all.

POSSIBLE SOLUTIONS TO THE LACK OF ACCESS

This situation clearly needs to be remedied. As Spanish-speaking patrons increase in numbers across the United States, access to information for this population must be improved. Budget cuts, lack of resources, and administrative inconvenience do not justify this intolerable state of affairs. Especially since there are tools such as *Bilindex* readily available to supplement *LCSH* for subject cataloging of Spanish books. In 1984 *Bilindex*[14] was first published as a bilingual Spanish-English subject heading list with equivalents to the ninth edition of *LCSH*. *Bilindex* is not, however, a direct translation of *LCSH*; rather, Spanish-speaking scholars have endeavored to arrange a subject heading list geared toward native speakers and even account for regional variations of Spanish. The Spanish list gives full syndetic structure.

Curtis Lavery argues that part of the problem in achieving good subject access for Spanish-speaking patrons is the lack of a "well defined national information policy upon which to base" programs that will urge professional catalogers to "actively promote positive attitudes . . . relating to cultural minorities,"[15] which in turn enhance access. In other words, he contends, the more that catalogers know about their communities, the more they are likely to describe their accumulated achievements by way of appropriate subject headings.

Lavery points out that in 1984 the National Commission on Libraries and Information Science (NCLIS) released a report with forty-two recommendations concerning the provision of information services to meet the needs of cultural and ethnic minorities.[16] He adds, however, that the recommendations highlight only what small successes there have been rather than offer concrete solutions. The report states: "Libraries must promote the continued use of subject headings that those whose primary language is not English may understand, and avoid prejudices, confusion, and a tendency to discourage potential patrons from using the library."[17]

According to Lavery, this general recommendation did not go far in achieving the goal of providing adequate subject access to Spanish-speaking patrons. To Lavery, access in native languages would be ideal, and he finds the NCLIS statement frustrating and unclear as to whether it is promoting cataloging in the native tongues of cultural groups as a means to "reverse the effects" of poor subject headings in traditional lists like *LCSH* and Sears. Lavery's own recommendations for better subject heading access range from the technical services librarian being more involved with the communities they serve to raising private funds for programs that advance multicultural services at the technical services level. He also urges cooperation among libraries via the bibliographic utilities by using *Bilindex* and its supplements, which are also available online.

Lavery's emphasis on the technical services librarian as the instrument for improving the subject headings system is echoed by Berman, who states that the responsibility to change current subject heading practices rests solely in the technical services personnel and the people setting policy for our libraries.[18] I agree. It is no longer tolerable that this profession hides behind the understandable but worn-out excuse of budget cuts and lack of resources in general for the slow pace in which subject headings change at the Library of Congress and in the field. As a profession, we must take seriously the responsibility that rests upon us as guardians and codifiers of information and as the keyholders of easy access to that information. Changes do not come easily and typically require great sacrifices in time and money. This is the kind of commitment that management and technical services librarians must be willing to exhibit in this noble endeavor.

While it is true that the Library of Congress has made efforts to change subject headings that are offensive and that block access to information by certain groups in our society, it is also true that LC makes these efforts mostly in response to pressure from individuals or groups which typically have clout. I believe that, instead of waiting for this kind of pressure, the Library of Congress should affirmatively take the initiative to change subject headings that do not promote access to information for all, particularly now that *LCSH* is computerized and there are models such as *Bilindex* to use. Not only do I believe that the Library of Congress should undertake this initiative, but I believe also that LC has the responsibility to do so. It is time for the Library of Congress and other libraries that do original cataloging to stop passing the buck and assume the responsibility, together with the commitment to do whatever is necessary to see that information is easily accessible to everybody.

NOTES

1. Em Claire Knowles and Linda Jolivet, "Recruiting the Underrepresented: Collaborative Efforts between Library Educators and Library Practitioners," *Library Administration & Management* 5:1 (Fall 1991): 189.

2. Mary Huston and Joe Williams, "Research Response to the Politics of Information," *Research Strategies* 5:2 (Spring 1987): 90-93.

3. Hans Wellisch, "Bibliographic Access to Multilingual Collections," *Library Trends* 29:2 (Summer/Spring 1980): 223-244.

4. Robert Haro, *Developing Bibliographic Access to Multilingual Collections* (Metuchen, N.J.: Scarecrow Press, 1981).

5. Wellisch, "Bibliographic Access," 223.

6. This paper focuses on *LCSH* only. It should be noted, however, that Sears does have a Spanish language version.

7. Quoted in: Sheila S. Intner and Jean Weihs, *Standard Cataloging for School and Public Libraries* (Englewood, Colo.: Libraries Unlimited, 1990), 80.

8. See, for example: M. L. McQuiston, "The Problem of English Subject Headings in the Bi-Lingual Library," *Texas Library Journal* 51:4 (Winter 1975): 189-190; American Library Association, *The Public Library Mission Statement and Its Imperative for Service* (Chicago: ALA, 1979), 13, 15-16; and "Code of Ethics for Librarians," adopted by the ALA Council on June 30, 1991. Although different kinds of libraries have different mission statements, librarians have a responsibility to provide equal access to all users of their libraries.

9. Sanford Berman, "Stop Playing Hide-and-Go-Seek with Ethnic Materials!" *Wilson Library Bulletin* 52 (May 1978): 691, 719; and *Prejudices and Antipathies* (Metuchen, N.J.: Scarecrow Press, 1971), 22-88.

10. Huston, "Research Response," 92.

11. In addition to citations in notes 1-5: see also Elizabeth Bole Eddison, "Limited Library Service for Spanish-Speaking Americans" (Typescript, Simmons College, 1972).

12. Berman, "Stop Playing," 52.

13. See Wellisch, "Bibliographic Access," and Eddison, "Limited Library Service." Eddison found in her study that many librarians expressed the desire to find a list with Spanish subject headings. The implication was that catalogers would use it if they had it. In fact, such a list did exist then, but it was not being used. There is now a much better subject heading list called *Bilindex*, which, apparently, is also not being used. A search in OCLC shows that the Boston Public Library and all other libraries in Massachusetts, save three, do not own a copy of *Bilindex* and its supplements.

14. *Bilindex* has had two supplements: *Bilindex Supplement I, 1985-1986* (Oakwood, Calif.: California Spanish Language Database, 1986) and *Bilindex Supplement II, 1987-1990* (1992). It is currently being maintained online.

15. Curtis Lavery, "The Commitment to Spanish Language Services," *Lector* 2:4 (January/February 1984): 8-9.

16. U.S. Task Force on Library and Information Services to Cultural Minorities, *Report of the Task Force on Library and Information Services to Cultural Minorities* (Washington, D.C.: U.S. Government Printing Office, 1981).

17. Lavery, "The Commitment to Spanish Language Services," 7.

18. Berman, "Stop Playing," 691.

Index

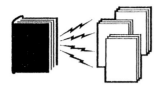

Haworth
DOCUMENT DELIVERY
SERVICE
and Local Photocopying Royalty Payment Form

This new service provides (a) a single-article order form for any article from a Haworth journal and (b) a convenient royalty payment form for local photocopying (not applicable to photocopies intended for resale).

- *Time Saving:* No running around from library to library to find a specific article.
- *Cost Effective:* All costs are kept down to a minimum.
- *Fast Delivery:* Choose from several options, including same-day FAX.
- *No Copyright Hassles:* You will be supplied by the original publisher.
- *Easy Payment:* Choose from several easy payment methods.

Open Accounts Welcome for . . .
- Library Interlibrary Loan Departments
- Library Network/Consortia Wishing to Provide Single-Article Services
- Indexing/Abstracting Services with Single Article Provision Services
- Document Provision Brokers and Freelance Information Service Providers

MAIL or *FAX* THIS ENTIRE ORDER FORM TO:

Attn: **Marianne Arnold**
Haworth Document Delivery Service
The Haworth Press, Inc.
10 Alice Street
Binghamton, NY 13904-1580

or **FAX:** (607) 722-1424
or **CALL:** 1-800-3-HAWORTH
(1-800-342-9678; 9am-5pm EST)

PLEASE SEND ME PHOTOCOPIES OF THE FOLLOWING SINGLE ARTICLES:

1) Journal Title: _____
   Vol/Issue/Year: _____ Starting & Ending Pages: _____
   Article Title: _____

2) Journal Title: _____
   Vol/Issue/Year: _____ Starting & Ending Pages: _____
   Article Title: _____

3) Journal Title: _____
   Vol/Issue/Year: _____ Starting & Ending Pages: _____
   Article Title: _____

4) Journal Title: _____
   Vol/Issue/Year: _____ Starting & Ending Pages: _____
   Article Title: _____

(See other side for Costs and Payment Information)

COSTS: Please figure your cost to order quality copies of an article.

1. Set-up charge per article: $8.00
   ($8.00 × number of separate articles) _____

2. Photocopying charge for each article:
   - 1-10 pages: $1.00 _____
   - 11-19 pages: $3.00 _____
   - 20-29 pages: $5.00 _____
   - 30+ pages: $2.00/10 pages _____

3. Flexicover (optional): $2.00/article _____

4. Postage & Handling: US: $1.00 for the first article/
   - $.50 each additional article _____
   - Federal Express: $25.00 _____
   - Outside US: $2.00 for first article/
   - $.50 each additional article _____

5. Same-day FAX service: $.35 per page _____

6. Local Photocopying Royalty Payment: should you wish to copy the article yourself. Not intended for photocopies made for resale. $1.50 per article per copy
   (i.e. 10 articles x $1.50 each = $15.00) _____

GRAND TOTAL: _____

METHOD OF PAYMENT: (please check one)

❑ Check enclosed ❑ Please ship and bill. PO # _____
(sorry we can ship and bill to bookstores only! All others must pre-pay)

❑ Charge to my credit card: ❑ Visa; ❑ MasterCard; ❑ American Express;

Account Number:_____ Expiration date:_____

Signature: *X*_____ Name: _____

Institution: _____ Address: _____

City: _____ State:_____ Zip:_____

Phone Number: _____ FAX Number: _____

MAIL or *FAX* THIS ENTIRE ORDER FORM TO:

Attn: **Marianne Arnold**
Haworth Document Delivery Service
The Haworth Press, Inc.
10 Alice Street
Binghamton, NY 13904-1580

or FAX: (607) 722-1424
or CALL: 1-800-3-HAWORTH
(1-800-342-9678; 9am-5pm EST)